SARA HA

CHARLES DENYER was in Washington on 9/11 when terrorists attacked the Pentagon. The events of that day and seeing how the nation responded inspired a new mission for Denyer. Since 2001, he's worked with hundreds of organizations throughout the globe in helping them obtain a true competitive advantage with cybersecurity, data privacy, and regulatory compliance, while also providing essential national security and advisory services to some of the world's most recognized brands.

He consults regularly with top political and business leaders throughout the world, including former vice presidents of the United States, White House chiefs of staff, secretaries of State and Defense, ambassadors, high-ranking intelligence officials, CEOs, entrepreneurs, and others. His time with these transformational figures and the insights they've shared have afforded Charles a front-row seat into many of the world's most consequential events of the past five decades, and what lies ahead.

Learn more at charlesdenyer.com

"Charles Denyer provides a riveting look at the endearing friendship between two great Americans who together changed the world. Well-written, captivating, and highly engaging, *Texas Titans* examines two of the most consequential statesmen of the 20th century and how their lives were inextricably linked personally, politically, and in public service."

— THE RIGHT HONORABLE BRIAN MULRONEY,
Former Prime Minister of Canada

"George H.W. Bush and James A. Baker, III were the best of friends; two men who, for six decades, worked together to make the country and the world a better place. *Texas Titans* offers readers a well-deserved and inspiring portrait of the lives of these two men, their mutual respect and shared loyalty to our nation."

— DICK CHENEY,
46th Vice President of the United States of America

"George Bush and Jim Baker had what many consider the most consequential friendship and partnership in the history of American politics. *Texas Titans* captures the true meaning of this extraordinary relationship."

— DAN QUAYLE,
44th Vice President of the United States of America

"One of the great honors of my life was having a front-row seat to the legendary friendship between George H.W. Bush and James A. Baker, III. With *Texas Titans*, Charles Denyer captures the essence of a friendship that changed the world."

— JEAN BECKER,
Chief of Staff to Former President George H.W. Bush (1994–2018)

"*Texas Titans* tells the story of a deep, multi-decade friendship between two loving, smart, patriotic, and effective leaders . . . of how they trusted and supported each other and how each one's success helped the other. When Dad spoke of the importance of faith, family, and friends, Jimmy Baker was at the top of the friends list."

— NEIL BUSH,
Son of George H.W. Bush

"*Texas Titans* captures the essence of two strong figures in American history. More importantly, it teaches us how two strong and capable individuals achieved much more at the highest levels of government working together than they would have accomplished without the support of each other."

— CRAIG FULLER,
Secretary to the Reagan Cabinet (1981–84)
Chief of Staff to Vice President George H.W. Bush (1985–89)

"*Texas Titans* is the story of a historic friendship — of two friends who together made history. It goes beyond the well-known public achievements of George H.W. Bush and James A. Baker, III to the less well-known (or appreciated) personal qualities that made both men the leaders and the friends that they were. There are lessons here for all who aspire to leadership or to simple friendship. And there is much here to give heart to Americans in difficult times, reminding them that our land is richly blessed with good people who, when called upon, serve their country with honor, selflessness, and success."

— CHASE UNTERMEYER,
United States Ambassador to Qatar (2004–2007)

TEXAS TITANS

TEXAS TITANS

George H. W. Bush and James A. Baker, III :
A Friendship Forged in Power

Charles Denyer

FOREWORD BY
VICE PRESIDENT DICK CHENEY

CAMBRIDGE KLEIN PUBLISHERS

Publisher's Cataloging-In-Publication Data

Names: Denyer, Charles, author. | Cheney, Richard B., writer of supplementary textual content.
Title: Texas titans : George H.W. Bush and James A. Baker, III : a friendship forged in power / Charles Denyer ; foreword by Vice President Dick Cheney.
Description: Austin, Texas : Cambridge Klein Publishers, [2020] | Includes bibliographical references and index.
Identifiers: ISBN 9780998764221 (hardcover) | ISBN 9780998764238 (paperback) | ISBN 9780998764245 (ebook)
Subjects: LCSH: Bush, George, 1924-2018--Friends and associates. | Baker, James Addison, 1930---Friends and associates. | Politicians--Texas--Biography. | United States--Politics and government--20th century. | LCGFT: Biographies.
Classification: LCC E882 .D46 2020 (print) | LCC E882 (ebook) | DDC 973.928092--dc23

Unless otherwise noted, all photos have been provided courtesy of the George H.W. Bush Presidential Library & Museum and Rice University's Baker Institute for Public Policy.

Book design by Michael Kellner / Edited by Shelley Holloway

Printed in the United States of America

For more information, contact:
Cambridge Klein Publishers, LLC
Austin, Texas 78738
info@cambridgeklein.org

To my daughter Caroline Harper Denyer.
I love you so much, my sweet angel.
Go conquer the world, my little Einstein!

Contents

Foreword

GEORGE HERBERT WALKER BUSH AND JAMES A. BAKER, III embody the very spirit of the meaning of friendship. Both men shared a love for tennis, the sport that brought these two fierce competitors together on the courts of the Houston Country Club. Serves and volleys were just the beginning for Jim Baker and George Bush. Soon, their families became close friends — Baker and his boys, and Bush and his growing family.

Jim, admittedly, wasn't very political when his lifelong friendship began with George Bush, but that changed as tragedy struck with the passing of his first wife, Mary Stuart. At Bush's insistence, Jim threw himself into the political arena in 1970 by managing Bush's US Senate race. Bush lost, but what he gained was without question his most valuable political ally for the next quarter century.

Looking back to when I was chief of staff for President Ford, I remember how hard Jim worked to secure the delegates we needed to fend off Ronald Reagan for the Republican nomination in 1976. Jim was our delegate hunter, a demanding job that required around-the-clock attention to get us the votes we needed. Jim delivered for us, and Ford won the nomination. He then helped close the double-digit gap between Ford and Governor Carter to bring us to a statistical dead heat with the Georgia governor on Election Day 1976.

Jim was tenacious, never giving in or giving up on a race that many had written off. Though we had to pack our bags — politically speaking — with the loss to Carter, it was only a temporary hiatus for Jim, George, and me. I returned to Washington just two years later as Wyoming's lone congressman, and Jim signed on to Bush's 1980 presidential campaign, upsetting Reagan in the Iowa caucuses, though eventually losing the nomination. Bush accepted Reagan's invitation to join the ticket, and they swept to victory over Jimmy Carter. It was the first of many victories for George Bush as a candidate and Jim Baker as a campaign chairman.

In 1988, following Reagan's two terms, Jim ran George Bush's presidential campaign, one of his finest political achievements — in my opinion — as he helped his good friend win the presidency in a landslide. Jim and I found ourselves working together yet again for another Republican president as I became secretary of Defense, with Jim serving as secretary of State. Little did we know the events that would unfold — and the tidal wave of change that would sweep through various regions of the world — all as we served President George H.W. Bush during his single term in office.

Those were consequential times that called for unquestioned leadership from our commander in chief, who, in turn, sought advice from Jim and me, as well as Brent Scowcroft and many others to help navigate the ever-changing global geopolitical landscape. Time and again, President Bush showed the world what true leadership was, and with Jim Baker by his side, made some of the most significant decisions of his — or any — presidency, shaping a post-Cold War world. The president trusted Jim's advice immensely on virtually every foreign-policy matter we were confronted with.

But more than just foreign policy, Jim had a great read on all things political, and it was Jim who returned to the White House to help resuscitate Bush's flagging presidential campaign for a hopeful second term. Bush lost a tough re-election race, but make no mistake, Jim gave it his all for his best friend in 1992.

Eight years later, I was honored to be chosen as the vice-presidential running mate for Texas governor George W. Bush on the Republican ticket. I was more than ready to go to work and serve a second President Bush, but before that could happen, we needed Jim's help securing the critical twenty-five electoral votes in Florida. Jim signed on immediately, taking complete command and control of the Florida recount, outworking and outmaneuvering Al Gore's campaign with a brilliant display of political acumen. Thanks to Jim's legendary efforts in Florida, I was sworn in as America's 46th vice president of the United States on January 20, 2001, ready to serve another president named George Bush. And much like his father, George H.W. Bush, George W. Bush was a man of character and integrity. He assured me that I would have a significant voice in his presidency, and for eight years, he was true to his word.

As for George H.W. Bush and James A. Baker, III, these two men stood side by side in countless battles, sharing both their victories and defeats. President Bush's handpicked team for foreign policy, national security, and defense — which Jim and I were so proud to be a part of

— was one of the finest ever. We all worked well together; we understood our roles and responsibilities , never encroaching on each other's turf as we worked for one of the greatest presidents to ever serve our nation. Jim calls Bush the greatest single-term president ever, and one of the best of all time. I couldn't agree more. If ever a person was ready for the presidency and the profoundly important responsibilities that come with the office, it was George H.W. Bush.

When I think of George Bush and Jim Baker, words come to mind that reflect traits inextricably shared by both men — determination, courage, selflessness, wisdom, optimism — and more.

These two men are without question Texas Titans. Best of friends — legendary figures from the Lone Star State — and two of Houston's most revered citizens.

— Vice President Dick Cheney

Author's Preface

George H.W. Bush and James A. Baker, III. Rarely, if ever, have I witnessed two individuals who, in the political spectrum, accomplished so much together during such consequential times for not only America, but the world. I'm often asked why I wrote *Texas Titans*, and the answer is really quite simple. I wanted to express my immense gratitude for these two men — for their commitment to making our world a better place — and to pay tribute to two of the world's most important statesmen of modern times. True Texas Titans, they were towers of leadership and strength, as much of this book will bear out. As for their friendship, I've shared the thoughts of those who knew them well, along with some of their own words and experiences that exemplify what real and lasting friendship means.

ON BUSH

When I think of the word patriotism, I'm reminded of the sacrifices George Herbert Walker Bush made on behalf of this great nation.

While born into privilege, he took the road less traveled, a winding, treacherous, yet adventurous and fulfilling road that ultimately landed him at 1600 Pennsylvania Avenue as America's 41st president of the United States. But his life was about so much more than the presidency. His was a life of courage and a relentless drive for overachieving, but he never forgot the importance of dignity and humility. Bush wasn't a gloater, so let me take this opportunity to gloat on behalf of a man whom I've come to admire so much in my adult life.

As World War II broke out, Bush could have easily bypassed military duty in favor of the collegiate experience followed by a lavish life of Wall Street riches, which is exactly what many sons of privilege did. After all, they were following a family lineage of bankers and financiers that had been instrumental in creating the world of capitalism as we know it today.

Bush chose a different path, one that began by defending this great nation in the treacherous Pacific as a naval aviator during World War II. He was shot down and rescued, yet suited up again, flying a total of fifty-eight missions during his service. Decades later, when asked about his service during the war, he often spoke with sorrow and sadness about how he survived being shot down over Chichi Jima, when his crew had perished. And when he entered the political arena, it seemed logical that a candidate with Bush's military background would use it for political gain in campaigns. After all, Americans admire our patriots, and rightfully so, but Bush wouldn't have any of it. His congressional, Senate, and presidential campaigns were largely void of talk regarding his unquestioned valor and service, because as Bush saw it, it wasn't right. His take on it was that millions had died, so honor them, rather than thanking him. It was an incredible display of humility, possibly one of Bush's greatest traits.

After the war, Bush once again chose not to return to the East Coast and a life of country clubs, endless social activities, and countless job opportunities afforded to the men of Ivy League schools. Instead, he headed west to the oil fields of Texas, with dreams as big as the Lone Star State. He gave it his all in the oil business, finding success early and often, ultimately moving from Midland to the boomtown of Houston, Texas, where he found friendship with none other than James A. Baker, III. Bush's entrepreneurial spirit earned him financial success, but his drive toward public service took him from the oil rigs to the rigors of the campaign trail, finding victory — yet also defeat at times — during his political races from 1963 to 1970 in Texas.

In the decade that followed, Bush held several posts under the Nixon and Ford administrations: ambassador to the UN, chairman of the Republican National Committee, chief of the US Liaison Office in China, and director of the Central Intelligence Agency. He learned a great deal about politics during that time, which worked out well, because he brought that knowledge as well as his integrity, diplomacy, and character to bear in the years to come.

Bush became well-known on the Washington scene during the seventies, but the country first came to know Bush when he decided to run for president in 1980. That's when America got its first real taste of the man who, when facing defeat in the primaries, stepped aside for the good of the party, making way for California governor Ronald Reagan to head the ticket. Reagan, well aware of Bush's reputation and political talents, didn't lose a beat, or an opportunity, and named Bush as his running mate, and they soundly defeated incumbent president

Jimmy Carter. Bush became America's 43rd vice president, serving his one-time archrival with absolute loyalty during Reagan's two terms in the White House. That Bush would seek the Oval Office in 1989 was almost a given.

On November 8, 1988, George Herbert Walker Bush became President-elect Bush as he waltzed to the White House with a landslide victory over Massachusetts governor Michael Dukakis. His achievements during his single term in office were simply astonishing, prompting his dear friend Jim Baker to call it what it was — an extremely consequential presidency. I couldn't agree more.

Yet the political winds began to shift direction in 1992, and suddenly, America's commander in chief was in danger of losing re-election to Bill Clinton. Bush's campaign team called for a shakeup, one that included possibly removing embattled Vice President Dan Quayle from the ticket. Bush would have none of it. He chose Quayle in 1988, and was sticking with him again in 1992, regardless of what the political pundits had to say. To me, it spoke volumes about another of Bush's greatest traits, loyalty.

He ultimately lost re-election to a man he regarded as politically inferior and lacking character. Regardless, Bush looked beyond the election loss and years later, found a personal friendship with Clinton, becoming a father figure to the man who denied him re-election. But that was Bush, always finding the goodness in people, no matter the circumstances. Many wondered if his friendship with Clinton was really as close as it seemed to be, and the answer is a resounding, "Yes." Bill Clinton loved George Bush, and Bush loved Clinton. Strange how politics can change a man, even stranger how one-time political enemies can become such close friends. It's a lesson in civility that we should stop and consider when living in today's contentious political climate.

As Baker told Chris Wallace of Fox News, Bush was the very best one-term president, and perhaps one of the greatest presidents to ever serve this nation. While I'm saddened that he passed before this book project began, I've been blessed to have received letters over the years from him and his wife, Barbara. They were personal, funny, and so uplifting.

ON BAKER

I've always found Jim Baker a fascinating individual. He never cared much for politics in his early life, but the one-time Democrat found his calling when a dear friend by the name of George Herbert Walker Bush asked him to help run his 1970 US Senate campaign. Bush may have lost that race, but what he gained with Baker was a man who became one of the most consequential figures in American politics for the next three decades. Baker was bitten by the political bug and never looked back. He's been called the Velvet Hammer, the Miracle Man, Mr. Cool, and probably dozens of other lofty titles. I, myself, refer to him as a Smooth Operator, a man who knows what he wants and gets what he wants, yet rarely — if ever — does he do so by upsetting or belittling his adversaries. Now, that's a talent that very, very few political operatives have learned to master, but Baker has, arguably better than anybody else ever has, or will.

The true success of politicians is not measured by the races they win or the positions they're appointed to, but rather how they perform their jobs. It's really that simple. Do they get things done and make a difference, or are they merely standby gear, an insignificant player relegated to the back room?

When history tells the story of James A. Baker, III, his successes will be many. In every — and I mean every — position he's held in the political spectrum since his appointment as President Ford's delegate hunter in 1976 — one hell of a tough job, by the way — his performance has been nothing but legendary.

How does a man go from practicing law in Houston in the summer of 1975 to running the general-election campaign for the sitting president of the United States of America, Gerald Ford, just twelve months later? Let's just say that's when the Miracle Man — the nickname the media gave to Baker after he secured Ford's delegates to push him over the top for the GOP nomination in 1976 — was born. That's where it all began. People in the Ford campaign — and the countless delegates he secured to fend off Ronald Reagan — witnessed first-hand the Baker magic. Words that come to mind to describe Baker during this critical period for President Ford — tough, strategic, relentless, courteous, persuasive, and many more. Said Peter Roussel, who worked under Baker, "When I couldn't close on somebody, I'd give the delegate to him. Believe me, if anybody deserves the credit for winning the nomination, it's James A. Baker, III."[1]

Evidence of his powers to strategize and persuade: He was given the almost unachievable and improbable task of trying to erase a massive, double-digit lead (some estimates as high as 30 percent) held by Georgia governor Jimmy Carter over President Ford. And he almost pulled it off as polling had Ford and Carter in a dead heat on Election Day. Ford lost in a closely contested race, but Baker's magic was evident once again. Undeterred, he was back at it again, running Bush's 1980 presidential campaign, and derailing Reagan once again — yet only temporarily — with Bush's surprise victory in Iowa.

The man who twice tried to defeat Reagan then became his chief of staff — imagine that — and will go down in history as perhaps the finest gatekeeper to ever serve a president. Later joining Reagan's Cabinet as secretary of the Treasury, Baker asserted himself in the most impactful ways. Then following his service to Reagan, he successfully directed Bush's presidential campaign in 1988, trouncing Michael Dukakis, and then served as Bush's secretary of State. His best friend called him back to duty in the summer of 1992 to help revive a dysfunctional re-election campaign that was spiraling downward.

And who can forget Baker's performance in the Florida election dispute of 2000, the [George W.] *Bush vs. Gore* debacle that consumed the nation for thirty-seven long days? If not for Baker's sterling performance, the son and namesake of his dear friend George Herbert Walker Bush would not have become the 43rd president of the United States. See a pattern here, folks? Baker gets things done. He leaves a mark wherever he goes, and a hell of a good one.

Yes, he's a fascinating man; a man with many victories — and noteworthy accomplishments — in the rough and tumble world of politics. When he wasn't running campaigns, he was running the White House, overseeing financial matters for the country, spearheading international diplomacy, and more. Each of these assignments was unique, requiring an arsenal of skills for getting the job done. Many people have failed to make the transition from one political position to the next. Not Jim Baker. Drawing from his East Coast education and his Texan roots and upbringing, he could influence and persuade across the aisle and across the world.

Since 1975, the Houstonian with the slight, yet at times, heavy Texas drawl, has run with the best of them, running circles around the East Coast gentry who have dominated much of Washington since the founding of our great nation. He took to Washington a perfect combination of intelligence, grace, a fierce work ethic, and so much more — all delivered with a little Texas attitude.

I've been honored to spend time with one of the most iconic figures in modern American politics, and he's everything and more than you'd expect. He's witty, loves a good laugh, yet can be incredibly serious and introspective when our conversations turned to the likes of national security, the future of America, and naturally, the current political climate.

Mr. Secretary, it's been an honor getting to know you.

Introduction

"AND FOR NEARLY FOUR YEARS NOW, I HAVE HAD THE PRIVILEGE of introducing him as the President of the United States. Ladies and gentlemen, there is only one way to introduce the president of the United States, and that is to say to you, ladies and gentlemen, the President of the United States."[2] And with that, James A. Baker, III then stepped away from the podium at the Houston Westin Galleria ballroom to make way for George Herbert Walker Bush, America's 41st president, to deliver his concession speech, having just lost the bid for his second term as president of the United States to a little-known governor from Arkansas.

It was 1992, and by then, Bush and Baker had become close personal friends — perhaps the closest — and exceptional political allies who displayed diplomacy at its best during their decades of service to the American people. Together, they rose to the top of the American political spectrum, both men working tirelessly during Bush's single term as president of the United States from 1989 to 1993. Their challenges were mammoth. The tensions in Tiananmen Square. The fall of the Berlin Wall. The invasion of Kuwait by a ruthless dictator. The destruction of the Iraqi army — at that time, the fourth largest in the world — by a carefully crafted coalition of nations, militarily spearheaded by the United States. The collapse of the former Soviet Union, and much more. It all happened under the watchful eye of George H.W. Bush — with Baker skillfully helping architect many of Bush's international policy directives.

Both men's résumés were legendary. Bush served as a United States congressman, ambassador to the United Nations, chair of the Republican National Committee, US liaison to China, director of the Central Intelligence Agency, 43rd vice president, and 41st president of the United States.

Baker served as undersecretary of Commerce, secretary of the Treasury, secretary of State, and White House chief of staff — twice — and also chaired or played a lead role in five successive presidential elections for three different candidates from 1976 to 1992.

As successful as their political careers were, both men also knew what it felt like to lose on election night. Bush twice lost races for the US Senate of Texas, once in 1964, when he lost to Ralph Yarborough, and again in 1970, losing to Lloyd Bentsen. Baker ran unsuccessfully for attorney general of Texas in 1978, losing to an eventual governor, Mark White.

Recalled White, "I remember at a conference while I was governor, while he [Baker] was in the Reagan administration and had come to Texas for some reason, he thanked me for beating him in the race for attorney general. . . . He said, 'Otherwise, I'd still probably be attorney general in Texas. I'd never have had the opportunity to do what I have in Washington.' . . . As I did then, I have the highest regard for him — and his contributions to public service have meant a great deal to Houston and Texas and the nation."[3]

But possibly the toughest defeat for both Bush and Baker to endure was that loss in November 1992, when Arkansas governor Bill Clinton ended a twelve-year Republican reign of the White House. Clinton, driving a relentless message to voters that the economy was in the doldrums — and Bush was to blame — became the first baby-boomer president, just forty-six years old, defeating a man more than two decades his senior.

It was fitting that Baker introduce his good friend on such a difficult night. The president gave a concession speech that reflected the man he was — honorable, diplomatic, and a loyal American. Acknowledging that America had spoken, Bush promised that he and his administration would work with President-elect Clinton to ensure a smooth transition of power. A scene unimaginable just nineteen months earlier, when Bush had achieved a politically unheard-of 91 percent approval rating following the 1991 Gulf War.

And there was Baker telling the crowd, "It's real hell to lose these squeakers, isn't it?" A gentle reminder to all that the election had been winnable, indeed, and more could have — should have — been done to secure Bush's re-election. In good times and bad, both personally and in the challenging world of politics, both men stood by one another, comrades in arms who savored the victories and consoled one another after the defeats. They both rebounded from that 1992 loss, returning to Houston, Texas, Baker's birthplace and Bush's adopted home state since 1948. Bush was proud to call Houston his hometown. As for Baker, he was a Texan — a fourth-generation Houstonian — through and through, and going home was as easy and natural as watching the sun set on a hot Texas day.

Bush became one of America's most beloved former presidents, involving himself in countless humanitarian efforts throughout the world — a kindly reminder of his "Thousand Points of Light" mantra. Baker soldiered on. After all, that's what tough, gritty Texans do. He ultimately helped another Bush win the White House in 2000, and he continued to play a role on the world stage. Baker, while never elected to a political office, is nonetheless revered as one of the most influential politicians of his time. "There's not a world leader who wouldn't take Jim's phone call," according to America's most powerful vice president ever, Dick Cheney.

This is a story of George Herbert Walker Bush and James Addison Baker, III, two of America's most consequential statesmen of the past fifty years. Two men from opposite areas of the country who found friendship on the tennis courts at the Houston Country Club. Two men who helped transform a world during an era of immense challenges and change. Two men who became — and still are — Texas titans.

TEXAS TITANS

CHAPTER ONE

Different Worlds

G EORGE HERBERT WALKER BUSH WAS BORN ON JUNE 12, 1924, in Milton, Massachusetts, to his father, a prominent Wall Street banker and future United States senator, Prescott Sheldon Bush, and his mother, Dorothy Walker Bush. The second son of Prescott Bush, he was named after his maternal grandfather who was known as "Pop," which resulted in George Bush being called "Poppy," a tribute to his namesake.

The Bush family moved to Greenwich, Connecticut, in 1925, where young Bush attended the prestigious Greenwich Country Day School, followed by Phillips Academy in Andover, Massachusetts. Tall, handsome, outgoing, well-liked, and an excellent athlete, Bush served as president of his senior class, as well as captain of the varsity baseball and soccer teams. Bush's devotion to his alma mater was evident throughout the decades, visiting the school often, even serving on the Board of Trustees for sixteen years, while sending three sons to Andover — George W. in 1964, Jeb in 1971, and Marvin in 1975.

Bush's last visit to Andover was on September 30, 2015, when he made a surprise appearance. Though a bit frail at ninety-one years old, the former president was energized by the standing ovation from the students and faculty that filled Cochran Chapel. "Thank you for that warm Andover welcome back to the school that has meant so much to me in my life," he said.[4] Reflecting on that special day after sharing a private lunch with students, Bush said, "It always gives me great joy to return to Andover. . . . The lessons learned and the relationships forged here have meant so much throughout my full and adventurous life, and I could wish nothing more for every student who is so blessed to walk on this campus."[5]

Following the bombing of Pearl Harbor in 1941, Bush decided to forgo college — temporarily — to enlist in the United States Navy. Shortly thereafter, Bush headed to flight-training school, earning a commission as a naval pilot assigned to the aircraft carrier USS *San Jacinto* (CVL-30). He flew his first combat mission in May 1944 and was soon promoted to lieutenant on August 1, 1944. Flying a Grumman TBF Avenger, a torpedo bomber, Bush saw the horrors of war firsthand.

Just one month later, in September, as part of a combat mission against the Japanese on the island of Chichi Jima, Bush's plane was hit and seriously damaged. Though his plane was on fire, Bush courageously completed the mission, but he and the crew were forced to bail out. His crewmembers did not survive, but Bush was rescued when the USS *Finback*, a Gato-class submarine, miraculously appeared. Bush stayed with the crew of the *Finback*, helping rescue more Navy pilots who'd been shot down, but others were not so fortunate. Many of them were captured by enemy forces and executed, some even barbarically eaten by their captors.[6]

In an exclusive interview decades later, Bush relived the dreaded moments of that day, September 2, 1944. "I told the crewmen to get out. I dove out onto the wing . . . hit my head on the tail . . . and bleeding like a stuck pig, I dropped into the ocean and I swam over and got into this life raft. I was sick to my stomach . . . scared. If somebody didn't pick me up, I would have been captured and killed. They were very brutal on Chichi Jima. . . . Suddenly I saw this periscope, and it was the USS *Finback* . . . Nothing heroic about getting shot down. And I wondered, why was I spared when two friends in the plane with me were killed."[7] He returned to the skies, flying fifty-eight combat missions during World War II that included 128 carrier landings and 1228 hours of recorded flight time, an unbelievable achievement for a man who just a few years earlier had been attending basic preflight training in North Carolina.[8]

While still enlisted in the Navy, Bush met Barbara Pierce during the Christmas holidays of 1941, and they wed on January 6, 1945, in Rye, New York. Together, they had six children: George Walker, Robin (who was born in 1949 and died in 1953 of leukemia), John Ellis "Jeb," Neil, Marvin, and Dorothy "Doro." Bush's eldest son, George W., followed his father into the world of politics, first serving as governor of Texas and ultimately as the 43rd president of the United States, with son Jeb serving two terms as governor of Florida.

Following the Japanese surrender, Bush was honorably discharged in September 1945, allowing him to enroll in Yale, where he graduated in 1948 as part of an accelerated academic program. Much like at Andover, Bush was active in all parts of school life at Yale, serving as captain of the baseball team, while also being selected to join the secret society known as Skull & Bones. While at Yale, Bush's baseball team played in the first two College World Series, with Bush even meeting Babe Ruth before a game during his senior year.

Curt Smith, a former speechwriter for President Bush, said, "It is fair to say that he [Bush] loved the game as much or more than any president. . . . He played the game, he coached the game, he captained the game, and he celebrated the game. The first time he swung a baseball bat was at age five. I once asked him how he felt, and he said, 'Baseball has everything.' That's a wonderful encapsulation of what the game is and means."[9]

GEORGE HEADS WEST

With a Yale degree now added to his impressive list of credentials at such a young age, Bush didn't choose the path of least resistance. Bush wrote: "I am not sure I want to capitalize completely on the benefits I received at birth — that is on the benefit of my social position."[10] The restless, anxious Bush wanted something more in life, perhaps adventure, so why not Texas? "I have this chance to go . . . to Texas," Bush wrote. "Texas would be new and exciting for a while — hard on Bar perhaps — and heavens knows many girls would bitch like blazes about such a proposed move — Bar's different though. She is wholly unselfish, beautifully tolerant of my weaknesses and idiosyncrasies, and ready to faithfully follow any course I choose."[11]

It was set, then. The East Coast Ivy Leaguer was heading to Texas, working for Dresser Industries, and starting at the very bottom of the ladder, an equipment clerk. Their first family home to which he and Barbara brought young George W. Bush was a tiny two-bedroom duplex with just one bathroom, which they had to share with what

Bush described as "a woman and her daughter, both of whom seemed to make their living by questionable means."[12]

Texas was indeed new to Bush. A fascinating place to be, especially when he saw what he remembers as his first real, powerful West Texas sandstorm. He also marveled at the first time he saw golfers using a small jeep-like vehicle and holding umbrellas up because, as Bush tells it, "It was so damned hot that they really couldn't have made it around without this car. We [he and Barbara] both laughed over the looks of the damn thing but had to secretly admit the ingenuity of the gents."[13]

But Texas was no laughing matter. It was about hard work, finding a new way of life, being on his own, and making new friends thousands of miles away from the comfort of his family. In the early period of his new career, Bush found his employment merely satisfactory, admitting that much of what he initially did required little brain power. He was eager to get out to the oil fields, and also eager to read anything he could about the booming West Texas oil industry. Bush was steadily progressing, and with Barbara by his side — along with the ever-rambunctious George W. — he was becoming a fast learner in the oil industry. From helping change clutches and brakes on a rig to pitching a bed on the front seat of a car for hours, Bush was getting his hands dirty, indeed, often working seven days a week, but never complaining.

Bush came to like Midland, calling it a fine town with many young people. He admired Texas but expressed his restlessness in many of his letters to friends and family. He called himself a poor salesman, but he was learning a tremendous amount about the oil industry, and for that, he was happy and appreciative of the opportunities afforded him. But the anxiousness got the best of Bush, writing in the spring of 1951: "I became too restless in my job . . . and decided to strike out on my own. I joined up with our good friend and neighbor John Overbey, and together, we founded Bush-Overbey Oil Development Co. Leaving my job was a tough decision, not only because it meant lost security, but especially because of my great respect for Neil Mallon [CEO of Dresser Industries]. However, he was supportive and even encouraged me to try to start my own business."[14]

For Bush, the early fifties were an exciting time to be in the oil business and in West Texas, but he always kept his finger on the pulse of the political scene. His father — Prescott Sheldon Bush — was elected in 1952 as a United States senator from Connecticut, a seat he held until January 1963. Bush remembers introducing himself to then senator Lyndon Baines Johnson as Bush was walking out of a hotel in Midland. LBJ told Bush that he and Bush's father shouldn't be looked upon as Democrats or Republicans, rather as good Americans. Surely, that was yet more encouragement to try his hand at politics. But he had to set aside his business dealings and his growing interest in the political circles, to mourn the death of his daughter, Robin, who died from leukemia in October 1953. He knew he had to soldier on with life, once noting, "In time, we will only have pleasant memories to look back on."[15]

In 1953, Bush co-founded Zapata Petroleum Corporation, an oil company that drilled in the Permian Basin in Texas. The following year, Bush was named president of Zapata Offshore Company, a subsidiary that focused primarily on offshore drilling. Bush, no doubt proud of his new company — and position — wrote to Barbara's father, Marvin Pierce, "I am sending you a copy of our recent press release on our offshore drilling project and a glossy print of the proposed barge. Zapata has taken this deal, and we have hired the personnel and set up the organization. We will end up with partners undoubtedly, in fact we are now talking about a public financing since it's too big for us to handle alone."[16]

Bush proclaimed 1954 a good year for Zapata, with the company holding a one-third interest in seventy wells, and a hundred more wells to drill in 1955. Four years later, in 1959, Zapata was split into two companies, and though Bush loved his life in Midland, he acknowledged years later, "Midland is nowhere near the Gulf of Mexico, where all our drilling rigs were operating. So, a very pregnant Barbara, myself, and four boys packed up and moved to Houston."[17]

Bush's next few years were hectic, indeed, settling into a new town, while also managing the many challenges of his new business. That's when it began. . . . What he called the political itch. "I decided to start small — very small — by running for chairman of the Harris County Republican Party."[18]

Small but victorious. Bush won in February 1963, writing that his "opponent withdrew before the election, so I recorded an overwhelming victory at the polls." With a paid staff and 270 precincts in the county, Bush found his job consuming, though incredibly worthwhile. He made it clear in his diary that one of his goals as Harris County GOP chairman was to reach out to minority voters, believing strongly that the Republican Party should "make room for every American."[19]

Baker recalled, "He [Bush] ran for county chairman, started right where he — I guess you should start, right at the bottom, and worked his way up to president of the United States. He was Harris County chairman of the Republican Party. In those days, it was a hanging offense to be a Republican in Texas. I'm not kidding you!"[20]

Bush set his sights much higher the following year, running for the United States Senate in 1964 against Liberal Texas senator Ralph Yarborough, a contest he ultimately lost.

BAKER — BORN ON BISSONNET

James Addison Baker, III was born on April 28, 1930, in Houston to James A. Baker Jr. and Ethel Bonner. Baker's early childhood was a crash course in the world of polite manners, hard work, and respect for adult authority. He was born into a family of means. His mother's father was a very successful businessman, and the Baker family managed the state's most prestigious law firm and had engaged in various successful business endeavors with each generation. Baker said his parents didn't spoil him, courtesy of a frugal father who had little regard for the material things in life. There were no fancy automobiles or lavish spending allowances, rather a comfortable two-story home and membership to two country clubs. If there was any monetary value assigned to a promise, it was for Baker to collect a $1,000 reward for not smoking or drinking until the age of twenty-one. "I didn't collect," he recalled, "though I managed to wait until I was eighteen for my first taste of hard liquor."[21]

Baker departed the Lone Star State and headed east to attend the Hill School. Going from Houston, Texas, to Pottstown, Pennsylvania, in his junior year of high school was an adjustment, but by the following year, he was elected to the student government, captained the Hill tennis team, and established friendships that he still has to this very day. His grades were good, but not great, yet he gained admission to Princeton University — a school he calls the "destination of choice for many young American men of Scottish heritage, particularly those from the South."[22]

His competitive streak meant a continuation of tennis, but with so many nationally ranked players, Baker opted for the rigors of rugby, which led to a spring break trip with his teammates to Bermuda in 1950 where he met Mary Stuart McHenry, also on spring break from Finch College in New York. While Baker's first few years at Princeton were more geared toward social activities than academic life, he found his passion leaned toward history and the classics, admitting to having no interest whatsoever in math and science. He earned his bachelor's degree in history in 1952.

The study of history seemed to go hand in hand with an eventual law degree. After graduation, young Baker fully believed he would attend law school and then return to Houston to the very firm founded by his family. But before law school could be entertained, American boys were being shipped to the Korean Peninsula for the ensuing conflict that lasted for three long years, taking the lives of more than 40,000 American soldiers, while wounding more than 100,000. Baker wanted to enlist, but it was too late to join the ROTC program at Princeton, so instead, he opted for the Marine Corps Platoon Leaders Course.

Baker was stationed in the Mediterranean for six months, returning home to wed Mary Stuart in her hometown of Dayton, Ohio. Following his discharge from the Marines, he and Mary Stuart moved to Austin, Texas, in 1954, where Baker enrolled in law school at the University of Texas at Austin, graduating with honors. The next move? Houston, naturally. According to Baker, "We never considered settling anywhere except Houston. My family was there. So, too, was Baker Botts, the firm where three James A. Bakers before me had hung their shingles."[23] But with the family firm having a strict anti-nepotism rule, Baker joined Andrews, Kurth, Campbell & Bradley in 1957, working under the close supervision of Harry Jones, which Baker admits was a tremendous opportunity.

Business was booming, and life was grand for Baker as he approached the age of forty. He was happily married and in love, and had a family that had grown considerably in recent years — now with four boys: James IV (Jamie), Mike, John, and Doug. "Houston was my world, and I never dreamed of living anywhere else or doing anything besides being a lawyer," Baker once said. "Politics was not in the picture. The most that can be said of me politically is that I voted . . . in some elections anyway."[24]

But life can have its twists and turns, and for Baker, losing his wife Mary Stuart to breast cancer was a crushing reminder of just how delicate and precious life can be. He turned to his family and faith for strength during that time, and also to his friend George Bush, who stayed by his side. Other than close family members of Mary Stuart, Bush and his wife, Barbara, were the last friends to visit with Mrs. Baker before she fell into a coma, never to regain consciousness.

A FRIENDSHIP IS BORN

James A. Baker, III first met George Herbert Walker Bush in 1959 in Houston, Texas. Bush had just moved his family and his company, Zapata Offshore Company, from Midland, Texas. In talking about their long friendship, Baker is quick to point out that over the years, he's had a plethora of names for Bush — first George, then Bushie,

Mr. Vice President, Mr. President, and most recently, *Jefe* (that's Spanish for *the boss*).

Their mutual passion for tennis and their back-to-back victories as the Houston Country Club men's doubles champions in 1966 and 1967 led decades later to both being inducted into the Texas Tennis Hall of Fame. As Baker tells it, "Neither one of us had a partner for the doubles matches. And so, they put us together. And that's how we became friends. . . . We first became tennis doubles partners."[25] Baker's recollection of Bush was how genuine, personable, caring, and considerate of others he was — traits that Baker said really come through when you spend one-on-one time with Bush. According to Baker, "What sometimes doesn't come through is his competitive spirit and steely determination, which I first encountered on the tennis court and which strengthened him for success in business and politics."[26]

Their friendship carried over to the political arena as Bush sought — once again — one of Texas's US Senate seats in 1970. He brought Baker on board, and despite Bush's loss to Lloyd Bentsen, the experience further strengthened their personal and professional relationship. Baker is very open about his friendship with Bush. "I have admired his success in everything he'd undertaken in his life . . ."[27] Baker refers to their careers in the political arena as "inextricably linked, and to a large degree, mutually reinforcing since 1970."[28]

CHAPTER TWO

Man on the Move

W ORK HARD, STUDY . . . AND KEEP OUT OF POLITICS." THAT'S the advice given to Baker by his grandfather, Captain James Addison Baker. And for the first four decades of his life, Jim Baker did just that, shunning any political ambitions and aspirations. He was a practicing lawyer in his beloved hometown of Houston, a born-and-bred Texan deeply entrenched in the Lone Star State's elite professional and social circles. Life was good for Baker, and politics seemed like the furthest thing from his mind as a new decade approached in 1970. But tragedy struck when his wife Mary Stuart was diagnosed with breast cancer at age thirty-eight.

The renowned surgeon Dr. Denton Cooley, a close friend of the Baker family, performed a mastectomy on Mary Stuart, after which Baker, sensing Cooley's apprehension, began to prepare for the worst. The couple did not openly discuss death with one another. According to one family member, Baker was adamant about not discussing the doctor's prognosis with his wife, instead choosing to live their lives fully, even building a new home and throwing a surprise birthday party at the Bayou Club in Houston for Mary Stuart's thirty-eighth birthday.

Baker recalled, "From the time I met her in Bermuda in 1950, I never dated anyone else. She was a gorgeous and bright woman, a devoted wife, and a loving mother." After her death, Baker found a letter written to him by Mary Stuart, addressed to "My dear sweet loving and lovable Jimmy."[29]

Her passing left Baker without a spouse, and their four young boys, ages eight to fifteen, without a mother. Baker, already by then a self-admitted workaholic, worked even longer and harder in the early years following Mary Stuart's death, yet also committed himself to do whatever he could for his children. With four hard-charging sons — full of anguish and pain over their mother's passing — Baker fell back on the values his father had taught him: faith in God; a work ethic that doesn't waver; and quite a bit of hunting to bond his family in their time of need.

Baker found love again, marrying Susan Garrett Winston in 1973, one of Mary Stuart's closest friends. But before their marriage, he dipped his hat into politics and never turned back. However, Baker confesses, "I sometimes wonder whether, if Mary Stuart had stayed healthy, I would have kept out of politics for my entire life."[30]

Bush had flirted with politics in the early sixties, with a run for one of Texas's US Senate seats in 1964, a seat he lost to liberal Democrat Ralph Yarborough. But he found success when he won Texas's 7th Congressional District in 1966, becoming the congressional representative for a district that encompassed western Harris County. But he still had his eyes on the Senate.

With his US House seat secure, Bush reached out to former president Lyndon Baines Johnson (LBJ) for advice. While Bush told LBJ he had virtually no opposition for his current seat, had a powerful seat on the House Ways and Means Committee, and would likely continue to move up the ranks, he still didn't mind taking a gamble. The straight-talking LBJ told Bush that the difference between being a United States senator and US congressman is the difference between chicken salad and chicken shit![31] Six weeks later, Bush called on President Richard Nixon to discuss the possibility of running for the Senate. Nixon wanted him to run. So, it was done. Bush tried yet again — the second time in six years — for one of Texas's US Senate seats, running against Lloyd Bentsen.

Aware that Bentsen was a worthy opponent, Bush recruited his Houston Country Club doubles partner — now a close friend — Jim Baker to work on his campaign, knowing he needed all the resources available to secure a victory over the well-known Democrat. Baker recalled, "I had no idea whatsoever that I would ever be involved in politics or public service. All I intended to do was be a first-rate lawyer with a big law firm here in Houston. After my first wife died, my friend and tennis doubles partner George Bush came to me and said, 'Bake, you need to take your mind off your grief and help me run for the Senate.' I told him, 'George, that's a great idea except for two things: number one, I don't know anything about politics. Number two, I'm a Democrat.'"[32] It was Baker's wife's influence that eventually led him to politics and the Republican Party.

Baker told CBS's *60 Minutes* in 2018, "There were a lotta people who helped me along the way, but the guy who really got me going, got me started, turned me around at — at a time in my life [when]

I've said if I were ever gonna become an alcoholic, it's when I lost that wife, and [she] left me with those four small kids. And he [Bush] was there for me and he's been there for me ever since."[33]

Baker himself had briefly considered the idea of running for the 7th Congressional District seat Bush was vacating when it was clear Bush would be running for the Senate, but with his wife battling breast cancer at the time, he opted out. Baker's involvement with Bush's campaign began an almost quarter-century-long political marriage between the two, starting with rural cites in Texas then campaigning all the way to the White House in 1988. They became the best of friends, a political duo that Bush described as a "big brother – little brother" relationship, one that both men have acknowledged often over the years.

As the 1970 Senate election drew closer, Nixon descended on the Lone Star State in hopes of rallying support for the man he told to give up his US House seat to run for the Senate. With one Republican already in the US Senate — John Tower — Bentsen argued, "Texas needs a Democrat in the Senate," and with heavier-than-expected voter turnout in rural areas, Bentsen edged out Bush, winning 53.5 to 46.5 percent.[34] This second loss for the Senate was crushing to Bush, and it begged the question — what was his political future? After the election, Bush wrote to friends: "The future — I don't know, maybe public life in DC, maybe back to Texas. . . . We're torn between staying in politics in some way or moving back to Houston and getting fairly immersed in business. Whatever we do, I'm sure it will be challenging."[35]

NEW MAN IN NEW YORK

Nixon, aware of Bush's political gamble when he gave up his US

House seat to run for the Senate, offered Bush a post as senior advisor to the president, which he dutifully accepted. But Bush wasn't content with an advisory role, he wanted more, pushing his case for the ambassadorship to the United Nations.

According to Bush, "I told him [President Nixon's chief of staff H.R. Haldeman] that I thought the UN would have some real appeal because I could spell out his [President Nixon's] programs with some style. . . . I felt I could really put forward an image there that would be very helpful to the administration."[36]

Nixon was intrigued. As he saw it, if he could have Bush, a man deeply entrenched in East Coast society — push forward his agenda to those who Nixon felt were nothing more than Ivy League educated ideologues at the State Department, then all the better. "Wait a minute, Bob, this makes some sense. George would be in the Cabinet. . . . He'd be coming down here [the White House] every couple of weeks, getting briefed and having an input on domestic policy, and all of this makes a good deal of sense to me."[37]

Nixon made no attempt to hide his disdain for the East Coast establishment society, feelings of contempt he still bitterly harbored after losing to John F. Kennedy in 1960. He was a product of Whittier College from the suburbs of Los Angeles, thousands of miles away from the likes of Harvard and Yale and preparatory academies that fed into America's elite Ivy League institutions.

On December 11, 1970, Nixon officially announced Bush as his nominee to be ambassador to the United Nations, stating Bush's "distinguished service in the House, his years of experience before that in activities in private enterprise, which took him abroad to many countries, and most important, his enormous interest in the United

Nations, his support of the United Nations and its objectives, not only its peacekeeping objectives, but also its objectives in the field of the environment and all of the others that will be so exciting in the next decade — these are the qualities that led us to the conclusion that he was the best man who could now go to this very important post."[38]

So now, one of the biggest political questions of 1970 after Bush's loss to Lloyd Bentsen in the Texas Senate race — "What would George do next?" — had been answered. Bush soon settled into the ambassador's residence at the Waldorf Towers, performing duties completely different from those of a United States congressman. Prior to officially taking the oath, Bush reached out to the likes of Henry Kissinger, former president Johnson, and others for advice on his political appointment. Bush recalled LBJ being somewhat dismissive of the UN ambassadorship, yet the former president told Bush to use the position to entertain diplomats from around the world, show them the good in America, and give Nixon exposure when needed.

Never one to forget his roots, Bush wrote a letter to many of his colleagues in the US House, urging them to come to New York City to learn more about the United Nations and his roles and responsibilities as a newly minted ambassador. Wrote Bush: "This is just a note to have you know that the welcome mat is out for you here at the United States Mission to the United Nations. I know from my own experience in the House that I never really took a good look at the operations here in New York, and I want to be sure you realize that I would like to have you stop in at any time."[39]

Bush, a political novice in terms of international diplomacy, nevertheless savored the opportunities and challenges brought on by his new job. From dealings with the UN Security Council, along with what Bush called a social whirlwind — endless lunches, cocktail parties, and going-away events for dignitaries, and more — the ambassadorship gave the now self-declared Texan a raw view of politics through a new prism.

During his relatively brief tenure as UN ambassador, Bush found his most difficult issue was China's representation in the United Nations, particularly when it came to who would be sitting in China's seat on the powerful UN Security Council. Bush found his work fascinating, yet worried about his lack of accomplishments on both the political and diplomatic side. He also found New York City an "unrealistic place" and was amazed at the arrogance of the "intellectual elites in New York," claiming they feel they're "so darn right" on everything.

As hectic as Bush's schedule was, family always came first, and his private diary reflects a politician who was always a husband and father first. Bush even attended his father's seventy-sixth birthday party in May 1971, calling it a very touching occasion and saying "how lucky we are as a family to feel so very, very close."[40]

During his ambassadorship, Bush was well aware of the political chatter about him as a possible replacement for Spiro Agnew in 1972, yet he quickly downplayed it. After all, he had a job to do and was doing it well. "This kind of speculation is no good at all," he said. The vice presidency for Bush was not to be in 1972.

Richard Nixon's re-election victory was nothing short of a landslide; he carried 49 states and garnered 520 electoral votes, crushing his opponent — George McGovern — in the popular vote by a whopping eighteen million votes. Nixon's failed 1960 presidential run against John Kennedy as well as his relatively close win over Hubert

Humphrey in 1968 all seemed like a distant memory to him, and the American voters.

Immediately following his re-election, Nixon directed H.R. Haldeman to inform all Cabinet members that their letters of resignation were to be sent to the White House as soon as possible, where the president would then meet with each member individually. Bush didn't want to leave his UN post, but he also knew very well that it wasn't his choice. His service to the Nixon administration came at the pleasure of the president, and Nixon wanted him to run the Republican National Committee — a position Bush admitted was no fun at all. In a letter to Nixon, Bush said, "As to the Republican National Committee, access to you is all important, trying to gear up for the '74 elections is important . . . You visualize a very different role — getting all politics out of the White House and into the Republican National Committee through its chairman. This I find really challenging. . . . My thanks to you for your friendship and loyalty. I will repay it with hard work and loyalty in return."[41]

Privately, Bush had hoped for another diplomatic post, perhaps the number-two person at the State Department. He had brought himself up to speed rather quickly as UN ambassador when it came to politics on the global stage, relishing his role and determined to continue to expand upon his newfound foreign-policy credentials. But Nixon needed one of his own at the RNC, somebody he could confide in and trust, and he turned to Bush. Initially, it seemed like a relatively safe political appointment; Nixon's landslide victory in 1972 gave him immense political clout, and with Bush being Nixon's personal choice, it gave Bush himself a considerable amount of clout at the RNC. When Bush began his job, the Watergate break-in had already occurred (June 17, 1972), yet the Nixon White House had not been deeply implicated. But it was all about to change as revelations of a cover-up began to surface, putting Bush in an incredibly challenging situation. As Nixon held on for his political life, Bush was in charge of what some called an almost sinking ship, helping to get Republicans elected in a time of great peril for the GOP.

By June 1973, it was becoming clear that the Nixon White House was under siege from the Watergate drama. Senior aides H.R. Haldeman and John Ehrlichman resigned, as did Attorney General Richard Kleindienst, and White House counsel John Dean was fired. Bush agonized over the events, at one point writing to General Alexander Haig, a key Nixon confidant: "People want to believe in the president and the presidency . . . but particularly in party circles, there is a feeling that they must have more information. This is especially true in light of [John] Dean's testimony. I therefore recommend . . . that the president hold a press conference soon. The president should move around the country as much as possible speaking on major issues, meeting party leaders . . ."[42]

Bush remained loyal to Nixon, still hoping the president was not involved in any aspect of Watergate. In a letter to his four sons in July 1974, Bush wrote: "I retain a basic confidence in the president's ability. I respect him still — not at all for the tapes [recordings that implicate Nixon in Watergate] . . . but for his courage under fire and for his accomplishments. I will never feel the same around the president after all of this, but I hope he survives and finishes his term. I think that's best for the country in the long run."[43] Bush's optimism — for Nixon and the country — was dashed as articles of impeachment were adopted by the House Judiciary Committee on July 27,

1974. Nixon was now politically boxed-in, forcing his resignation on August 9, 1974.

Saddened and in disbelief, Bush remembered how President Nixon looked "just awful" the day he left the White House, how the day was covered with an aura of sadness, almost like somebody had died, and how a lot of people probably weren't sure of their political future. With Nixon's resignation and the swearing-in of Vice President Gerald Ford as America's 38th president, speculation immediately began as to who would replace Ford as the new number two. Bush was without question in the thick of it, along with a healthy list of other candidates, including Nelson Rockefeller, New York's long-serving governor. As Ford recalled, he had one overriding criterion for a vice president: it had to be a person fully qualified to step into his shoes should something happen to him as president. Ford tasked Bryce Harlow, one of his political advisors, to evaluate all potential vice-presidential candidates based on points, then to rank them numerically. By the end of Ford's first week as president, the list of candidates that had begun at sixteen, had been whittled down to five.

According to Harlow's evaluation, Bush came in first with forty-two points, Rog Morton, a former chairman of the GOP was second, House Minority Leader Rhodes was third, Tennessee senator Bill Brock was fourth, with Nelson Rockefeller coming in at fifth place, with thirty-five points. Though Rockefeller was technically last out of the five candidates, according to Harlow, he was professionally the best qualified by far with the added strengths of bringing in a strong presence as vice president, having superb resources, while also broadening the president's political base. According to Harlow, the choice narrowed to Bush and Rockefeller, claiming, "For party harmony, plainly, it should be Bush, but generally, that would be construed as a weak and depressingly conventional act, foretelling a presidential hesitance to move boldly in the face of known controversy. A Rockefeller choice would be hailed by the media normally most hostile to Republicans, would encourage estranged groups to return to the party, and would signal that this new president will not be a captive of any political faction."[44]

After assessing Harlow's analysis, Ford ultimately decided on Rockefeller, but made a courtesy call to Bush in Kennebunkport, informing him of his decision. Bush confided in Baker what an enormous personal disappointment it was to not be selected, nevertheless saying, "That was yesterday. Today and tomorrow will be different for I see now, clearly, what it means to have close friends — more clearly than ever before in my life. The sun is about to come out and life looks pretty darn good."[45]

Two days after Ford announced Rockefeller to be his vice president, Bush was in the Oval Office meeting with the president, who acknowledged the decision was very close, and therefore, asked Bush, "What do you want?" A clear gesture that he'd be open to politically accommodating one of the GOP's top figures. Bush spoke about the possibility of chief of staff but was more than willing to continue to broaden his foreign-policy skills.

Bush and Ford eventually settled on China. Bush became a special envoy to China, officially the chief of the US Liaison Office to the People's Republic of China, because at that time, the US did not yet have full diplomatic relations between the two countries, hence, no ambassador to China. Bush recalled, "After much thought, and discussing it with Barbara, I decided what I really wanted to do was represent the United States in China. . . . I felt like China was so important to our future, and a bigger diplomatic challenge than even Great Britain or France."[46]

Bush, eager to learn as much as he could about China, turned to who he called the unquestioned expert on the country — former president Richard Nixon. Bush found Nixon reserved and somewhat distant — understandably so, having recently resigned in disgrace. Nevertheless, the former president acknowledged the importance of China and how it would become a superpower in the next twenty-five years, but he cautioned Bush that the job would be lonely and isolated. On September 16, 1974, Bush officially submitted his resignation as chairman of the National Republican Committee. Soon thereafter, Bush and his wife, Barbara, began preparing for the big move thousands of miles away.

Bush's first thoughts of China were the curiosity of the people — no hostility at all — rather, a true curiousness toward him and Barbara. He spoke about how vastly different life was in China — no expression of freedom, no dissent, a closed society, yet one that Bush acknowledged had made significant progress from what he called "the bad old days with people dying on the streets. . ."[47] In his diary, Bush described the tiny church he attended in a run-down part of town, his climb up Western Hills with Barbara, the beautiful weather, and how pretty the scenery was.

Bush began each day at 6:30 a.m. with a short jog and was provided with a better-than-expected Chrysler car and a driver. America's special envoy to China was busy in the early weeks of his job, making countless calls on Chinese officials — formalities as Bush called it. He made special note of how hospitable the Chinese had been to him since his arrival. Never one to cease communicating with family and friends, Bush stayed in touch through letters. One in 1974, telling Baker, "We're here. We have been for almost four fascinating weeks — weeks filled with a variety of emotions. This is a land of great beauty but also a lot of gray dirt and drabness. . . . It's great and we are very happy here, though both Bar and I miss family, friends, news, even politics. . . . I have been far busier than I thought I'd be — diplomatic calls, calls on Chinese officials. . . . We are well-received here. Kissinger comes in a week or so. . . . We sure miss the Houstonians."[48]

As an American diplomat in China, Bush's mail — especially anything sent internationally — was opened and checked by what he called "some very sophisticated methods. . . . I find this is not unusual."[49]

As envoy to China, it was important to Bush that the Chinese came to understand and trust the United States. Though their two countries were thousands of miles apart and completely different in terms of culture, Bush, ever the optimist, thought it important for both sides to deal openly and honestly with one another. Bush wrote: "We must be Americans. We must be what we are. We must be sure they understand what we are. . . . I think they would appreciate it if we are more frank."[50]

Bush took time to study the history of Chairman Mao and the Chinese way of life, realizing that they are not only open and outgoing but warm and friendly people, and "we should convince them . . . that Americans are not stuffy, rich, and formal."[51] It was quintessential Bush — giving praise to the other side, no matter what the differences were. As his mother told George and his teammates when he was a young boy: always be respectful of the losing team.

Bush's children made their way to China to visit their parents, even engaging in some friendly games of tennis and Ping Pong. America's special envoy to China was beginning to truly understand the Chinese culture, remarking in his diary: "Beginning to feel that the informal style, riding on the bike, the informal dress, the openness with the diplomats and the Chinese may pay off."[52] Bush wrote how one gentleman told him, "You are getting to be a legend in your dress." Another mission man from Italy stated how he couldn't even imagine his ambassador riding a bike (which was one of George and Barbara Bush's primary forms of transport).

Bush voiced frustration with his political post at times, being thousands of miles away from Washington. He wrote that there was admittedly no credit in his work, but he continued on — believing it was possibly an "accumulative thing and you've got to keep digging" — pushing hard to put forth the right impression of America. He had a good staff with him and was highly appreciative of their work helping to develop countless suggestions and recommendations that were dispatched back to the State Department. And though he confided in his diary: ". . . it is hard to 'do' anything. And yet I wouldn't trade it for England, Paris or any of the other posts. . . . I think this is more substantive in one sense and certainly more interesting."[53]

Bush's time as special envoy to China was cut short in 1975 when President Ford reshuffled his administration in a big way. What became known as the Halloween Massacre resulted in seismic shifts in the administration, which included: the firing of Secretary of Defense James Schlesinger who was replaced by Chief of Staff Donald Rumsfeld; the appointment of Dick Cheney — Rumsfeld's deputy and protégé — as the president's new chief of staff; the removal of

Henry Kissinger as national security advisor, which was given to Brent Scowcroft; and the forced early retirement of William Colby, director of the CIA. Colby was replaced by Bush, who first heard the news in a telegram from Henry Kissinger. It read: "The president is planning to announce some major personnel shifts on Monday, November 3rd at 7:30 p.m. Washington time. . . . Among those shifts will be the transfer of Bill Colby from the CIA. The president asks that you consent to his nominating you as the new director of the Central Intelligence Agency."[54]

From special envoy to China to director of the CIA was a political transformation that caught Bush by surprise, and understandably so. Bush wrote back to Kissinger: "Your message came as a total and complete shock. I have followed from afar some of the debate on the agency [CIA]." Bush was well aware that it was, once again, time to "serve his country and his president," now in a much different role, but he was up to the challenge, expressing to Kissinger various professional and personal concerns that should be considered if he was to be confirmed as director of the CIA.[55] Specifically, Bush wanted to be able to freely pick his top deputy and support staff, as well as have "free and direct access" to President Ford, along with assurances that the agency continue to be well financed, even as it was presently suffering a public-relations nightmare as many of its activities were made public through a series of leaks and the work of investigative journalists. In closing, Bush asked Kissinger to thank President Ford for such an honor, stating he would "work his heart out" for the agency.

As Bush wrote in his diary: "Although I would not become director of the CIA until January [1976], it immediately overwhelmed our lives. Everything else became almost secondary, even finishing my job in China. The CIA was awash in controversy, accused of everything from assassination plots to attempts to overthrow governments. And suddenly, I was to be in charge."[56]

The CIA crisis in the mid-1970s was simply extraordinary. The office of the director of Central Intelligence (DCI) had been a revolving door, with Bush set to become the sixth DCI in just eleven years. The crisis began when then CIA director James Schlesinger — responding to reports of CIA misconduct — commissioned a series of reports known informally as the "Family Jewels." Almost 700 pages of responses from CIA employees to a 1973 directive from DCI Schlesinger asking them to report activities they thought might be inconsistent with the agency's charter.[57] The report ultimately found its way to investigative journalist Seymour Hersh, who revealed some of its content in the *New York Times*. The result was a series of congressional inquiries led by US House member Otis Pike and Senator Frank Church that severely damaged the CIA's public image and its pride.

As the inquiries from Congress continued, the Ford administration came to believe that William Colby — DCI from September 4, 1973 to January 30, 1976 — had disclosed more information to Congress than was necessary. The missteps and ensuing scrutiny had left the agency paralyzed, unable to effectively execute its responsibilities. This was the very agency George Herbert Walker Bush was now being asked to serve as its director.

Bush prepared for his confirmation hearings, which were to take place just before Christmas 1975, clearly aware of some of the charges that would be leveled at him: he was too partisan; he would not stand up to the pressures of the White House; and he had no experience in the intelligence world.

As to being too partisan, Bush wrote in a draft of his opening statement, "I think it is wrong to suggest that a person who has participated in purely partisan politics cannot set that aside and be fair and independent of partisan politics when he or she embarks on a new undertaking."[58]

Bush also wrote that he would ensure that the CIA would be free from domestic politics, and while director, he would not attend political meetings, nor would he discuss domestic politics as it related to himself. He stated that he viewed being head of the CIA as a "negative factor in terms of one's own political future."

President Ford had promised Congress that Bush, if nominated and confirmed as DCI, would not be selected as a candidate for vice president of the United States in 1976, something Baker felt was unfair and politically boxed-in his good friend. Yet Bush agreed, writing in his prepared statement: "I will say that I am not a candidate for vice president. I will not discuss this matter with my political friends. I will not encourage any such talk directly or indirectly, and I state here and now I am not seeking the vice presidency, and to the degree there has been public speculation about it, that speculation should end. I am not available."[59]

As to the charge of no experience in the intelligence world, Bush wrote that he might "have to plead part guilty to this charge." Nevertheless, he had served in what he called two important diplomatic assignments, both of which afforded him access to CIA analysis materials. "I think I have a clear picture of what good intelligence can do and should do." Bush also pointed to his two terms in Congress and his business experience as worthy credentials, stating he intended to provide strong and forceful leadership to the agency.

Bush noted in his diary that just prior to his confirmation hearings, he received a letter from former president Nixon offering some advice. "What you have been through before will look like a cakewalk to what you will now be confronted with." He told him not to over-promise, and thereby "give away the store" during his hearings. According to Bush's diary, Nixon told him "to stand up for the CIA and its important work."[60]

On January 30, 1976, the United States Senate confirmed Bush as director of Central Intelligence by a vote of 64 to 27, and he was sworn in immediately. While Bush's confirmation hearing produced no meaningful controversy, it was the largest ever "cast against" votes [27] for a DCI's nomination to date, but it had nothing to do with Bush, and everything to do with the disenchantment that Congress had with the agency itself.

BICENTENNIAL BLUES

Baker was just five months into his new job as undersecretary of Commerce, having left behind his law practice in Houston for the politics of Washington, when he started working on Ford's re-election fight against Ronald Reagan for the GOP nomination.

Baker said he got his first taste of campaign trench warfare — on the national level, at least — during the primary campaign. "I went on the campaign trip to Texas with President Ford, and on the way back, he asked me to go over to the PFC, the President Ford Committee, to become the delegate hunter in the nomination fight with Ronald Reagan. And that was because his delegate hunter Jack Stiles had been killed in an automobile accident." As Ford's new delegate hunter, Baker succeeded in the most important way possible —

garnering just enough votes to fend off Reagan and ultimately secure the nomination for the president. It was the last contested nomination decided at a national convention.

Baker, a political novice, performed admirably, something that didn't go unnoticed by the president, or his chief of staff at that time, Dick Cheney, who was instrumental in bringing him on as the delegate hunter. A close friendship was forged, both personal and political. Baker admits that Cheney taught him everything he ever needed to know about fly fishing — and quite a bit about politics.

Rogers Morton, then the secretary of Commerce for whom Baker worked, was transitioning out of his Cabinet position to become the PFC's second chairman, leading the president's re-election efforts. But it was a bumpy road from the beginning for Morton due to a series of not-so-flattering media stories and quotes by Morton himself. And Morton's health was failing; he died just three years later from prostate cancer.

By late August 1976, with President Ford down by as many as twenty-five points against Georgia governor Jimmy Carter, he announced a campaign shakeup. Baker, who just twelve months earlier had been practicing law 1,400 miles away in Texas, was to replace Morton at PFC, giving Morton a symbolic role as the leader of a new campaign steering committee. As Ford recalled, "Rog Morton had been ailing for months, and he didn't feel that his health would allow him to continue on as chairman of the PFC. Jim Baker had demonstrated an outstanding organizational capability as our chief delegate hunter, so he would be a fine replacement to run the campaign."[61]

How badly was Ford trailing Carter when Baker took over as PFC? In Ford's memoir, he wrote how the top brass for the campaign huddled together in Vail, Colorado, for a week-long working session to reboot the president's election efforts, noting: "The latest Gallup poll put Carter ahead . . . 56 to 33. The Harris survey gave him an even wider lead of 61 to 32. Our pollster, Bob Teeter . . . projected that I could lose the election by 9,490,000 votes. There were seventy-three days left until November 2nd. All I had to do to win . . . was convert 130,000 Carter supporters every day."[62]

As that team strategized together in the basement of their rented chalet, Baker led the efforts to help stop the bleeding by trying to derail Carter's momentum that seemed to continue to increase. Baker had a more than competent team to assist in his efforts — Bob Teeter for polling, Bill Greener as campaign spokesman, Dick Cheney as the liaison between the White House and the PFC, Doug Bailey and John Deardourff to create Ford's ads, and Dean Burch for campaign-debate negotiations. Additionally, with new election campaign spending limits in place for the general election — which were set at $21.8 million (a meager sum by today's standards) — Baker confided to the media in Vail, "The candidate who makes the wisest use of dollars is going to win the election."[63]

Carter's massive lead was attributed to a number of well-known reasons. Ford's pardoning of Nixon was controversial to many voters, to say the least, and Carter had effectively positioned himself as an outsider in the post-Watergate era. The Ford White House had also stumbled at times in terms of presenting an image of a president in full command as the administration found itself besieged by congressional hearings time and again. But perhaps one of the biggest reasons, as Ford wrote in his memoirs, was that the "Reagan challenge [for the 1976 GOP presidential nomination] had required an awful lot of time, money, and energy. It had forced me to take some positions that I suspected would hurt me in November and it had delayed some substantive achievements."[64]

When once asked if Reagan's campaign challenge ultimately made Ford a better candidate, Baker replied, "I think you could argue that it might have, yes. . . . He [Ford] became a damn good candidate. I thought he was an extraordinarily good candidate."[65]

Baker's strategy for Ford was multifaceted. First, create a campaign theme built on trust, and under this umbrella, talk about jobs, affordable healthcare, and reducing crime — issues that American voters cared deeply about. Second, create an effective strategy built on campaign appearances and media advertising to ensure the messages resonate with voters. Third, find a viable path to 270 electoral votes — the number needed to win the election — and allocate resources to states that Ford had to win. As Ford himself recalled, "Carter's strategy was to campaign in the North . . . while retaining his strong southern base. Somehow, we had to find a crack in that strategy. For us, the South was a long shot. Florida was touch and go; the only southern state we felt sure we could win was Virginia. The West, with the exception of California, where we were far behind in the polls, seemed strong for us. Ohio was a question mark, but the Middle West appeared to be friendly. Our problems were in the Northeast and the Middle Atlantic states."[66]

For Baker, it was an electoral challenge, indeed, something made even more problematic as Carter, governor of a southern state, was polling extremely well in reliably Republican southern states. For starters, Baker spearheaded the campaign strategies that were agreed to during the meeting in Vail, one of which was to challenge Carter to a series of debates. As Baker recalled, "I think that was a successful campaign strategy, I do. I think he [Ford] had to do something to shake it up. As I told you, when I took over as chairman of the President Ford Committee, we were twenty-five points behind. That was in August. It was there at that session in Vail where I think he threw the challenge out [to debate Georgia governor Jimmy Carter]."[67]

Baker ultimately led the efforts to organize the all-important presidential-campaign debates — the first since Senator John F. Kennedy debated Vice President Richard Nixon in 1960. As became a central strategy in Baker's debate demands, Carter's camp agreed to Baker's request to have both candidates standing throughout the debates. Baker wanted to portray the physical difference in height between the two men — President Ford was just over six feet while Carter only five-foot-nine. Baker used the same strategy in all future campaigns from 1980 to 1992 for Reagan and Bush. Interestingly, Baker had the taller candidate (Ford in 1976 and Reagan at six-one in 1980 and 1984) until 1992 — as both Bush and Bill Clinton were six-foot-two.

As Ford recalled the first debate, "These were to be the first debates between party nominees since 1960 and the first ever to involve an incumbent president. All of us knew the stakes were high — an audience of between 80 million and 100 million Americans would be watching — and all of us realized that first impressions would be critical. Millions of votes could be decided during the first half hour of the first debate. I was confident that I could win."[68]

Baker vividly remembers Election Day 1976. "We knew the Gallup was even going into Election Day. . . . We started getting the exit polls and they didn't look real good. We went over to share them with the president at 4:30, 5 o'clock in the Oval Office . . . And the president didn't seem to be too upset about that. He said, 'Well, those are just exit polls.' . . . We were very hopeful . . . but we still lost so very narrowly. I remember thinking to myself at 3 o'clock in the morning, the morning after Election Day, 'This is the most bizarre thing in the world. Seven years ago, I was a Democratic lawyer in Houston, Texas, and now I have run a campaign or been chairman of a campaign for an incumbent Republican president in the closest presidential election of my lifetime.'"[69]

Baker bluntly noted: "Look where he came from in the general election, twenty-five points behind in August and dead even on Election Day. Lost by only 10,000 votes out of 81 million votes that were cast. You'd turn 10,000 votes around in Ohio and Hawaii and Ford would've been elected."[70]

POLITICAL GRAVEYARD

Reflecting on the tumultuous political climate of the mid 1970s in Washington, much has been discussed about Bush being sent to what he called "the political graveyard" at the CIA, a move supposedly orchestrated by one of his chief rivals in the Republican Party, Donald Rumsfeld. Both men had served in the US House of Representatives and risen through party ranks in various positions, and both were on the short list of potential candidates to be Ford's vice president in 1974. Ford had also chosen Rumsfeld to be his chief of staff, a position Bush had lobbied for, but lost.

They were, in many regards, the future of the Republican Party, so a certain element of competition between the two men was obvious. Rogers Morton, the secretary of Commerce at that time, flatly told Bush, "I think you ought to know what people up here are saying about your going to the CIA. . . . They feel you've been had . . . Rumsfeld set you up . . ."[71] Yet in meetings with both President Ford and Rumsfeld himself, both men denied the allegations.

Baker knew all too well that Bush wanted to run for president someday, so taking the position as director of the CIA seemed to be a major detour. He wondered if Americans would ever accept a former spy chief as chief executive. Bush ignored his friend's advice and took the job, noting that it was a profoundly important position, and that President Ford had personally made the request. On the rumor that Rumsfeld had sent Bush to the CIA, Baker said, "If true, removing George from the scene [of one day running and becoming president] could only have helped his [Rumsfeld's] chances."[72]

Bush's perceived exile to the CIA, in all fairness, was more a part of the complexities of the Ford White House than anything else, and not the doing of Rumsfeld, the young, brash political operative of the Nixon and Ford administrations. In fact, it was just one of the many changes President Ford decided to make, including a move to help diffuse a potential political spat in the making with Henry Kissinger. Kissinger had just been stripped of his title as national security advisor, that role going to Brent Scowcroft. Ford had initially decided to nominate Bush as secretary of Commerce and Elliot Richardson as director of the CIA. At first, the reshuffling made sense. Bush had a strong business background, an essential ingredient for running the Commerce Department, and Richardson had served in a high-ranking Cabinet position already as attorney general, and briefly before that as secretary of Defense. But Ford changed his mind when Kissinger made it known he preferred Bush at the CIA and Richardson, with whom he was not particularly warm, at Commerce, an agency with which he [Kissinger] had little interaction. Fine, according to Ford, so the switch was made.[73]

Bush found his new role fascinating and demanding. Well aware that the CIA had suffered incredible indignities in recent years, Bush knew he had to change the image of one of America's most revered agencies. In a memo to all CIA employees, dated March 12, 1976, Bush wrote: "As Director of Central Intelligence, I am determined that the Central Intelligence Agency conduct its activities in strict adherence to its legislative charter, to applicable laws, Executive Orders, and appropriate National Security Council Directives. Only by such adherence both to the spirit and letter of the law can the Agency continue to serve the People of the United States by properly carrying out its mission to contribute to the national security."[74]

In an excerpt from a speech Bush gave early into his tenure as DCI, admitting that while not a seasoned intelligence operative — he had only been DCI for a mere six weeks — he gave immense praise to the dedication and competence of the CIA employees. Bush called them "professionals in the finest sense of the word," men and women with remarkable skills.

Bush also spoke of the need to work with Congress at all times but emphasized the importance of not divulging certain pieces of information that could jeopardize the agency. Just as Americans respect confidentiality at the ballot box, the country also needed to understand the importance of secrets for the greater good of the country in terms of safety and security.

He went on to say, "The agency indeed made some mistakes in the past. I am not here to defend them. But I am here to tell you that the agency itself rooted out those errors and put an end to them well before they were publicly revealed. . . . Let me tell you another thing I have learned about the CIA," he continued. "Its employees have very deeply ingrained pride and loyalty. They also have an extraordinary sense of duty."[75] He led by example, and his dedication and diligence garnered him great loyalty.

Sadly, the public never came to know many of the great successes of the CIA. "We do battle with kidnappers abroad; we struggle against a network of narcotics peddlers who try to spread their poison in our country. . . . Every one of those things could affect you personally as well as our greater national interests. . . . I wish you could all have the chance to feel the spirit and pride I feel in the intelligence community."[76] Charged with getting the CIA back on its feet, Bush worked long and hard to restore the integrity of the world's most famous spy agency.

Six months in as director, Bush had kept himself extremely busy, making thirty official appearances before various committees in Congress, along with an additional thirty-three meetings with congressional members. Bush wrote to the president of his activities, stating that while working very diligently in an effort to cooperate with Congress, having to report to seven different congressional committees was simply too much. Though eager to accommodate Ford's request for congressional oversight of the CIA, Bush found both chambers of Congress generally unwilling to work with him. But even with all the bureaucratic distractions of dealing with Congress, Bush confidently reported to President Ford the agency's many accomplishments early into his tenure as DCI.

First, relations between the CIA and the State Department had improved noticeably, thanks in large part to Henry Kissinger's and Larry Eagleburger's involvement. Second, Bush gave a thumbs-up to the president regarding CIA morale, which was greatly improving, as twelve changes were made in the top sixteen slots at the agency. According to Bush, the changes helped revitalize top management, all "with a minimum of personal and institutional heartburn."[77]

As DCI, Bush met regularly with all station chiefs — the top CIA officials in charge of operations in the US embassies abroad — something fundamentally important for boosting morale and also learning more about the inner workings of intelligence. With the agency now getting what Bush called "first-class support" and also building an excellent working relationship with the National Security Council (NSC), the CIA was changing course under its new director, yet there were still major concerns plaguing America's premier spy agency.

Bush was gravely troubled about disclosure — giving up too much of the CIA's secrets. He expressed concern about the never-ending congressional oversight measures, and the "continuous erosion which gives away classified materials at home and complicates our liaison relationships abroad." Bush wrote that he was "frustrated by our inability to deal with the leaking of classified information."[78]

Extremely worried about the negative press coverage of the agency, Bush wrote: "I want to get the CIA off the front pages and, at some point, out of the papers altogether; thus, I have turned down many national media opportunities. . . . It is still almost impossible to have a speech containing positive things about CIA given prominent coverage."[79]

Lastly, Bush wrote to Ford regarding the congressional mood toward the CIA, explaining that, while improving, there were still lingering effects from the recent scandals, even noting, "There is still a staff-driven desire to 'expose' and to 'micro-manage.' . . . The staff at the House Appropriations Committee, on the other hand, gives appearances of wanting to run the CIA."[80]

As DCI, Bush found himself working longer hours than ever before, and unlike his prior appointments, which allowed him to speak openly with Barbara as he unwound from the day, this was not the case as the CIA's top official. Who was running for what political office was in sharp contrast to what telephone lines the Soviet Union spy agencies were tapping, such topics being off limits at home, causing Barbara — with all the children grown and gone — to suffer from a severe bout of depression that tested her resolve like never before.

While Bush soldiered on as DCI, the 1976 presidential election seemed to come out of nowhere for him. With the Republican Convention underway in Kansas City, Bush spoke of a certain nostalgia in seeing all of his political friends gearing up for the much-anticipated fall election, admitting, "I have a twinge of regret — but only a twinge, for this work [director of CIA] is fundamentally important, and I comfort myself with the fact that I am very lucky to be here and to be surrounded by so much excellence."

At Governor Carter's request, Bush, as director of the CIA, was asked by President Ford to brief his prospective rival on various intelligence matters, a rather unusual request, as Carter had not officially received the Democratic nomination. Presidential candidates had been given intelligence briefings *subsequent* to their nomination for decades, but not before. Ford agreed to Carter's request and dispatched Bush to meet with the soon-to-be nominee. In writing about his meetings with Jimmy Carter, Bush spoke of how the briefings had gone quite well, how the CIA officers with him during the briefings had done an excellent job, and how Rosalynn Carter, the governor's wife, "fixes sandwiches for us. Amy [governor's daughter] runs around playing with the cat. It's all very homey, but there is no nonsense about the governor. I am having difficulty trying to figure out what the heartbeat really is there."[81]

Bush found time to write to friends who simply didn't understand why he was briefing Carter on intelligence issues. Bush spoke of following orders, and how President Ford had instructed him to give Carter a series of meetings to bring him up to speed on sensitive matters. "I am strongly in favor of this presidential decision. We are living in tough times and any candidate for president must be up to speed on where things actually stand in the world. If we don't have these kinds of briefings, Governor Carter would have to rely on the [news]papers and other sources."[82]

Carter ultimately prevailed over President Ford in the 1976 presidential election, forcing Bush to ponder his own future — once again. Bush called to congratulate Carter after the win, recognizing he was no longer speaking to just a candidate, but to the president-elect, the man who would be commanding America's nuclear arsenal — and all of its intelligence secrets — in just over two months. Bush reluctantly tendered his resignation at that time, agreeing to step down when the new administration took office. Shortly thereafter, Bush headed to Plains, Georgia — Carter's hometown — on November 19, 1976, with a half-dozen CIA agents for a comprehensive briefing that also included Vice President elect Walter F. Mondale.

After the exhaustive briefing, Bush found it strange that there had been no comments or questions from either Carter or Mondale. Carter "registered no emotion of any kind, asked for little follow-up, and frankly, seemed a little impatient at the end of my presentation of these items. Perhaps it was because he knew that there was a full plate waiting for him in the next room of several more hours of briefings." In closing, Bush gave Carter one last piece of intelligence that could only come from the nation's top spy official. "I emphasized the need to be very careful using the telephone. I gave him some indication of the Soviet capabilities to read phone calls . . . and to penetrate in many ways."[83]

Though Bush had accepted the political fact that his resignation as director was a foregone conclusion — he began to second-guess that presumption when the issue came up again during their meeting. Though he chose to make a case for continuing as director of the CIA, Bush ultimately agreed that it was the president's decision, therefore, he would officially resign. Why the change of heart from Bush? Because he realized that he truly loved the job, craved the knowledge he was gaining of the intelligence world, and believed he was making a sincere difference.

In a parting letter to the CIA, Bush thanked the countless men and women for their efforts, stating, "It's time to go now, and yet it seems as if I have just begun. I am leaving, but I am not forgetting. I hope I can find some ways in the years ahead to make the American people understand more fully the greatness of the CIA."[84]

Next stop for the Bushes? Back to Houston, Texas, for some soul-searching on what George Herbert Walker Bush would do next. Barbara couldn't have been happier to return to Houston, which they did in January 1977, but she also knew the boundless energy of her husband and wondered what would be next for him. What would make George happy? Bush wrote in his diary: "After being gone for ten years, Barbara and I moved home to Houston. I was sad to leave the CIA, a job that I loved. But it was great to get back to Texas. Now my main challenge was to figure out what came next in my life."

By 1977, Bush's political résumé and service to his government were noteworthy, indeed, thus, finding business opportunities was the least of his concerns. Bush found himself turning offers away — board seats and advisory roles (he ultimately joined the boards of Eli Lilly and Texasgulf) — and musing about not wanting to "slip into that three- or four-martini late dinner, rich social thing. There is too much to learn still."[85]

What did Bush ultimately want? He wanted the presidency. Of that, there was little doubt. "I think I want to run or at least be in a position to run in '80 — but it seems so overwhelmingly presumptuous and egotistical; yet I'll think some on that."[86]

Between January 1977 and well into April 1979, Bush was a man on the move, traveling the world, meeting with foreign dignitaries, speaking on the growing economic concerns of the country — activities you do when considering a run for the nation's highest political office.

Barbara couldn't help but notice the enthusiasm and spirit of her husband, noting as they entered 1978 that it had become even more apparent that George would eventually run for president. She wrote to several media contacts: "What a man is my great George, he is getting better about 'blowing his own horn' — a thing we were taught as children never to do. But a thing you must do if you want this job. He is uniquely qualified, and I am sure more than willing to tell people why. The one thing that he has done that none of the rest of them have done is he founded and made a success of a company that has business around the world. He knows what it means to meet a payroll, work with all government rules and regulations, and he also knows how to wrestle with tough problems and make it work. You don't need a lecture about my George, but when you add his business experience to his many government jobs that he did well, it just adds up to the right person at the right time for the job."[87]

During Bush's tumultuous travels and activities as he prepared himself for the 1980 presidential campaign, his eldest son, George W. Bush, and his close friend Jim Baker entered the political arena with their own names on the ballot. George W. had never held elected political office, yet decided to make a run for Congress in 1978, ultimately challenging a well-known and well-liked Democratic state senator, Kent Hance. George H.W. Bush expressed great hope for his son's race, writing to a GOP consultant that George W. Bush "is off and running in Midland. The party poohbahs are not too thrilled, but the guy is energetic, attractive, he grew up in Midland and has lots of friends. I'd say he is an underdog now, but he'll acquit himself well, I'm sure. I'm tickled pink about this."[88]

In the waning days of the campaign, thousands of voters received a letter in their mailboxes from Lubbock attorney George Thompson III. It began, "Dear Fellow Christians," then went on to describe a Bush campaign ad in a university newspaper that promised free beer at a Bush campaign rally. "Mr. Bush has used some of his vast sums of money . . . to persuade young college students to vote for and support him by offering free alcohol to them."[89]

Five days later, Hance bested Bush in the 19th Congressional District, 53 percent to 47 percent, a bruising campaign that George W. Bush remembered as, what he called, his first confrontation with cheap-shot politics, but also the last race the eventual 43rd president of the United States would ever lose.

Though George W. Bush may have lost to Hance, according to longtime friend Don Evans, "What stands out in my mind was the extraordinary amount of energy he was able to generate. . . . I remember driving through the neighborhood and seeing a sea of campaign signs. They didn't just show up by themselves. That takes a lot of organization and a lot of volunteers."[90]

That very same energy shown by son George was soon exhibited by the father himself as he began his march toward the GOP nomination for president in 1980. Endless campaign events, twenty-plus-hour days, hundreds of interviews — and more — it was all headed George H.W. Bush's way as he crisscrossed Iowa in the early primary season.

In 1978, Baker was also running and gunning for his first politically elected seat — attorney general of Texas. He ultimately lost to eventual Texas governor Mark White, who beat Baker 55 percent to 44 percent.[91] Bush had wanted him to run for Texas governor, instead — something Baker, having formerly been a declared Democrat, opposed as he was not confident he could raise the money needed as a Republican. Furthermore, it was going to be difficult to defeat a conservative incumbent Democrat, Dolph Briscoe. Yet Briscoe went down in defeat in the primaries, losing to John Luke Hill, who ultimately lost to Bill Clements — the first Republican governor in one hundred and five years.

Baker had assumed his run for attorney general would be against Price Daniel Jr., a liberal Texas Democrat with a long political lineage in the Lone Star State. That didn't happen as Mark White, who resigned as Texas secretary of State to run for the attorney general office, defeated Daniel in the Democratic primary. Ever the organizer, Baker had letters ready to mail to all Mark White supporters who had contributed $50 or more, asking them to back Baker and not Daniel, but with White's surprise victory, the letters had to be destroyed. As Baker recalled to a reporter from *Texas Monthly* in 1982, "The same thing happened to me that happened to George Bush in 1970. . . . He filed to run against [liberal] Ralph Yarborough and wound up running against [moderate] Lloyd Bentsen. I planned to run against Daniel and wound up against White. We were both aiming for liberals, because in Texas, a Republican still has a hard time against a conservative Democrat — unless you're Bill Clements and you throw in four and a half million dollars of your own money."[92]

With a different opponent than originally expected, Baker pushed forward, campaigning against a man who shared similar political views — and friends — in the Houston area. With his new baby daughter Mary Bonner Baker often by his side at the endless campaign events and fundraisers, Baker quipped: "I'm one of the few politicians who brings his own baby to kiss." The race ultimately came down to party identification. Baker also brought in the biggest of the GOP big guns. Ronald Reagan, Gerald Ford, Jack Kemp, Bob Dole, and of course, George H.W. Bush all made campaign appearances for Baker.[93]

Other big-name Republicans also gave their support to Baker — John Connally and Reagan aide Lyn Nofziger. Baker respectfully thanked them and took their support, but also made it clear that his loyalty was to George Herbert Walker Bush, if Bush indeed decided to run for president in 1980. Though Baker lost to White, he was good-spirited about it; a true gentleman throughout it all, someone who got to "see what it's like on the other side" as a losing candidate.

He accumulated campaign debt, something he regarded as a stain against his name and credit, but it was quickly paid off, thanks to generous donors who were more than willing to help their fellow Texan. In fact, the donations exceeded his campaign debt, giving Baker the opportunity to send partial refunds back to his donors. Baker's wife, Susan, recalled, "When those checks went out, it was one of Jimmy's proudest moments in politics. . . . I've never seen anything make him happier."[94]

Baker may have lost what was the only campaign for elected office with his name on the ballot, but what he gained was undeniable. His thirst for the political world was growing, and it came calling again when his close personal friend threw his hat in the ring for the presidency in 1980.

George H.W. Bush, circa 1925.

James A. Baker, III, circa 1930.

George Bush, Summer 1940.

Lt. James A. Baker, III, USMC, circa 1952.

Jim Baker (at far right) poses with fellow members of his tennis team, circa 1945.

Doubles Champions Jim Baker and
George Bush smile for the camera
at Houston Country Club, circa 1967.

Bush addresses reporters at the opening
of his Harris County Bush for Senate
campaign headquarters. 1970.

Jim Baker with his wife Susan. August 1973.

Jim Baker works on his volley shots. June 1981.

George Bush sneaks in a bit of topspin on his opponent at Walker's Point. August 1989.

Vice President Bush shakes Alexander Haig's hand as he arrives at the Situation Room, joining Ed Meese (L), Jim Baker (R), and others after the assassination attempt on President Reagan. March 30, 1981.

President Reagan, recovering in the hospital after the assassination attempt, signs papers for Jim Baker. April 1981.

Jim Baker, carrying his daughter Mary Bonner, enjoys the events at the White House Easter Egg Roll. April 1982.

President Reagan walks the White House Colonnade with James Baker, George Bush, Ed Meese, and Michael Deaver. June 1982.

Three former presidents join President Reagan and James Baker at the White House prior to Ford, Carter, and Nixon going to Egypt to represent the US at Anwar Sadat's funeral. October 8, 1981.

Jim Baker reviews documents with President Reagan in the Oval Office. February 1984.

President and Nancy Reagan pop some champagne with Jim Baker to celebrate winning their campaign for reelection. November 1984.

President Reagan announces that Chief of Staff James A. Baker, III and Secretary of the Treasury Don Regan are trading positions in his administration. January 1985.

President Reagan and Jim Baker engage in conversation in the Oval Office. July 1987.

CHAPTER THREE

No. 2

GEORGE HERBERT WALKER BUSH ANNOUNCED HIS CANDIDACY for president of the United States on May 1, 1979. By then, he had built a formidable résumé — US congressman, ambassador to the United Nations, chair of the Republican National Committee, special envoy to China, and the 11th director of the CIA. Yet with all the political accolades, he was not considered the front-runner for 1980; that went to former California governor Ronald Reagan, who lost a very close contest to then incumbent president Jerry Ford for the 1976 GOP nomination. In losing to Ford, Reagan had ultimately set himself up as the unquestioned front-runner for 1980, and with miserable economic numbers and a presidency in peril for Jimmy Carter, it was becoming increasingly clear that whoever the Republicans nominated for president, Carter was a relatively easy target in the general election.

Bush may have officially launched his campaign on May 1, 1979, but he'd been planning a run for president years earlier. According to

Baker, while he had been resting and unwinding in Florida following his loss in the 1978 Texas attorney general race, Bush called him and said, "Let's get cracking," asking Baker to start working on Bush's 1980 presidential run. It meant cutting back on his law work. And why not, he asked rhetorically. "I was ready for a change from the grueling . . . and, at that point in my life, less challenging practice of law."[95]

The man who just two years earlier had been the top operative in President Ford's quest for re-election became Bush's campaign manager. Though Ford had ultimately lost, the grit and dogged determination shown by Baker throughout the general-election season became well-known in Washington. Bush had his man for the top slot, his close friend, but more important, a tried and proven campaign manager who'd been through the toughest of political battles at the highest level.

Ever the disciplined professional, Baker's first task was to put forth specific budget projections, which he completed in January 1979. A year later, following Bush's upset victory over Ronald Reagan in the Iowa caucuses, Baker confidently showed his aides how his fundraising projections had fallen within 0.7 percent of the actual first-year revenue, with spending off by only a scant 9 percent. The Houston lawyer-turned-political-operative turned out to be an operational maestro, and quite the accountant.[96]

Baker described the extraordinary relationship that these two men had built by 1980, one that became even stronger as the years went on. "I've always given him my unvarnished advice. . . . I think he said that I'm the one person who always told him exactly what I think — even when I knew he didn't want to hear it."[97]

Bush had limited national appeal and minimal campaign funds, but he poured every ounce of energy into the Iowa caucuses, visiting all ninety-nine counties, many of them more than once. If there was an event in Iowa, you could almost count on Bush being there. From countless chamber of commerce meetings to county fairs, picnics, barbershops, and more, Bush gave Iowa his all, outworking and out-hustling the Reagan campaign. As son and former president George W. Bush recalled, his dad "held dozens of campaign events. He talked about the struggling economy, rising inflation, and declining American power abroad."[98]

Dorothy "Doro" Bush, George H.W. Bush's daughter, remembers Baker telling her, "It took one hell of a lot of courage after having done the jobs he did to step out and run for president when you have no name ID, no ability to really raise a lot of money. A candidate is sometimes the lowest form of human life. Everybody's an expert in politics, and it just took one hell of a lot of courage, and your dad had that courage."[99]

Presidential historian Jon Meacham, looking back on George H.W. Bush's career, underscored the relentless drive, determination, and selflessness that we've all come to appreciate of the former president. "Can you name a former director of the CIA who's a plausible presidential candidate? No, you can't. George Bush knew what he wanted to do and never gave up. To be chairman of the Republican National Committee during Watergate . . . to lose two Senate races, which is so painful. To emotionally keep going — to keep getting back up. The great politicians always do that. . . . George Bush kept getting back up and running, always with dignity, always with grace. He had no enemies, which is amazing when you think about it . . . with both

Nixon and Ford . . . it was always, what important job can we find for you? Because he was a very loyal, intelligent man."[100]

Iowa was a family affair, with Barbara Bush also visiting all ninety-nine counties, along with enlisting the Bush children whenever they could. Marvin, Bush's youngest son, spent an entire year in Iowa doing all he could to help his father's campaign by giving speeches to crowds anywhere he could speak, sometimes to groups no larger than a dozen people.

In the fall of 1979, Bush began keeping a campaign diary, documenting the rigors of being on the road. As the Iowa caucuses loomed, Bush wrote: "I think I'm putting on a little weight. I got to run only once this week, and that was in Iowa. The food varies. . . . What I like are the barbeques. . . . I saw Barbara twice this week: once in the middle of the night at Des Moines, Iowa, and once briefly in Indianapolis. She's working hard and getting good press. I am awfully proud of the children and what they are doing."[101]

In another campaign diary entry, Bush wrote: "I'm so digging in, so tense . . . I have no time to think about relaxation. Just this one goal . . . no time to think at all. . . . Drive, drive forward. I'm surprised my body can take it. The mind is still clear, although I totally lose track of where I've been and whom I'm with. I've given up on names. . . . determined to push on. . . . I don't want to look back and find that I've left something undone."[102]

Even with Reagan being anointed the front-runner status for the primaries, Iowans seemed to like what they heard from Bush, enough so that he won the caucuses with approximately 32 percent of the vote, edging out Reagan. It was a huge victory for a candidate who had limited national name recognition when compared to the actor-turned-politician Reagan, and overnight, it changed the dynamics of the race. Bush was reinvigorated, claiming he now had the "Big Mo" [momentum] on his side and was ready to take the New Hampshire primaries by storm. Reflecting back on Iowa, Baker notes: "Politics is beating expectations. It's one advantage we had; our expectations were incredibly low. Our candidate was an asterisk in the polls . . . I think he may at one point just before the Iowa caucuses have polled something like two or three percent, but that was all."[103] Bush turned himself from an asterisk into a major contender with his surprising Iowa victory over Reagan. An enthusiastic Bush proclaimed, "We'll do even better there . . . in New Hampshire . . . there'll be no stopping me." But one victory in the primaries doesn't equate to being the nominee, and with Bush riding high on his Iowa win, the Reagan camp dug in, hitting the ground and the airwaves in the Granite State in hopes of stealing Bush's Big Mo, while also plotting what Baker called a political "ambush" on Bush.

Bush was confident, writing to a supporter: "The Iowa results were tremendously heartening, but there's a long way to go yet before the convention. Still, I'm getting more and more confident of winning both the nomination and the election."[104]

With Reagan looking to regain momentum against Bush, both men agreed to a second debate in Nashua, New Hampshire — but with conditions. It would only be Reagan and Bush in attendance, a strategy devised by the Reagan camp to "cut George down to size." Naturally, the other GOP contenders objected to being excluded from the debate, and the Federal Election Commission (FEC) agreed, thus the Reagan camp suggested that they and the Bush campaign share the costs for the debate, $1,750 each. The Bush camp said no, ultimately a "big mistake," according to Baker.

As the debate in Nashua drew closer, now fully funded by the Reagan campaign, his staff told the other candidates — Howard Baker, Bob Dole, Phil Crane, and John Anderson — that if they came, they might be included in the debate. On the day of the debate, Bush was the first candidate on stage, then Reagan appeared — accompanied by the other four candidates. Caught off guard, Bush sat quietly as Reagan paraded the other candidates up to the stage, then amid the applause and momentary confusion, moderator Jon Breen requested that Reagan's microphone be turned off. What came next was one of the campaign's most memorable moments as Reagan snapped back, much to the delight of the crowd — and the four candidates behind him — "I am paying for this microphone, Mr. Green."[105] Interestingly, lost amid the cheers from 2,500 people in attendance was Reagan's misspeak of Breen's last name.

Regardless, as Bush sat stoically in his chair, Reagan's eight simple words gave New Hampshire voters a glimpse of his character. In a state that prides itself on its independence — as evident by its motto of "Live Free or Die" — Reagan regained the momentum that night. The results of the debate between Reagan and Bush as the other four candidates left the stage? As Bush press aide Pete Teeley told Bush afterward, "The bad news is that the media are playing up the confrontation. The good news is that they're ignoring the debate, and you lost that, too."[106] Bush also lost the New Hampshire primary to Ronald Reagan, with the former California governor garnering 49.6 percent, and Bush a distant second at 22.7 percent. Recalled

Andy Card, a close Bush operative, "There were false expectations that the Big Mo would sweep us past Ronald Reagan, who was the presumed front-runner. . . . The Big Mo lost its momentum in New Hampshire."[107]

Bush's Big Mo had been dashed, returning him to underdog status as the Reagan juggernaut picked up steam, winning a string of primaries and positioning the California governor to eventually secure the nomination. Bush fought back, taking critical primaries in Connecticut, Pennsylvania, and Michigan, but losses in Texas and other pivotal states simply put the nomination out of reach. The campaign was also low on funds. At one point, Baker came to Pete Teeley and said, "Pete, we're out of dough and I can't pay you." Pete flatly said, "I don't care. I'll just be a volunteer, and we'll just go through with it."[108] Teeley remembers getting a letter in the mail from Bush thanking him for all his efforts: "He's [Bush] on the road, he's working like hell . . . twelve, fifteen, eighteen hours a day — and yet he finds the time to write this lovely note to say thanks *again*. I was really touched by that."[109]

Ever the fierce competitor, Bush wanted to soldier on to California in hopes of somehow upending Reagan in his home state. Baker was adamant that Bush drop out, and soon. Baker told Bush that by staying in, he was hurting his chances of being chosen as Reagan's running mate.

Speaking with reporters, Baker said a win in California, Reagan's California, would be "goddamn tough." He then told David Broder and Bill Peterson of the *Washington Post*, "If you can't do California, then you can't argue to people that you still have a shot [at the nomination] in terms of the numbers. And once you concede that, why do you stay in?"[110] The media took that statement as a signal that Bush was withdrawing from the race. Bush was furious at Baker's comments, but even so, both the candidate and his campaign manager knew the reality of the race, and Bush had to make a decision, and soon. According to Baker, his message to his close friend was clear, "Look, we've got to fold this thing. We don't have any money; it's time. You've got to get out."[111] And with relations between the Reagan and Bush camps already tense, and also mindful that the vice presidency — if even offered — was no doubt appealing, Bush officially dropped out of the race on Monday, May 26, 1980 — one day before the California primary.

Never one to give up, in his prepared statement, Bush said, "I have never quit a fight in my life. But throughout my political career — as a precinct worker, a county chairman and national chairman — I have always worked to unite and strengthen the Republican Party. . . . In that spirit, earlier today, I sent the following message to Governor Reagan: CONGRATULATIONS ON YOUR SUPERB CAMPAIGN FOR OUR PARTY'S 1980 PRESIDENTIAL NOMINATION. I PLEDGE MY WHOLEHEARTED SUPPORT IN A UNITED PARTY EFFORT THIS FALL TO DEFEAT JIMMY CARTER. . . ."[112]

"What I'll admit to, but George never will," said Baker in 1981, "is that the Veep thing was always the fallback. It was always in my mind. That's why, at every opportunity, I had him cool his rhetoric about Reagan."[113]

With the Republican Convention just seven weeks away, Bush was unsure of his political future. He had gone from front-runner status after upending Reagan in Iowa to dropping out of the race. Regardless, he headed to Detroit to fully support Ronald Reagan and his platform. Bush's schedule at the convention was filled with receptions, meetings, lunches, and dinners — activities one would expect for a highly visible candidate who'd finished runner-up to Reagan for the GOP nomination. Yet he was still unsure as to what his chances were — if any — of being chosen by Reagan.

Bush was a logical choice for some obvious political reasons. He had battled Reagan toe-to-toe in the primaries, earning his own hard-fought victories against the former California governor, so he had name recognition and visibility throughout the country. His decision to withdraw from the presidential race was made out of respect for the party and himself, and because ultimately — truth be told — he knew the race had been lost.

Yet Reagan descended onto the convention with what Baker called an "Anybody But Bush (ABB) motto," and when talk of a Reagan–Ford ticket started leaking out, Bush knew his chances had just become even slimmer.

The idea of a Reagan–Ford ticket in 1980 seemed enticing, exciting, and from internal GOP polling data, an almost surefire way to defeat Carter and Mondale. But to some, including Baker, the idea of Jerry Ford — a former vice president-turned-president — returning to the vice presidency seemed almost absurd. Baker thought to himself, "How would I even address Ford? 'Hello, Mr. President–Vice President.' Or was it, 'Hello, Mr. Vice President–President?'" But for two men who'd had a less-than-amicable political relationship over the past four years, it seemed bringing them together for what many were calling a co-presidency — at least in Ford's mind — was a most improbable task.

The idea of a Reagan–Ford ticket met its doom quickly when Ford took to the airwaves in an interview with Walter Cronkite in which the former president declared, "If there is to be any change, it has to be predicated on the arrangements that I would expect as a vice president in a relationship with a president."

Baker recalled later, "As I watched the interview, it really hit me that we had some major problems with the idea [of Ford being vice president]. *Wait a minute,* I remember thinking, *this is really two presidents he's talking about.*"[114]

But Baker wasn't alone in thinking that a Reagan–Ford ticket made no sense. Nancy Reagan thought the idea was absurd. "I didn't see how a former president — any president — could come back to the White House in the number-two spot. . . . It would be awkward for both men and impractical, and I couldn't understand why that wasn't obvious to everybody." Nancy told her husband, "It can't be done. It would be a dual presidency. It just won't work."[115]

Bush's eldest son, George W. Bush, also believed the idea made no sense at all. "No former president had ever returned as vice president, and I did not see how the sitting president could agree to share power with a predecessor."[116]

Barbara Bush remembers walking over to the convention hall with Baker's wife Susan and witnessing all the commotion unfold as Ford completed his interview with Walter Cronkite. "Jerry hinted he would consider being the vice-presidential candidate, under the right circumstances. We were confused about what was happening," Mrs. Bush recalled.[117]

In his heart, and politically, Baker knew that his friend was the obvious choice. As Baker saw it, there were so many positives for Bush — a proven candidate who won more than three million votes in the primaries against Reagan, an exemplary record of public service, and also a moderate when compared to Reagan, something essential for balancing the ticket in the upcoming general election.

Listening to his closest advisors, most of all, his wife and most ardent protector Nancy, Reagan saw that this was his time, which meant a break from the past — and no co-presidency. He would choose his own vice president, on his own terms, and George Herbert Walker Bush fit the role naturally, but it wasn't a love affair initially. Reagan had a certain degree of skepticism as to whether Bush would fully embrace and adopt his policies if chosen as his running mate. The Reagan camp vividly remembered a day in April 1980 when then candidate Bush described the former California governor's economic plans as "voodoo economics."

According to Chase Untermeyer, who served as executive assistant to Vice President Bush, "This really put the Reagan camp up in arms, creating a level of resentment that never really went away," at least not until Reagan was shot.[118] Years later, when pressed by a reporter regarding "voodoo economics," Bush denied ever using the phrase. According to Untermeyer, it was a classic example of Bush moving beyond the past and not reliving moments that he now deemed insignificant. This was especially true when it came to anything associated with political positions taken during the 1980 GOP primary race against Reagan. "He didn't live in the past. He would move on and move forward."[119]

Reagan also felt Bush should have shown more resolve regarding the Nashua debate and letting the other candidates participate. That, according to Reagan biographer Lou Cannon. But that characterization wasn't shared by Baker, who would remind us all about Bush's accomplishments. Let's not forget the ideals of a man who became a young naval aviator, turning away a career of Wall Street riches to serve his country. And let's not forget a man who moved halfway across the country to start a business in an industry he knew little about. Bush had resolve, lots of it, but according to Baker, "these facts about the man [Bush] seemed to matter little" at the time of the 1980 Republican Convention.[120]

He could have easily fought to the bitter end, but why? And political pundits agree that this gesture alone was clearly on Reagan's mind when looking for a running mate. According to Untermeyer, "When Henry Kissinger's earnest effort to repeat past glories in shuttle diplomacy failed to achieve an agreement by which a former chief executive [Jerry Ford] could comfortably serve as vice president to another, Reagan turned to George Bush."[121]

Baker remembers what happened next. It was July 16, 1980, just after 11:30 p.m. and the phone rang in Bush's suite, room 1912 of the Pontchartrain Hotel. Baker answered the phone. It was Drew Lewis, a former Ford operative now working for Ronald Reagan. Lewis said that Reagan would like to speak with Bush, who, of course, accepted the call. After a brief discussion, Bush turned to Baker and others in the room, smiled, and gave a thumbs-up. Bush became the 1980 vice-presidential nominee for the Republicans, joining his former rival for the general election. Reflecting back on the night Reagan offered Bush the number-two spot, Baker recalled, "If he hadn't gotten that call, he has said, and I believe firmly, there wouldn't have been a Bush 41. And if there had not been a Bush 41, Bush 43 has said there wouldn't have been a Bush 43. And I believe that, too."[122]

BACK IN CAMPAIGN MODE

With Bush joining Reagan as his running mate, the Reagan camp wanted Baker on board. As they saw it, as the architect of many of Bush's victories against Reagan in the primaries, his political skills would be a valuable asset against Carter and Mondale. Reflecting in his memoirs, former president Jerry Ford commented, "Baker had little or no political experience — originally, he'd come to Washington to be Rog Morton's deputy at the Department of Commerce — but he possessed a superb mind, he was an excellent organizer who got along with everybody and worked around the clock."[123] William Casey, Reagan's longtime confidant, actually approached Baker in June 1980 in hopes of getting him on board for the general election, which he agreed to, but only on terms Baker considered acceptable.

Battle-tested by now, courtesy of running Ford's 1976 presidential campaign and Bush's 1980 GOP primary campaign, Baker proved invaluable in helping Reagan throughout the critical months of August to November 1980. Baker joined the team as a senior advisor to the campaign, with Bush's vice-presidential campaign run by Dean Burch.

Baker was not afraid to solicit advice early on in the campaign, regardless of his, at times, strained relationship with Reagan's campaign chairman William Casey. On one particular occasion, Baker wrote a letter to Governor Reagan, telling him, in part: "You have not asked for these comments, and having managed two presidential campaigns, I am well aware that the one thing a candidate receives too much of is unsolicited advice." Reagan, as Baker recalled, never took the advice as a criticism. He was comfortable and confident in himself as a candidate, always listening and welcoming such information.

Baker's role expanded during the general campaign to include serving as the debate negotiator with the Carter camp, as well as prepping Reagan for the debates. Though Carter decided to skip the first debate, both camps ultimately agreed to an October 28, 1980, showdown between Reagan and the president, but after a series of back-and-forth discussions in the Reagan camp, they were rethinking the idea. Polls were showing Reagan surging ahead of Carter, so why create a misstep with a debate against a sitting president that could trip up Reagan's lead?

But Baker wanted the debate and pushed for it. As he saw it, voters needed to be reassured that Reagan wasn't just an actor, someone who fell into the California governorship with nothing more than his celebrity-status image and memorable one-liners from films. Baker wanted to showcase to the American electorate the man he'd come to know in a short period of time; an intelligent, hard-working, thoughtful, and pragmatic man — someone who could be trusted with major domestic and international challenges that would no doubt come Reagan's way. Baker was also wary of an October Surprise, something consequential that could ultimately derail Reagan's quest for the presidency, such as the release of the fifty-two American hostages that had been kidnapped by the Iranians at the US Embassy in Tehran on November 4, 1979.

As the debate grew closer, America got a glimpse of both candidates on stage — but not the debate stage. It was the annual Al Smith Dinner in New York, a rich tradition where both parties' candidates for the presidency joke and lightly jab one another. Carter disappointed, coming off cold and distant, while Reagan warmed the crowd with his charming demeanor and famous grin. The dinner was a prelude to what played out at the only presidential debate between the two men less than two weeks later.

With the election just days away, all major polls showed Reagan ahead of Carter, and with Reagan's debate performance less than a week earlier, all signs indicated a victory for the former actor-turned-California governor. Reagan made no major mistakes, kept to his script of major themes, and hit Carter repeatedly on the economic malaise, at one point famously stating, "There you go again," after the president seemed to unnecessarily delve into details defending his domestic policies. While the average listener that night became lost in the complexities of Carter's analysis, they no doubt took note of Reagan's catchy one-liner aimed at the president.

In what's considered one of the stronger and more memorable closing statements in debate history, Reagan took aim at Carter by telling Americans, "Next Tuesday is Election Day. Next Tuesday, all of you will go to the polls; you'll stand there in the polling place and make a decision. I think when you make that decision, it might be well if you would ask yourself, are you better off than you were four years ago? Is it easier for you to go and buy things in the stores than it was four years ago? Is there more or less unemployment in the country than there was four years ago? Is America as respected throughout the world as it was? Do you feel that our security is as safe, that we're as strong as we were four years ago? And if you answer all of those questions yes, why then, I think your choice is very obvious as to who you'll vote for. If you don't agree, if you don't think that this course that we've been on for the last four years is what you would like to see us follow for the next four, then I could suggest another choice that you have."[124]

As for a vice-presidential debate between Bush and Mondale, it was not to be. Far from a political tradition (the first such debate had been just four years earlier in 1976, *Mondale vs Dole*), Bush, following a recommendation from the Reagan camp, chose not to accept the invitation from the debate sponsors, the League of Women Voters, labeling vice-presidential debates as strictly minor league: "We're the Toledo Mud Hens," he quipped. According to Bush's press secretary, "Let's face it: the only way we're going to make national headlines is if we screw up."[125] So America had to wait another four years for the next opportunity to hear a vice-presidential debate, when Bush debated Geraldine Ferraro, the first female vice-presidential candidate representing a major American political party.

On November 4, 1980, Ronald Wilson Reagan, age sixty-nine, became president-elect of the United States with a landslide victory over incumbent Jimmy Carter. Reagan's victory was stunning in terms of his margins, carrying a hefty forty-four states, a colossal 489 electoral votes, and a popular-vote margin of victory of 8.5 million votes. The election was a stinging rebuke of the Carter–Mondale era that just four years earlier had been elected in one of the closest presidential contests in recent memory.

But that was 1976 and this was 1980, and Baker was part of something special, very special. Not only had he become a central figure in the Reagan campaign of 1980, he also watched his close personal friend elected the 43rd vice president of the United States.

Inauguration Day — January 20, 1981 — witnessed yet again the peaceful transfer of power in our great democracy as Reagan was sworn in as the 40th president of the United States. Baker remembers Bush quipping to him that day, "Bake, whoulda thunk?" After all, just five and a half years earlier, Bush had reached out to Baker in a letter telling his Texan friend: "I just got a call from Rog Morton querying me on you for undersecretary of Commerce. The job would be a good one, and Morton would be good to work for in my opinion."[126] Five years later, Baker became President Reagan's chief of staff, a position regarded by many as the second most powerful job in Washington.

ONLY THE PRESIDENT LANDS ON THE SOUTH LAWN

Bush clearly understood his new role as vice president — supporting President Reagan's policies of lowering taxes, strengthening the military, and removing government as the obstacle to get the economy moving again. The first of Bush's five core rules while serving as vice president was *There is only one president.* The spotlight wasn't his — it was Reagan's, and Bush did all he could to ensure America's 40th president was successful.

Bush was initially looked upon with skepticism by the Reaganites. Was the East Coast transplant who now called Texas his home a true conservative? Was he simply chosen because Reagan and former president Ford could not agree on terms for a possible co-presidency scenario? That skepticism was erased in short order when President Reagan — having been in office for only seventy days — survived an assassination attempt on the afternoon of March 30, 1981.

Eager to catch a glimpse of the president of the United States, a group of onlookers — probably no more than fifteen feet away from Reagan as he exited the Washington Hilton Hotel — had gathered behind the security ropes. Walking in stride, with his Secret Service detail shadowing every step, President Reagan flashed his signature grin while happily waving to the crowd on a gloomy day in the nation's capital.

Seconds later, shouts of *Hello, Hi,* and *Welcome, Mr. President* from bystanders were completely drowned out by the horrific rapid fire of a .22 caliber pistol that unleashed a fury of bullets in under two seconds. Secret Service Agent Jerry Parr had trained for years, preparing for the unthinkable, the unimaginable — that an assassin would attempt to kill the president of the United States — and his instincts told him what to do. In an instant, Parr hurled Reagan into the heavily armored presidential limousine and headed to the safest place he knew, the White House.

"Get out of here! Go! Go! Go!" Parr shouted to the driver, fellow agent Drew Unrue. And with the rest of the motorcade still curbside, Unrue sped off. "Someone really tried to kill the president," thought Parr.[127]

Meanwhile, three other men lay wounded: Press Secretary James Brady, Secret Service Agent Tim McCarthy, and District of Columbia police officer Thomas Delahanty; all victims of a crazed gunman by the name of John Hinckley Jr. As trained, Parr quickly checked Reagan for possible wounds from Hinckley's barrage of bullets, and though he saw no visible bullet entry, purplish frothy blood began to appear in Reagan's mouth — oxygenated blood.

In a split-second decision — one that ultimately changed the course of history and saved the president's life — Parr told Unrue to head directly to George Washington Hospital. Reagan was in serious medical trouble, and Parr knew it.

Bush, just over two months into his term as vice president, was more than 1,500 miles away in Texas, undertaking various political events, when word reached him. He had just taken off from Carswell Air Force Base in Fort Worth when US Secret Service Agent Ed

Pollard informed him of the incident. "Sir, we've just received word about a shooting in Washington," he said. "There is no indication that the president has been hit."[128]

That proved false.

It wasn't until Bush received a coded message from Secretary of State Alexander Haig that he learned the grave news that Reagan had in fact been shot and was in serious condition. "Mr. Vice President: In the incident you will have heard about by now, the president was struck in the back and is in serious condition. Medical authorities are now deciding whether or not to operate. Recommend you return to DC at the earliest possible moment."[129] Air Force Two refueled in Austin and headed back to Washington, DC.

Stunned, Bush thought to himself, "How could anybody work up a feeling of sufficient personal malice toward Ronald Reagan to want him dead?"[130] Less than a decade earlier, President Ford had survived two assassination attempts, and less than eighteen years earlier, John F. Kennedy had been gunned down in cold blood — a stark reminder of just how real — and serious — the current situation with Reagan was.

Adding to the chaos and confusion of the day was Al Haig's rather awkward statement to a pressroom full of reporters: "I am in control here at the White House, pending return of the vice president [Bush]."[131] It appeared to portray Bush as seemingly irrelevant and insignificant in one of the nation's darkest hours, a blunder of epic proportions made by Haig that sent the completely wrong message to the country.

Bush was aware that all eyes were on him to assume control as Reagan underwent surgery to remove a bullet that had lodged dangerously close to his heart. Though security was an issue, indeed,

Bush did not have Marine Two land on the South Lawn. "Only the president lands on the South Lawn," he insisted, instead landing at his residence at Number One Observatory Circle and taking a relatively small motorcade to 1600 Pennsylvania Avenue. When he arrived, there was no scolding of Haig for his ill-advised comments, rather, he settled in and joined other senior White House officials to discuss next steps.

As fate would have it, President Reagan survived the attempt on his life, and Bush continued serving as America's vice president. But during those haunting hours on March 30, 1981, the country — and the entire world — learned something about Bush. They saw a man with principles, integrity, and a clear loyalty to his president. And a man ready to do whatever was necessary to lead the country, had President Reagan lost his life. The once doubtful Reaganites — always mildly suspicious of Bush — changed their tune. They saw a man with true candor, somebody who acted with honor and distinction when the survival of America's 40th president was in question.

Baker vividly remembers that fateful day. He had been so busy that he'd had to tell Mike Deaver, "I just can't go" to the AFL-CIO meeting at the Washington Hilton. Deaver went in Baker's place, later recalling, "The press started asking their usual questions. I turned and moved [Jim] Brady up because he was the press secretary. I took three steps. Then the first shot went over my shoulder. I knew what it was. . . . I smelled the powder."[132]

Baker first heard of the shooting from David Gergen, the White House staff secretary, but it was still unclear what had happened and who had been shot. That all changed when Mike Deaver called Baker, informing him that doctors had found a bullet hole in Reagan's coat, and according to Dr. Daniel Ruge, who was on the call with Deaver, the president had lost a tremendous amount of blood. Baker, along with Ed Meese, immediately headed to George Washington Hospital, arriving just after 3:00 p.m. Reagan was wearing an oxygen mask, yet ever the optimist, gave both men a wink and asked, "Who's minding the store?" Ever the jokester, then came the famous line he dropped on Nancy that made headlines throughout the world: "Honey, I forgot to duck." Regardless of Reagan's upbeat attitude, Baker was traumatized by how pale and feeble the president appeared, a stark difference from the man who'd shown so much stamina and vigor since the start of his presidential campaign.[133]

Once again, presidential succession was on the minds of millions of Americans, including Baker. Would Section 3 of the 25th Amendment have to be invoked? Ratified in 1967, Section 3 states: "Whenever the president transmits to the president pro tempore of the Senate and the speaker of the House of Representatives his written declaration that he is unable to discharge the powers and duties of his office, and until he transmits to them a written declaration to the contrary, such powers and duties shall be discharged by the vice president as acting president."[134]

As Baker saw it, "It would be difficult to transfer power to George Bush during the surgery. More important, we [he and Ed Meese] didn't think the transfer was medically required, even though the president would be under anesthesia."

In 2015, former president Bush agreed to an email interview with the *Dallas Morning News*, recounting the events of that ominous day. "I recall thinking about Nancy and the president when I first heard how bad the situation really was," Bush told *The News*. "Even though it was still early in the administration, I didn't think about them as president and first lady, but rather as friends." [135]

Alan Peppard, who wrote the extensive article on the events of that day, summed it up perfectly. "Vice President George H.W. Bush's pitch-perfect reaction to the crisis lies largely unexplored in the shadow of history. He had only recently been Reagan's energetic opponent, a fact that was fresh in the memories of Reagan loyalists. The steady hand he showed after the assassination attempt would linger in the minds of his admirers as one of the defining moments of his public career." [136]

THE BUSH VICE PRESIDENCY

On Bush's vice presidency, Baker notes: "He [Bush] was a very loyal vice president. He understood the job. He knew how it was supposed to be performed, and he performed it that way. He never let himself be juxtaposed against the president. He kept his advice to the president private. He didn't throw it out there in public means, because he knew that there's nothing that's secret here in Washington, DC." [137]

Baker also recalled, "Once I became the White House chief of staff, I was in a position to help him [Bush] because I was in a more powerful position than he was, and I made sure that he had the office in the West Wing there that . . . [Walter] Mondale had had. I made sure that he had a weekly lunch with the president. I was in a position to make sure that he was included in meetings that the vice president should be included in. And so, it was a case of little brother being able to repay big brother in fairly important ways." [138]

Baker shared with a reporter that Bush often said, "The one thing I like about Jim Baker is he'll tell me what he thinks, even if he knows

I don't want to hear it." Reflecting on the memory, Baker said, "I like that, and that's really quite a compliment. But the way that would play itself out is we would have these arguments, and finally, after we'd been going back and forth for a while, finally he'd look at me and he'd say, 'Baker, if you're so goddamn smart, why am I vice president and you're not?' I knew that's when the conversation was over." [139]

Bush was quite clear on his role as vice president, listing five core rules to abide by: (1) There is only one president; (2) No political opportunism; (3) No news leaks; (4) All interviews must be on the record; (5) The vice president owes the president his best judgment.

During his first two years as vice president, Bush's role was limited, and he kept a low profile as Reagan and Baker were busy hammering Congress for sweeping tax cuts for families and businesses. Yet he began to spread his wings, embarking on a seven-nation tour in hopes of persuading NATO allies to station ballistic missiles in their countries. Over a ten-day trip, Bush sprinted through West Germany, the Netherlands, Belgium, Italy, France, Great Britain, and Switzerland. It was an international success for the country, the Reagan White House, and for Bush, personally. The *Washington Post* heralded the consensus, running an article titled, "George Did It," on February 13, 1983.

While the economy was still struggling throughout much of 1982 and 1983, the tide turned in a big way as economic numbers began to drastically improve in early 1984, perfect timing for Reagan and Bush who were seeking re-election against Democratic nominee and former vice president Walter Mondale and his running mate, New York congresswoman Geraldine Ferraro.

With soaring economic numbers and America feeling very good

about herself, it seemed as if a landslide was in the making, possibly as big as — or even bigger than — Richard Nixon's 1972 victory. Yet Reagan stumbled badly against the fiery Mondale in the first debate. His sentences were broken at times. Long pauses and confusion seemed to set in as he tried to hit back at Mondale. The former vice president won the first debate hands down, but in the second and final debate, Reagan bounced back with one-liners and zingers that confidently set aside concerns regarding his age and health.

Bush looked forward to this vice-presidential debate. It was a historic event; the first-ever vice-presidential debate to include a female — Geraldine Ferraro — on a major ticket. "We tried to kick a little ass last night," said Bush, after the debate. In an era of conservatism and coming from someone usually known for his rather correct tone, Bush's remarks created some political drama, yet he refused to apologize. "I stand behind it. I use it all the time. . . . My kids use it. Everybody who competes in sports uses it." Bush quickly noted that Ferraro would understand because "she's a good competitor."[140]

To the American public, they saw a tough and determined vice president not afraid to step outside the political boundaries in hopes of giving voters a better taste of who George Herbert Walker Bush was — and could be. Throughout the spring and summer of 1984, and into the general election, Reagan and Bush enjoyed a comfortable lead in the polls — and it showed on Election Day. The victory was simply staggering. Reagan bested Mondale in the Electoral College 525 to 13 votes. The popular vote victory was just as impressive — Reagan defeated Carter's former vice president by almost seventeen million votes. It was a landslide of epic proportions, something rarely seen in presidential elections.

With Reagan and Bush being sworn in for a second term, the whispers began immediately in Washington. Would Bush be next? Could he secure the Republican nomination in 1988 and continue the Reagan Revolution as the 41st president of the United States? November 8, 1988 — the next presidential election — seemed like an eternity from January 1985, but not to Bush, and not to his new incoming chief of staff, Craig Fuller.

History wasn't on Bush's side; vice presidents of the past who then sought the presidency had failed miserably. While a handful had ascended to become America's president — the more notable being Teddy Roosevelt, Calvin Coolidge, Harry Truman, Lyndon Johnson, and Gerald Ford — it was because of the sitting president's death or resignation. Not since Martin Van Buren had a vice president actually won the presidency.

As Bush's second term as vice president began, he told his chief of staff, "I know I need to change," in reference to becoming a much more visible, transparent, and "presidential" face to the American electorate. For a man who, for many years, had aspired to be president, this ultimate political prize was now within reach. Fuller admitted that Bush himself had initial doubts about winning, but Fuller confidently encouraged him. "You'll be ready when the time comes, and you'll have all the opportunities to secure the nomination."

Fuller believed, as did Baker, that Bush had to step out of Reagan's shadow, essentially reintroducing himself to the American public. The economy was strong, and Bush had served Reagan admirably for their first four years, but he could not expect to ride the coattails of Reagan to victory in 1988. Baker explained, "So when he [Bush] started running for president, he had to separate himself somewhat.

It couldn't be seen to be a third — in effect, a Reagan term. And he successfully did that, the first time anybody has done it since 1836, a sitting vice president to get elected president."[141]

Baker extolled his friend's credentials, calling Bush's résumé unquestionably one of the best — ever — of any candidate for the presidency. From Bush's exemplary education to his service in the military, a successful oil executive, a US congressman, a foreign-policy liaison to China, director of the CIA, and a highly engaged vice president — Baker knew his old friend was more than ready for the challenges of the presidency. And Baker was proud of Bush, a man of immense decency. "They say that integrity is doing the right thing when nobody knows. It's also doing the right thing when the only person who knows is your friend. And in our countless hours of playing tennis or golf, shooting quail and dove, downing Otto's barbeque, visiting each other's families, and doing both politics and public service together, I never saw him cut a corner or do anything disreputable. He always went by the book."[142]

Baker knew Bush would have a list of challengers fighting for the nomination, including New York congressman Jack Kemp. Kemp was young, charismatic, and a former star quarterback for the then Los Angeles Chargers. Baker remembers giving a speech on Michigan's Mackinac Island in 1986 and being concerned about how organized Kemp was in Michigan. "There were Kemp fliers on all the chairs and everything else. When I got back to the White House — I was Treasury secretary — I called the vice president, and I said, 'I really want to talk to you about something — and bring Barbara.' The three of us met in his office, and I said, 'You know, it looks to me like this guy's really gearing up. I mean, I go out there, and this is a governmental event and everything — hell, there are Kemp campaign fliers all over.' It was something of concern to me. . . . That's the first time I remember talking to the vice president about the '88 campaign."[143]

Between '86 and '88, Baker was occupied with his responsibilities as secretary of the Treasury. There were some challenging initiatives on his plate, from fighting back protectionist legislation in Congress to various budgetary issues. Though he followed his friend's primary battles and offered advice when he could, he wasn't engaged in the campaign itself.

With all the noise surrounding the upcoming Democratic Convention, Baker suggested that he and Bush get away from DC. "We went on a pack trip on the north fork of the Shoshone River in the Absaroka Mountains in northwest Wyoming. We spent about three or four days up there fishing, so we didn't have to listen to Ann Richards talking about silver foot in the mouth and all that. It was really a very good thing to have done."[144]

Dukakis won the Democratic nomination, and Bush prevailed over Kemp, Dole, Dupont, Haig, and others — ultimately securing the 1988 Republican nomination for the presidency — but there were a few bumps and bruises along the way. Bush had begun the 1988 election cycle with a dismal third-place finish in the Iowa caucuses, losing to rival Bob Dole and even bested by televangelist Pat Robertson, who finished in second place. But Bush rebounded by trouncing Dole and all other rivals in the Super Tuesday primaries held on March 8, 1988. "George won sixteen out of sixteen primaries. . . . That sewed it up [the nomination]," recalled Baker.[145]

With the nomination essentially locked up for Bush, no one in the campaign expected any surprises at the convention in New Orleans, but a little drama unfolded as a little-known senator from the heart of the Midwest became Bush's running mate.

Prior to the convention, Bush had narrowed his list down to just a handful of candidates — Alan Simpson, Pete Domenici, Bob Dole, Elizabeth Dole, and Dan Quayle. Domenici pulled himself out and Simpson — being pro-choice, which was contrary to Bush's position — withdrew his name, but Bush still had plenty of choices. Picking Dole or Kemp made sense for a number of reasons, but probably first and foremost was that both men were candidates Bush had defeated for the nomination, much like Reagan defeated Bush eight years earlier. That would tell the American public that Bush, just like Reagan, had no problem picking a former rival.

Both Bob Dole and Kemp were well-known to the country. Dole a seasoned senator who had run — and lost — as the vice-presidential nominee in 1976. Kemp was the handsome, engaging, silver-haired former NFL quarterback-turned-US congressman with widespread appeal to the conservative base. Elizabeth Dole, an incredibly capable politician, would have been just the second woman ever chosen for vice president on a major ticket. Geraldine Ferraro had been the first, just four years earlier. And then there was Dan Quayle, the handsome, boyish-looking senator barely known to not only the American public, but many in the press corps.

The political pundits were confident they'd see a Bush–Dole or Bush–Kemp ticket, creating little drama and fanfare with Bush's selection. According to Baker, "The only time I remember weighing in [on the vice-presidential search] was during that Wyoming camping trip with George in mid-July [1988]. I remember that I thought Bob Dole and Dan Quayle were the most logical choices."[146] But Bush kept his pick to himself, all the way up until the final hours when a choice had to be made.

As Baker recalled, the choice made by then vice president Bush was his, and his alone. "The vice president made the selection. He made it clear he was going to make the selection. He made it clear he wanted to do it in a way that did not subject the potential candidates to undue prying or embarrassment or that sort of thing. So, we compartmentalized the review process that Bob Kimmitt ran. I picked Kimmitt for that. He did a great job, I think. But nobody saw the material that the potential candidates supplied Kimmitt, except the vice president. And he didn't make his selection until either the day before or on the airplane going down to New Orleans [for the 1988 GOP convention]."[147]

According to Craig Fuller, "We had a bet, and I chose Pete Domenici of New Mexico. James Baker, I believe, assumed it would be Kemp. But obviously, it ended up being Quayle."[148] They were both wrong. In fact, almost all the political experts were wrong.

Bush's surprise choice of Indiana senator James Danforth "Dan" Quayle made the forty-one-year-old Quayle the first-ever baby boomer on a major ticket, a pick that Bush kept private — from the American public — until right before Bush's announcement on the deck of the SS *Natchez* under the sweltering summer heat of New Orleans.

The convention in full swing by this time, Fuller had to find Quayle, who was reportedly having lunch at a restaurant in the French Quarter. Next, he remembers telling the head of Bush's Secret Service detail, "We're about to have a US senator that's going to need protection in about two hours."[149]

Quayle and his wife, Marilyn, had to muscle their way through the mob of cheering supporters to board the steamboat. Initially mistaken for onlookers, the Quayles were finally noticed by Bush supporters and joined Bush on deck for what many, including Quayle, considered a hasty announcement that "was not the best-planned episode in political history." As Barbara Bush recalled, "Dan and Marilyn had trouble getting to the platform because they looked too young, and no one realized why they needed to be up there."

Quayle's challenges were just beginning as he faced a blistering onslaught of media attacks not only during the '88 general-election campaign, but unfortunately, throughout his single term as America's 44th vice president.

And Baker, contrary to media reports that reported he was against the Indiana senator as Bush's running mate, had in fact felt Quayle was a solid choice, even stating for the record, "Let me get one piece of old baggage out of the way . . . Dan Quayle was a good choice in 1988. . . . Dan worked hard in the campaign, and more important, served effectively and honorably as vice president, just as he had as a senator from Indiana."[150]

Dukakis proved to be a lightweight in terms of political prowess. As the Bush camp slammed him with a barrage of ads depicting the Massachusetts governor soft on crime and weak on defense, Dukakis failed to counter. Orchestrated in part by Bush campaign strategist Lee Atwater, but always under the watchful eye of Baker, Dukakis found himself playing defense more often than not during the 1988 campaign. Sid Rogich's and Roger Ailes' attack ads resonated with the American electorate, and some were memorable, even downright laughable, especially when it came to depicting Dukakis weak on national security.

Early polling prior to the GOP convention had Dukakis ahead of Bush, but Baker knew that his old friend would regain the spotlight, and new momentum, with his acceptance speech — one that Baker called the "speech of his life." According to Baker, Bush's speech accepting the Republican nomination for president revealed "the George Bush whom I knew and respected, a modest man with the experience to serve as president, with deeply held values, and with a clear and inspiring vision of the role of government in the lives of Americans and the role of America in the world." [151]

The heavy lifting was about to begin in earnest, and Bush wanted his good friend to be steering the campaign. But that meant leaving his post at the Treasury Department. According to Baker, "The vice president and I agreed that I would approach the president [Reagan] and ask him to let me go over to the campaign to help the vice president get elected. The president basically said, 'Well, I think you can do him [Bush] more good by keeping the economy going. We have it going well now, and you're an essential part of that team, and I think it'd work better, perhaps . . .'" Baker recalls that Reagan didn't exactly say no, but nor did he endorse the idea. So, Baker went back and told Bush, "It didn't work, pal. It ain't going to work unless you do it." And he did. "We ended up having a meeting in the residential quarters with Vice President Bush, President Reagan, Nancy [Reagan], and myself. And the president ultimately said, 'Fine. If that's really what you want, George. If that's what you think, and you think you really need him over there that bad, then I'm willing to let him go.' I left in August [to run the campaign]." [152]

And with that, President Reagan and Baker held a press conference on August 5, 1988, in the White House press room to announce

Baker's resignation as secretary of the Treasury. Baker was once again back in the saddle of running yet another presidential campaign. It's a job Baker had done before, and he knew it well. Baker knew how to win, and he also knew that Bush needed a strong and forceful campaign manager to win against Michael Dukakis.

Baker remembers the challenges facing Bush when he joined the campaign as chairman in August. "We were about seventeen or eighteen points behind [Dukakis] in August [1988]. And the general thinking was we weren't going to win that campaign. No sitting vice president had been elected president since Martin Van Buren. It just wasn't done. And I must say that, looking at it objectively, we were rather pessimistic about our chances."[153]

TIME TO TAKE THE UPPER HAND

The Bush team was on a role, but it was determined that, in order to combat the Dukakis smear efforts, they had to fight back a bit. Bush's team put out one of the most memorable ads of the campaign — and arguably one of the most humiliating political attack ads of modern times. With footage showing a 68-ton M1AI Abrams Main Battle tank slowly maneuvering across a field, a laundry list of defense measures opposed by Democratic nominee Dukakis scrolls up the screen, from new aircraft carriers and anti-satellite weapons to the stealth bomber and even a ground emergency-warning system against nuclear attack, and more. Then suddenly, the tank heads straight toward the camera and the viewing audience. The driver — an awkward-looking Dukakis — smiles and points unnaturally before the image stills, the narrator closing with: "And now he wants to be our commander in chief. America can't take that risk."

The awkward outfit (made especially for Dukakis) and the ill-fitting helmet were simply too hard to ignore; a stark reminder of a candidate trying to be something he wasn't. Dukakis's scheduling director, Mindy Lubber recalled, "The second we saw that picture on the six o'clock news, we had pains in our stomach. . . . Regardless of anything that came out of the governor's mouth, we saw the picture, which was Mike Dukakis with his head sticking up in that goofy hat."[154]

While the Bush campaign of 1988 gets credit for crafting such a powerful commercial that resonated with voters, it's the Dukakis camp that wins the dubious distinction of creating one of the biggest campaign blunders in modern times.

How did Dukakis even find himself in one of America's mightiest fighting vehicles? It was a plan orchestrated by his own camp to create an image that simply backfired to unimaginable, laughable proportions. So why the tank ad? According to the Dukakis camp, the Massachusetts governor had a paper-thin résumé when it came to defense, particularly when compared to Bush's heavy-hitting résumé. According to Leslie Dach, Dukakis's communications director, they had to address the issue head on, yet that's about the only thing that campaign headquarters agreed on. A national survey taken by the *Los Angeles Times* prior to the tank campaign event debacle for Dukakis found that Bush bested him 54 percent to 18 percent on which candidate would do a better job of securing the country. According to Dach, "That needed to be addressed, and addressed strongly."[155]

Josh King, who worked on the Dukakis–Bentsen campaign, said, "The image of the diminutive Massachusetts governor pretending to be something he wasn't and, in the process, making a fool of himself on September 13, 1988, has haunted me, as it has every other advance person who has been entrusted — for a few hours or even a few minutes — with a candidate's fate."[156]

Rogich, Bush's chief media advisor, recalled, "We were comfortably ahead in the polls. . . . I questioned whether we should use the Dukakis commercial. I called [campaign chairman] Jim Baker and said, 'I'm just not sure we need it, and wouldn't it be better to close the campaign out on a real positive note?' He said, 'We took a vote, and you lost.'"[157] The commercial aired on October 18, 1988, during the third game of the World Series pitting the Oakland A's against the Los Angeles Dodgers.

The tank ad was just one of a series of blistering attack ads released by Baker during the campaign, proving he was willing to play hardball to get his fellow Houstonian into the White House. But not at all costs. There were lines not to be crossed, and Baker made it very clear the campaign had no association or affiliation with the infamous Willie Horton ad that targeted Dukakis's weekend-release program. It had been wrongly reported as an ad developed and released by the Bush–Quayle camp. Said Baker, "We did everything we could, if you'll look at the news accounts at the time, we did everything we could to get that *Americans for Bush* ad withdrawn. Everything we could. We filed a suit even. Because we didn't want to be associated with those creeps. And yet we were. A lot of the liberal press associated us with them because they didn't like the fact that this prison furlough business cut so hard against their boy [Dukakis]."[158]

Another memorable attack ad that *was* approved by Baker was the *Revolving Door* prison ad depicting Dukakis soft on crime. It showed footage of prisoners — some of them murderers not eligible for parole — literally coming and going through a revolving door as part of Dukakis's weekend-release program. The narrator describes how many of them committed more heinous crimes while on release, and others never returned, ending with the ominous message: "Now, Michael Dukakis said he wants to do for America what he's done for Massachusetts. America can't afford that risk."[159]

DEBATE DEBACLE FOR DUKAKIS

When it came time for the first debate, Baker, a master at staging his candidate, pulled one of his old tricks out of the hat. He insisted that both men walk to the center of the stage to greet one another, bringing to light the immense height difference between Bush at six-foot-two, and the much shorter Dukakis at five-eight. Bush almost had to lean down to shake the hand of Dukakis, an image no doubt remembered by millions of Americans who watched that night.

Baker got what he wanted when it came to the presidential debate negotiations because he quickly saw that Paul Brountas, Dukakis's campaign chairman, a man without a large ego, could nevertheless be wooed. Apparently, complimenting the man was "like throwing gasoline on a fire." According to Thomas Donilon, then a Dukakis aide: "Baker realized he could woo Brountas and did so masterfully. . . . He told Paul [that] he and Brountas were mega-lawyers with a code of honor that transcended the nastiness of mere politics. Paul ate it up."[160]

Baker even went as far as to convince Brountas that Bush was perfectly happy not to have any debates at all, which was never Baker's position. "Once Paul bought that," said Donilon, "the concessions flowed. Any chance we may have had to have Bush and Dukakis actually question each other without a panel was gone."[161] Reflecting back on the strategy used against Brountas to get what he wanted, Baker said, "Let's just say that whatever edge they thought they had, they convinced themselves they didn't have it."[162] According to Democratic operative Robert Strauss, a personal friend of both Bush and Baker: "Baker's absolutely the best I've ever seen at not making enemies. . . . It's not for nothing that he's called the Velvet Hammer."[163]

And all of the GOP top brass of the 1988 campaign knew very well that if they truly needed to get a message through to Vice President Bush, Baker was who they would turn to. "Once, when Bush thought he could go the kinder, gentler route exclusively [one of Bush's key campaign themes was a kinder, gentler nation], we asked Jimmy [Baker] to read him the riot act again," said Roger Ailes, Bush's media advisor. "That was one of the few times I've ever seen him blow up. He said, 'You call him yourselves. You're not the ones who have to carry that message and have him say, 'If you're so smart, Jimmy, how come I'm the one who's vice president?'"[164]

But perhaps one of the biggest blows to Dukakis's campaign came on October 13, 1988, in the second and final presidential debate with CNN anchor and debate moderator Bernard Shaw's opening question for Dukakis: "Governor, if Kitty Dukakis were raped and murdered, would you favor an irrevocable death penalty for the killer?" The question seemed to initially stun the audience as they went silent — even Bush was caught off guard, a serious expression on his face — yet Dukakis's passionless and dismissive response is what millions of voters will never forget.

A staunch opponent of the death penalty, Dukakis responded to the startling question by saying, "No, I don't, Bernard, and I think you know that I've opposed the death penalty during all of my life. I don't see any evidence that it's a deterrent, and I think there are better and more effective ways to deal with violent crime." Yet his body didn't move. He showed no agitation or anger with Shaw for putting such a provocative question into the debate.

Three weeks later, on November 8, 1988, Bush defeated Dukakis in a rout; 426 to 111 in the Electoral College, while also crushing him by more than seven million popular votes.

Later that night, the sixty-four-year-old vice president became president-elect of the United States as Dukakis called to graciously concede the election. For Bush, his victory was personal and fulfilling, indeed, but much like his mother taught him — and his wife Barbara had engrained into their children — humility and respect were paramount. While most politicians winning national elections typically speak of their great victory and the mandate they've been given, Bush reminded voters what mattered to him — family, duty, respect for others. As he stepped up to the podium, the handsome, lanky, six-foot-two president-elect gave out a few thank-you gestures, then told the crowd what they were waiting to hear. "I've just received a telephone call from Governor Dukakis, and I want you to know he was most gracious. His call was personal, it was genuinely friendly, and it was in the great tradition of American politics."[165]

Looking back, Bush's chief of staff, Craig Fuller, said he had expected challenges and surprises during the campaign, that's just the rough and tumble world of politics. From the selection of Dan Quayle as his running mate to fending off questions about his character — was he truly presidential timber? As history shows, the answer was yes. "He had the charisma, the credentials. This was his to win, and win he did."

Ask Baker what really got his feathers ruffled in 1988, and he'll say it was the anti-Bush rhetoric that ultimately backfired on the Democrats when Election Day came. They hit Bush with every possible smear line they could, from calling him a "wimp" to "blue blood" and being born with a "silver foot in his mouth," a phrase Ann Richards made famous. As Baker saw it, they forgot this was a man who passed up Yale to serve his country as the then youngest naval aviator in World War II (Bush was just nineteen years old). This was a man who faithfully served numerous previous Republican administrations in a wide range of roles — not because that's what Bush wanted — but that's what was asked of him. And this was a man who ventured out on his own, thousands of miles away from the comforts of his East Coast upbringing, to make a name for himself. In Baker's eyes, Bush was no wimp, no blue blood, rather, a kind, modest, yet resilient and resourceful man ready to lead the greatest nation on earth.

Many political pundits saw Bush's victory as a way to capitalize on his newfound image, thus, a grand victory speech was in order. But that wasn't Bush. He knew the great challenges that lay ahead, the almost certain perils of the presidency that were to come his way. He had survived political mishaps in the past, and having just ascending to the presidency on one of the most remarkable paths in recent memory, there was no time to gloat. It was time to get to work for the American people.

Years later, in a rather weak attempt to salvage what history would surely call a disastrous 1988 presidential campaign, Dukakis labeled Bush's attacks on him as unfair, a relentless barrage of negativity that ushered in a new wave of political tactics never seen before. The infamous tank ad will forever haunt Dukakis, but truth be told, it was one of the most brilliant political commercials ever devised, and Dukakis knows it. Baker's stance? "I make no apologies for going after Dukakis on prison furloughs, the Pledge, or anything else. He led with his chin on a lot of these issues, and we used them to take him out. Some described what we did as 'going negative.' A better term would be to say that we were showing the 'contrasts' between the candidates, a fair tactic as long as the ads were factual."[166]

As Baker saw it, "When the Democrats nominated Michael Dukakis, they all but elected George Bush." Dukakis "was in fact a classic Democratic liberal in the mold of George McGovern and Walter Mondale. Pick any topic — defense, the death penalty, tax policy — you name it — he [Dukakis] was off to the left. The more the American people knew about him and his core beliefs, the less likely they would be to vote for him for the simple reason . . . that the great majority of Americans don't agree with these policies. Eight years of Republican peace and prosperity made it even harder to pitch the liberal agenda."[167]

It was Bush's third straight general-election victory; two as a vice-presidential candidate, and the third as the GOP nominee. And they were all landslide wins from both the Electoral College and popular vote counts.

Two lost races for the US Senate in 1964 and 1970. Being passed over for vice president during the Ford presidency. The failed 1980 presidential campaign. Questions about his involvement in Iran-Contra. Fighting off the image of the Wimp Factor [a phrase fixated on by select *Newsweek* magazine reporters in 1987 and 1988]. Yes, Bush had his setbacks and challenges, as do all politicians, but with a little luck, timing, and some well-earned Texas toughness, he overcame the naysayers and pundits. On January 20, 1989, the Massachusetts-born, Connecticut-raised Yankee-turned-Texan was sworn in as America's 41st president of the United States.

CHAPTER FOUR

Reagan's Reinforcement

W HEN BUSH BEGAN HIS TENURE AS RONALD REAGAN'S VICE
president, an unlikely person took the reins as Reagan's
incoming chief of staff. That position — often regarded as one of the
most powerful in Washington — did not go to Ed Meese, Reagan's
longtime assistant and chief of staff while governor of California.
Instead, Jim Baker got the nod. The very same Jim Baker who
headed up Bush's failed 1980 presidential campaign for the Republican nomination and served as Ford's delegate hunter against Reagan
four years earlier. As Baker recalled, "I . . . was not only a newcomer
but also a former adversary who had fought hard, twice, to deny
him the presidency. . . . Some of Ronald Reagan's supporters would
have been happier if I had stood outside that door for the next eight
years. He was their hero. I was the enemy as they saw it — someone
from the dark side, lacking credentials as a loyalist to the man or his
ideas." [168]

But Reagan saw past all of this. He wanted someone with experience in Washington as he desperately looked to turn around the Carter era of double-digit inflation, rising interest rates, and an American electorate not feeling too terribly good about themselves.

Reagan and Baker had barely known each other during the 1980 GOP primary battles. Baker first met Reagan in Houston in 1972, when Baker was running fourteen Texas counties for Richard Nixon. Governor Reagan campaigned for him, also holding an event in Houston."[169] Then, in 1978, Reagan went to Texas to campaign for Baker in his race for attorney general against Mark White, which Baker ultimately lost.

Stu Spencer, a key Reagan campaign operative in 1980, told Reagan, "You don't really know him [Baker], so I'm going to put him on the plane, just so you two can talk." It seemed an improbable political partnership, but according to Hedrick Smith of the *New York Times*, "Reagan had seen Baker on the other side, fighting against him, very organized, very disciplined, and that's one way of checking your foe and saying, wow, I'd rather have that guy inside the tent."[170]

Baker recalls Reagan saying, "Jim, I'd like to talk to you before you go back to Texas." The morning after the election and Reagan's landslide victory over Carter, the president-elect offered Baker the job. Everyone in the Reagan camp — save for the top brass and Baker — was surprised. Baker had been tipped off early by Stu Spencer and Mike Deaver that Reagan wanted a political tactician who knew Washington. And as for Ed Meese, Sacramento was not Washington. In addition, both Spencer and Deaver, along with Reagan, felt strongly that Meese would be more valuable in another role. One political insider with years of experience working with Meese said the longtime Reagan confidant was no doubt effective, but he wasn't organized, noting he couldn't even keep his briefcase in order, calling it a bottomless pit.

Baker's wife Susan remembers, "I saw they were recognizing Jimmy's ability more and more during the campaign, especially after the way he handled the debates, and I thought he might be offered a job in the administration. But the chief of staff job is so demanding. I was afraid of it. We'd been married seven and a half years, and we'd just about settled in mixing the families. With the Bush campaign and then the Reagan campaign, well, it was like a whirlwind. I wouldn't trade a minute of it, but it was wearying. I wanted to see more of my man. I wanted him to see more of his children."[171]

Baker says that when he told Susan that Reagan had offered him the job, she broke down and started crying. Susan Baker remembers saying to herself, "I can't do this, I just can't do this . . . putting the family together . . . moving to Washington, coming back [to Houston], going back to Washington . . . juggling all these things with teenagers doing all kinds of things they shouldn't have been doing . . . and this toddler, this three-year-old . . . I just thought, I can't do this . . . but in the morning, I was thinking, God has been so good, he's gotten me through all this, I guess he'll get me through the next phase."[172]

Arriving at Reagan's home just two days after the election, Baker couldn't help but ask himself, "What are you doing here?" As he hesitated at the front door, Reagan spotted him and calmly said with his famous grin, "What are you doing out there, Jim?" As Baker and Reagan conversed, the politically astute Texan knew very well he was an outsider to the Reagan camp; certain factions were not happy with his selection, some even trying to undermine him from day one.

Regardless, Baker knew what Reagan knew: it's fundamentally more important for the president's chief of staff to be competent and loyal than it is for him to be a devout, true follower. Baker also notes: "He [Ronald Reagan] also understood that one of the most important tasks of a White House chief of staff is to look at policy questions through a political prism. After watching me at work in 1976 and 1980, he apparently believed I could do this."[173]

Reflecting back, longtime Baker aide and confidante, Margaret D. Tutwiler, said, "Ultimately, Reagan had to make a very tough decision . . . Not easy — and Reagan was not a mean person. This wasn't someone pulling something on somebody [over Ed Meese]. I give Reagan enormous credit for seeing the logic in it."[174] Further, Tutwiler noted, "I'll tell you this, and I believe it about Baker and I believe it about Reagan: the most successful managers are those that are secure enough to surround themselves with extremely strong-willed, talented people."[175] Tutwiler concluded, "Reagan was very secure in his own skin. I feel the same way about Jim Baker — that they're fine being alone. Reagan loves to go out there and ride that horse, chop that wood. Baker loves to sit in his turkey blinds — they're people who can spend time with themselves."[176]

Reagan, adamant that Baker and longtime friend and political ally Ed Meese cooperate as best possible, told Baker to work things out with Ed. Mindful that Meese had surely felt he would be Reagan's chief of staff, it became fundamentally important for Baker to build a true working relationship with Meese. Baker gives credit to Meese for his willingness to work with him. "Ed was a wonderful human being, someone whose word you could take to the bank, and a superb policy analyst."[177] Key to formalizing their respective roles within the Reagan White House was Baker drafting a memorandum on how the two men would work together.

"I was always struck by Reagan's ability to forgive and forget," Dick Cheney later observed. "When he hired Jim Baker to be his chief of staff, Jim had spent both the '76 election and the '80 election cycle doing everything he could to beat Ronald Reagan." Yet Cheney admits that the Reagan camp had the ". . . good sense to go to Jim and bring him on board as chief of staff." [178]

During the transition period after the election, Baker said, "All these things have been agreed to. In fact, Ed and I have a piece of paper where I wrote these things down, and we initialed it. I don't plan on releasing our memorandum, but it's all there, and we're all agreed to it, including the president-elect. I know that most policy decisions are made in that Oval Office with two or three people sitting around, and I'm going to be one of those people. The fact of the matter is that it's going to be Mike Deaver, Ed Meese, and myself." [179]

Remembers Baker, "Ed [Meese] and I went down to the coffee shop in Century Plaza, and we started talking about how we might be able to cooperate and divide up the responsibilities." Baker said he told Meese, "I think it would be appropriate if you had Cabinet rank, and I didn't." A gesture by the new incoming chief of staff to help make the relationship work. Meese accepted. [180]

Hedrick Smith of the *New York Times* said, "So he said [to Meese], 'You're the broad policy guy, I'm the practical politics guy.'" [181] Yet what Meese didn't know, and Baker did, was that the "practical politics" guy is the one who was really running the White House.

Recalled Cheney, "Baker came down [to see me] when he was in the midst of negotiating the chief of staff job. They had the difficulty of trying to sort out what Ed Meese and Mike Deaver were going to do. He [Meese] was very close to Reagan, had been with him in California . . . During the course of the negotiations, Jim came to see me, and he had a yellow pad that laid out what his duties and responsibilities were and what Meese's were. . . . Jim wanted to know if he had asked for all the key levers of power, and did he have the things he needed to be able to control the operation. He [Baker] had the right personnel, a solid schedule, and a long list of items — control of the military unit that supports the president and schedule and oversight of the press operations, congressional relations . . . and Meese . . . was policy . . . Jim had nailed it." Cheney told him, "You're dead on, it's exactly where you need to be." [182]

Baker admits that as far as he knew, something like this had never been done before, but again, with each new administration comes opportunities to break new ground. Meese became counselor to President Reagan and head of the Domestic Policy Council and was also given Cabinet status. He was essentially a part of Reagan's inner circle, which became known as the "Troika": Jim Baker, Ed Meese, and Mike Deaver — with Deaver as assistant to the president and deputy chief of staff. Baker found Deaver impressive. "He was a smart and talented guy, a great manager, and a genius at providing rich visuals — whether in the Oval Office or out in the country — to complement the Great Communicator's [Ronald Reagan's] speeches."

Margaret Tutwiler said both Baker and Meese initialed the one-page memo and dated it. She said there were times, albeit not many, when the letter was brought back out for reference. Dick Cheney thought what Jim had done was very perceptive because it put his hands on the levers, the controls that really run the White House. [183]

The fact that Meese was the only one of the "Troika" who had Cabinet-level status didn't concern Baker. As he saw it, people turn to those they can trust and who are competent, regardless of titles and roles. Presidents seek advice from those who have been in the trenches with them, fighting the battles each and every day, in good times and bad. While Baker had not spent nearly the amount of time with Reagan that Meese and Deaver had, he nevertheless had earned his stripes with Ford — something the Reagan camp was clearly aware of — and in time, the fiercely loyal Texan earned Reagan's unquestioned trust and confidence.

Some in the Reagan camp were still suspicious of Baker's more moderate policy views. Concedes Baker, "I was more moderate than Ed Meese, but when the press characterized me that way, that created problems for me." Problems that Baker needed to solve, and did, by winning over longtime Reagan loyalist and Nancy Reagan confidant Michael Deaver. Deaver was as close to the Reagans — both of them — as anyone, personally or politically. According to Tom Brokaw, "Michael Deaver is practically a member of the Reagan family. . . . He's especially close to the first lady [Nancy Reagan]."

Mindful of pitfalls that chiefs of staff had encountered in the past, Baker wanted to ensure that a solid understanding was in place regarding his role, and the roles of others when it came to paper flow in and out of the Oval Office, along with access to the president. Jerry Ford's "spokes of the wheel" model (one that chiefs of staff Donald Rumsfeld and Dick Cheney abruptly abandoned) essentially meant that a group of select advisors — approximately eight to nine individuals — reported directly to President Ford, none of them having any real authority over the others. Ford, the congenial president who always seemed to find the good in everyone, deemed the model an excellent break from the likes of Nixon's gatekeepers, especially H.R. Haldeman, who controlled access to President Nixon with an iron fist.

Reagan did not follow the "spokes of the wheel," clearly knowing the pitfalls of having competing interests vying for the president's time and attention. For starters, while Meese and Deaver may very well have had better offices with finer furnishings and nicer views, what mattered to Baker was having space to run meetings and discuss strategies. Baker grabbed the large office — just down the hall from the Oval Office — which had traditionally been used by previous chiefs of staff. Second, Baker controlled what's known as the "paper flow" to President Reagan, along with all presidential scheduling and appointments, except in the case of emergencies. Regarding access to Reagan, while Baker — and Meese — could walk into the Oval Office freely to meet with the president, Baker was the gatekeeper to all others. Getting to the president meant going through Jim Baker.

Being chief of staff had many responsibilities, but ultimately, it was about protecting the president as much as possible. As Baker saw it, the chief of staff is a "catcher of javelins aimed at the president — by political adversaries, by the press, and, surprisingly, perhaps, by members of his own political party. I also had to protect the president from traps."[184] In an interview with the *Washington Post* during the transition period between Carter and Reagan, Baker acknowledged, "First and foremost, a chief of staff has to be an honest broker. My job is to make the train run, and I go in disclaiming any intentions of formulating policy because you can't be an honest broker and push policy. But part of my job is also to cover the political side of the White House on the Hill for the president, and to implement policy jointly with Ed Meese. You cannot separate politics and policy."[185]

Dick Cheney, who had held the chief of staff position for President Ford called Baker "a classic pick. He has no ax to grind. He'll give the president a straight shot." Reflecting back on Baker's time as chief of staff, Cheney said, "Jim was a master of never letting a phone call to a congressman go unreturned. Every single day, he'd return every one. He was also very, very effective as a spokesman with the press."[186]

Baker believed in hiring the best and the brightest in terms of support personnel. The men and women who worked with him while he served as Reagan's chief of staff ultimately became an A-list of who's who in Washington throughout the years. Dick Darman, Jim Brady, Larry Speakes, Elizabeth Dole, Fred Fielding, and many others. As Baker saw it, "I recruited the best I could find. A leader who is afraid of hiring strong people is usually a leader on a glide path to failure."[187]

LEARN FROM THE BEST

Baker wasn't afraid to seek advice on how to prepare himself for arguably one of Washington's most grueling jobs. During the transition period between November 4, 1980, and January 20, 1981, Baker sought the advice of former chiefs of staff, and high on that list was Dick Cheney. As the youngest chief of staff ever to serve a president (Cheney was just thirty-four years old), he suggested to Baker that restoring power to the executive branch was vital. After all, Cheney had watched firsthand how an overzealous Congress greatly curtailed Ford's ability to govern.

Cheney also suggested that controlling the paper flow and having an orderly schedule was key to the president's success, and key to stopping leaks. And not surprisingly, Cheney believed in keeping a low profile, often reminding himself not to try to become a public figure. He was not the president — he was the chief of staff.

To this day, Jim Baker and Dick Cheney remain close personal friends. Baker tells the story of when he met Cheney. "I met Dick Cheney for the first time in 1975, just a few days after I'd been sworn in as Rogers Morton's deputy at the Department of Commerce. Rog wanted me to meet President Ford, so I tagged along with him to the White House one afternoon. . . . I was ushered into the Oval Office. . . . I was introduced to Dick — who very graciously offered me a chair. . . . That same human decency and down-to-earth style characterizes Dick to this day. It's hard to keep your sense of equilibrium in Washington, but the power game has never gone to his head."[188] Baker saw Dick as more of a cold warrior than he was, and they sometimes disagreed about Soviet policy and arms control, but this, too, never got in the way of a strong friendship, mutual respect, and a close working relationship.

Baker tells another story of those early days in the White House, when Cheney bailed him out of a political slip up with none other than the venerable Henry Kissinger. "During the 1976 Republican primary campaign, Dick bailed me out from my first embarrassing moment in government service, after I inadvertently announced Henry Kissinger's resignation from the government for him." As Baker recalled, "I got to the home of a banker down there [in Oklahoma] and it's a nice, quiet little group of . . . [people] . . . around the pool, and I'm told there's no press in attendance. So, I give my little pitch and then take questions. And one of the questions was, 'Will Henry Kissinger be in the second Ford administration?' I said, 'I can't conceive of that happening.' Well, it turns out there was a stringer for the *Daily Oklahoman*, the college paper there, and he wrote this stuff." [189]

According to Baker, a few days later, he was asked to drop by Chief of Staff Cheney's office — one Baker himself would occupy just five years later, and again sixteen years later. Cheney told Baker his statement about Kissinger's resignation was being picked up by the press and causing quite a stir. While another chief of staff would have torn into Baker, Cheney gave it a laugh, telling him, "Just make it right with Henry." Baker has always remembered how "Dick had taught me a lesson about being cautious in a very graceful fashion." [190]

Baker also solicited the advice of Donald Rumsfeld, once President Ford's chief of staff and secretary of Defense. Rumsfeld, typical of his CEO persona, gave Baker a twelve-page memo he had written years earlier, titled "Rumsfeld's Rules." The first section, "Serving in the White House," was directed to chiefs of staff and senior staff. It provided Baker with valuable insight for taking on one of Washington's most demanding jobs. Below are a few of the key points from that section.

» Don't accept the post or stay unless you have an understanding with the president that you're free to tell him what you think "with the bark off" and you have the courage to do it.

» Visit with your predecessors from previous administrations. They know the ropes and can help you see around some corners. Try to make original mistakes, rather than needlessly repeating theirs.

» Don't begin to think you're the president. You're not. The Constitution provides for only one.

» If you foul up, tell the president and correct it fast. Delay only compounds mistakes.

» Be precise. A lack of precision is dangerous when the margin of error is small.

» Preserve the president's options. He may need them.[191]

Politically, Baker knew his loyalty was first and foremost to the president of the United States, and nobody else. Yet his position as White House chief of staff afforded him the opportunity to keep the vice president — his close personal friend — in the loop on critical policy issues. But he knew the boundaries. As Baker saw it, "Any appearance that my real goal was only to help my old friend would have been inappropriate . . . would have undermined my effectiveness."[192]

A BALANCING ACT

As Baker saw it, both his personal and professional lives were focused on crossing the t's and dotting the i's, being disciplined and diligent each and every day. He was a workaholic, and while the president made every effort to keep Baker out of the White House in the evening and home with his family, the hard-working Texan found himself routinely pulling sixteen-hour days. The job was chief of staff to the president of the United States of America, a job Baker knew would not be 9-to-5. Fine by him. After all, he admittedly craved politics and greatly admired President Reagan, but perhaps more than anything, he knew what he was doing was important for the country, and he loved public life.

A closer look at Baker's daily early-morning schedule as Reagan's chief of staff reveals a regimented workflow that proved highly successful in terms of communication, control, and efficiency:

» 6:30 a.m. – Baker is picked up by his driver and heads to the White House. While in route, he reads the daily White House news summary that's prepared by the press office.

» 7:00 a.m. – Baker arrives at White House. Catches early morning news reports from major stations, while also reviewing top stories from the *Washington Post*, *Wall Street Journal*, and more. Update agenda for meeting with Michael Deaver and Ed Meese.

» 7:30 a.m. – Daily Troika meeting with Deaver and Meese to discuss all important matters — schedules, media, policy issues, etc.

» 8:00 a.m. – Meeting in the Roosevelt Room with President Reagan's assistants and deputy assistants.

» 9:15 a.m. – Media briefing from the White House press secretary. This would ensure that no other agency was out in front of the White House in terms of news.

» 10:00 a.m. – Return to the office or accompany Reagan to his next event.[193]

While no doubt his laundry list of skills — many engrained in Baker from his days as a corporate lawyer, and some, newly acquired — can be attributed to his success as Reagan's primary gatekeeper, the savvy Texan knew this:

» Maintain a good working relationship with Congress.

» Return all calls from reporters and lawmakers.

» Try to understand and see your oppositions' viewpoints.

» Place great value on courtesy and civility at all times.

» Give the president material in a manner he can best digest and understand it.

» Know when to discuss politics and when not to!

» Maintain control over the White House as best as possible, but more important, maintain control over the paper flow in and out of the Oval Office.

Though these challenges would make the position appear daunting to most, it wasn't all work when it came to being chief of staff to Reagan. There were days when Baker and the president rode horseback together through the Virginia woods, discussing mostly personal issues, leaving politics at the Oval Office. "We would ride for an hour or more . . . usually at a slow pace. . . . I used a Western saddle and rode in blue jeans and cowboy boots. . . . The president preferred an English saddle . . . and polished riding boots." [194]

For a man who had once seemed the unlikeliest candidate to be Reagan's chief of staff, Baker was a quick study at his new job, effectively becoming one of the most influential and powerful gatekeepers to ever serve a president.

According to then White House communications director David Gergen, "Baker would usually put things into three categories, the things that are easy to do, the things that are impossible to do, and the things that you might get done, but are really hard. . . . And he always said, 'We're going to focus on hard, but doable.'" [195]

Reagan would leave the Oval Office at 5:00 p.m., returning to the residence to be with his closest confidante and life partner, Nancy. Baker, keenly aware of Mrs. Reagan's influence on her husband, became quick friends with the first lady. While he was the president's gatekeeper at the Oval Office, the true guardian of Reagan was none other than Nancy. Baker admired the relationship between the president and his wife. They were "best friends" and so deeply in love, often spending their evenings in pajamas while having dinner and watching television. Having the first lady's trust and confidence was critical for Baker, and as their relationship flourished, Nancy grew fond of the once rival who tried to squash her husband's presidential ambitions — twice!

Reflecting on his tenure serving as Reagan's chief of staff (1981 to 1985), Baker said, "Ronald Reagan really was an incredible and beautiful human being. He was loyalty up, loyalty down. He was hope and optimism all wrapped up in one. And that was one of the reasons, I think, for his success. . . . He wanted the views of everybody, and I remember so many meetings that were divisive, but the way Reagan handled them, the party who lost never felt like he or she hadn't been given a full shot. It was really a wonderful experience and almost amazing. I don't think it's gonna happen again in American politics, where a president-elect will ask the campaign manager of two opponents of his to be his White House chief of staff. But they wanted somebody who knew Washington and who knew how things operated up there."[196]

Baker, revisiting his time as Reagan's chief of staff with Fox News reporter Eric Shawn in 2011, had this to say about his former boss: "His greatest impact, or legacy perhaps, is that he restored America's pride and confidence in itself. We were at a really low-point in this country when he came on the scene as president. He governed us with great dexterity for eight years. We had eight years of peace and complete prosperity. We ended up, as a matter of fact by virtue of his policies, having eighteen years of sustained, non-inflationary growth. And he just turned out to be a wonderful two-term president. Part of that, I think was due, or a great deal of it was due to his sunny nature and his optimism, and the fact . . . that he was just simply a beautiful human being."[197]

According to Chris Whipple, author of *The Gatekeepers: How the White House Chiefs of Staff Define Every Presidency*, "There's no secret sauce, but Jim Baker, everybody says — Republicans and Democrats alike — was the guy with the sauce. He was the gold standard. He had that combination of political skill and the ability to turn Ronald Reagan around on a dime when he had to on policy or tactics. He was the closest confidant, the most powerful advisor, the consigliere and the guy who keeps everybody on the same page. It was a hell of a tough job."[198] All for a job that, according to former vice president Dick Cheney, "has more authority and more power than the vice president."[199]

In a 2017 interview with NPR, Baker was asked if he had more influence running an agency as a Cabinet member or being chief of staff to two presidents of the United States. His reply:

"Well, it depends on which of my presidents you're talking about. I was of course personally closer to George Bush because we'd been friends for forty years. I had run all of his presidential campaigns, so nobody was going to ever get between me and my president. And when I went out as secretary of State and said something, they knew

I was talking for the president of the United States, and nobody questioned it.

"With Ronald Reagan, it was a little different. I was the outsider. I had run two campaigns against Reagan before he asked me to be his chief of staff. But he invested me with great authority and great responsibility and gave me great loyalty. I've said oftentimes that being White House chief of staff is perhaps the second most powerful job in Washington, DC. I think that's true. But so much depends upon your relationship with your [president]."[200]

According to longtime political journalist Leslie Stahl, "Interestingly, a lot of what Jim Baker accomplished and forced through were compromises, and yet people didn't think that Reagan compromised. It was brilliant."[201]

"Baker is not perfect, but he can handle pressure. He's a Steady Eddie. And he's a realist. It's almost clinical. He doesn't lead with emotion. He can handle a whole lot of incoming and just not get rattled," recalls Margaret Tutwiler.[202]

Ken Duberstein, who served briefly as Reagan's chief of staff toward the end of his two-term presidency, said, "Presidents sometimes make the mistake of hiring for the White House chief of staff somebody who brought them to the dance, rather than the person who needs to be the dance partner once you're governing. In campaigning, you try to demonize your opponent. In governing, you make love to your opponent. That's how you put coalitions together. Jim Baker understood campaigning, but he was a real pro at governing."[203]

As Reagan's political victories were adding up, Washington was taking notice of the man who had only arrived in 1975 but was now one of the Beltway's most persuasive and powerful operatives. Said

Baker, "It's not that you're trying to acquire power for power's sake, power really accretes to those who get things done."

But with a demanding job schedule growing tougher each day and tensions running high in the White House, Baker and Michael Deaver suggested a plan for Baker to assume the role of national security advisor. Reagan agreed, but then was talked out of it by insiders in the administration in a meeting not attended by Baker or Deaver. Recalled Baker, "There was a revolt on some . . . of the more ideological members of the administration, and the president changed his mind." It caught Baker off guard, but it was also a lesson learned — always have the last word with the president.[204]

TIME FOR A CHANGE

Sixteen-hour days and endless White House infighting were taking a heavy toll on the tough Texan. Recalls Baker, "It's a goddamn difficult job in the best of circumstances, and because I had to deal with Meese and the ideologues shootin' at me all the time, that made it even tougher. Four years and two weeks was longer than anybody else had ever held that job and not gone to jail!"[205] Baker was looking for an out, and he found it with Donald T. Regan, the president's Treasury secretary.

Baker and Regan had gotten into a brief spat over an alleged story that Regan blamed on being leaked by the White House. Eager to smooth over the issue, Baker went to see Regan, at which point Regan suggested they swap jobs. It no doubt caught Baker by surprise, but he flatly told Regan to be careful what you ask for, because "I might damn well take you up on it."[206]

Baker had unexpectedly found his way out of the White House

— and into an elite Cabinet position. And with President Reagan's approval, Baker and Regan effectively swapped jobs. It caught most of Washington by surprise as two power players were trading jobs that were equally different.

Regan had been President Reagan's Treasury secretary since January 22, 1981, while Baker had dutifully served as Reagan's chief of staff since day one of Reagan's presidency. Regan, the former president of Merrill Lynch & Co., was known as pragmatic, disciplined, a sharp operator, and a skilled manager who was demanding of himself and his staff.

In Baker's letter of resignation to President Reagan in early February 1985, he wrote: "You have accorded me the greatest privilege of my life: the honor of serving as your chief of staff over the past four years — years which historians will undoubtedly view as a period of much-needed and striking accomplishment. I know you are fond of saying that such achievements are a team effort, but if that is so, it is also true that rarely in our nation's history has a team been so ably led and inspired. . . . Susan and the rest of my family agree that you have given us many fine and fond memories. In the years ahead, we will look back on this special time in our lives with a deep sense of appreciation and pride. You have my heartfelt thanks and my pledge of continued loyalty and service to you and your administration."[207]

The man who ran the White House for Ronald Reagan would now be running the country's finances, and to many Washington insiders, the swap caused little to no angst among Republicans or Democrats. Then House speaker Thomas P. "Tip" O'Neill Jr. (D-Mass.) called Baker and Regan "very able and talented public servants who always do a job well. . . . I am looking forward to working just as constructively with them in their new positions as I have in their previous assignments. The country has been well-served by their past efforts, and I expect that the country will be just as well-served by their efforts in their new jobs."[208]

Then Senate majority leader Bob Dole acknowledged, "It's something I wouldn't have thought of, but it turns out it's a good switch. Two good men will remain in government. . . . I believe Don Regan will be a voice of reality and reason as Jim Baker has been. . . . I don't see any losers in this. . . . The president gets a strong hand in the White House. He gets a trusted hand and a strong hand at Treasury. Don Regan apparently wanted to do it. Jim Baker is tickled to death."[209]

Baker's position as secretary of the Treasury was his first of two Cabinet-level positions (he served as secretary of State from 1989 – 1992), yet it was a completely new role for the campaign gun-slinger-turned-presidential gatekeeper. By stepping into what some might deem one of the loftiest of Cabinet positions, Baker was removing himself from the daily operational grind of the White House and into the world of financial affairs for the United States. Early-morning staff meetings in the West Wing to review the daily agenda for the White House became discussions about a myriad of economic concerns — the nation's rising debt, simplifying the excruciatingly complex tax codes, stabilizing the American dollar, and countless other financial issues. To be clear, Baker may have left the White House as chief of staff, but he left behind key players that proved critical while he served as secretary of the Treasury. And Regan was not Baker. All of Washington knew it, and Reagan probably did also, but the president had capable hands by his side, giving Regan the support he needed to perform adequately.

Regan had helped spearhead many of the president's economic policy directives that were paying dividends as the economy was thriving by the time of Reagan's re-election victory in 1984. But budget deficits were beginning to increase, and with Reagan determined not to raise taxes, Baker found himself walking a tightrope of continuing to advance the president's policies, while also keeping the country in top financial shape.

Reagan was gunning for even more cuts in social spending for his second term, but Democrats — even some Republicans — were ready for a fight. Democrats were crying foul on cuts to what they considered important social services, while fiscally conservative Republicans were beginning to voice concerns about growing deficits. The lethargic economic malaise of the 1970s was still fresh on everyone's mind, yet the fiscally conservative Baker was also mindful of deficits that could create long-term economic paralysis for the country.

Both Baker and Regan had begun their new jobs with high hopes — and confidence. Baker delivered time and again as Treasury secretary, cementing monumental policy victories for the Reagan White House. Baker soon came to realize that Regan's stiff, no-nonsense, demanding demeanor was a hindrance to the president. He was found to be cold, aloof, and indifferent, and unable to warm to the president's closest confidante, Nancy Reagan. The phrase "dead on arrival" was quite fitting for a man who dared hang up the phone on First Lady Nancy Reagan, twice.

The swap proved to be a bad choice for Regan — he was eventually pushed out after two years — but it was even worse for the president. Reagan, without having Baker overseeing White House operations, became engulfed in the Iran–Contra affair, which almost destroyed his presidency. Ultimately, it took another Baker — former Tennessee senator Howard Baker — to resuscitate and save Reagan's second term from unquestioned disaster. Many in Washington have said that if Jim Baker had still been chief of staff, Iran–Contra wouldn't have happened. Though Baker can't say for sure, since the past is in the history books, he nevertheless has said, "It's easy and potentially self-serving, I suppose, to say I don't think so."[210]

Years later, while serving as secretary of State and also sitting on the National Security Council, he learned that John Poindexter, Reagan's national security advisor, had purposely excluded Baker from NSA meetings that discussed the arms-for-hostages deal.

BAKER THE BANKER

Baker's tenure as secretary of the Treasury began on February 4, 1985, a position he held until resigning in August 1988, as he shifted back into political-campaign mode for Bush's 1988 presidential run.

As Treasury secretary, Baker had a laundry list of items to accomplish, and as usual, not enough political time to get them done. He sought to propose policy initiatives to keep the economy growing, find a way — once and for all — to simplify the overly complex federal tax codes, devalue the dollar that was hurting many US industries, propose measures to halt the growing Latin American debt crisis, and much more.

Less than eight months into his new job, Baker negotiated a landmark international monetary policy to help rein in an overly aggressive US dollar. Throughout the first half-decade of the 1980s, the American dollar had seen rapid appreciation against the likes of the British pound, French franc, German Deutsche mark, and the Japanese yen — the respective currencies of the next four biggest economies. And while various areas within the financial sector were profiting from the rising dollar, a large number of American industries — automotive, manufacturing, high-tech, and others — were feeling the pain. Sensing the issue, Baker brought the G5 to the table to begin negotiations toward an agreement to depreciate the American dollar.

One of the real issues was Japan's economy. It was growing rapidly, allowing them to sell a wide range of products to the rest of the world. Many of these products being what the United States used to sell. The plan was to sell a lot of dollars, lower the value of it, thereby strengthening the yen and other currencies, while also making American exports cheaper. And the plan worked well — exceedingly well — with the dollar falling by as much as 40 percent over a two-year period.

On September 22, 1985, the minister of finance and central bank governors of France, the Federal Republic of Germany, Japan, the United Kingdom, and the United States met on a wide range of economic issues, leading to what became known as the Plaza Agreement. As for the United States, Baker committed the US to policies designed to ensure steady, non-inflationary growth, maximize the role of markets and private-sector participation in the economy, reduce the size and role of the government sector, and maintain open markets.

In order to achieve these objectives, the United States government would have to do the following:

» Continue efforts to reduce government expenditures as a share of GNP in order to reduce the fiscal deficit and to free up resources for the private sector.

» Implement fully the deficit-reduction package for fiscal year 1986.

» Implement revenue-neutral tax reform, which would encourage savings, create new work incentives, and increase the efficiency of the economy, thereby fostering non-inflationary growth.

» Conduct monetary policy to provide a financial environment conducive to sustainable growth and continued progress toward price stability.

» Resist protectionist measures.[211]

According to Takatoshi Ito, PHD, Professor of International and Public Affairs, School of International and Public Affairs, Columbia University, "The Plaza Agreement of September 1985 was the beginning of a brief period of policy coordination among the G5. It was led by Treasury Secretary Baker, but Japan was a very willing participant."

Furthermore, Ito said, "The Plaza Agreement is remembered as one of the most significant events in the history of international finance in the post WWII era. Witness accounts show that Japan was [a] more than willing participant of the Plaza Agreement, being prepared to accept yen appreciation. The objective of the Plaza Agreement, depreciation of the dollar, was achieved much faster than expected, with less intervention amounts than expected."[212]

One of the keys to success of the Plaza Agreement, according to David Mulford of Credit Suisse, was Jim Baker. Says Mulford, "Secretary Baker was an entirely different personality from Don Regan. He was a skilled and experienced lawyer, an outstanding political operator, and very good with people of all kinds. He was always remarkably well-prepared for the many and diverse meetings required of a Treasury secretary and seemed able to read every situation in a way to achieve maximum results. In short, he exercised power judiciously but with maximum effect. The more subtle and thoughtful approach to G7 issues was apparent immediately."[213]

In Reagan's 1984 State of the Union speech, he had stated, "I am asking Secretary Don Regan for a plan for action to simplify the entire tax code, so all taxpayers, big and small, are treated more fairly. . . . I've asked that specific recommendations, consistent with those objectives, be presented to me by December 1984."[214] With Regan and Baker swapping jobs, it was up to Baker to fulfill Reagan's mandate for tax reform. Yet as secretary of the Treasury, Baker did not have the access to Reagan he'd had when serving as chief of staff.

No different from any other Cabinet member, Baker needed an appointment to see the president, but Baker was confident that his years in the trenches with Reagan would give him the access he needed, when he needed it. Key members of Congress also knew Baker had a unique relationship with the president, another key factor in driving the success of tax reform.

But that's not to say there weren't other challenges. There were many obstacles and landmines along the way, but Baker effectively navigated the world of backroom politics, which was full of demands from congressional leaders, lobbying groups, special-interest parties, and more. There were Republicans hesitant for change, including Senator Bob Packwood, chairman of the Finance Committee, who said, "I sort of like the tax code the way it is." And there were endless negotiations with Democratic power brokers Dan Rostenkowski, the chairman of the House Ways and Means Committee, and Speaker of the House Tip O'Neil.

Sensing optimism for the tax reform bill, Baker, in late September 1986, recited to a group of lawmakers, reporters, and lobbyists "The Tax Reform Shuffle," a takeoff on the Chicago Bears' now-famous rap video, "The Super Bowl Shuffle."

They said tax reform was dead. Now it's alive.
Here's its story, it began in '85.
We drew up a plan and sent it out in May.
But the special interests said, "Ain't no way."
Rosty started hearings before the fall.
They were Gucci to Gucci out in the hall.
December came, reform was off track.
So, to the Hill rode the Gipper to bring it back.
All along, it's been a big tussle.
But we keep doing "The Tax Reform Shuffle."

Baker, who "had a hand in writing the Shuffle," was asked if he had any plans to make a videotape. A Treasury Department spokesman quipped, "I guess it would depend on the size of the advance."[215]

On October 22, 1986, exactly thirteen months — to the day — after the signing of the Plaza Agreement, the Tax Reform Act was passed by the 99th Congress, a hugely significant achievement for Baker that was monumental in many ways. First, it illustrated once again Baker's uncanny ability to get things done in a town that thrived on partisan politics, bickering, and talking points with little substance at times. Secondly, the law was truly a watershed moment in terms of what it gave the American taxpayer, which was a lot. It lowered federal income tax rates (from 50 percent to 33 percent), decreased the number of tax brackets, yet also expanded personal deductions and exemptions. It also exempted millions of low-income families from a federal income tax with the earned-income tax credit. There was more, but at its heart, the act — a clear priority for Reagan's second term — that had once been only a political pipedream, became a reality, thanks in part to Baker's skillful negotiations.

In the end, both sides of the political aisle seemed to emerge victorious, a bill that all of America would benefit from. Said Baker, "As I watched the ceremony [of President Reagan signing the legislation into law] — even now as I look back — I was amazed that we pulled it off. It was something of a miracle, frankly."[216]

Following many successes as Treasury secretary, Baker returned to the familiar territory of the campaign trenches to help Bush in his quest for the granddaddy of all political prizes — the presidency.

Baker and Bush enjoy a stroll and a chat on the grounds of the vice president's residence. September 1988.

Baker and Bush (and two unnamed) during a camping trip in Wyoming to escape the noise of the Democratic National Convention. July 1988.

Jim Baker visits Vice President Bush at his official residence, Number One Observatory Circle. October 1988.

With their wives, Marilyn and Barbara, at their sides, Senator Dan Quayle accepts George Bush's invitation to be his running mate. August 1988.

Jim Baker and Vice President Bush address an audience. August 1988.

With a young George W. nearby, Vice President Bush laughingly tries to dodge a playful hand to his face from Jim Baker. September 1988.

Jim Baker and President Bush in the Oval Office. June 1989.

Vice President Quayle, US Ambassador to Italy Peter Secchia, and then secretary of State James Baker attend a state dinner in honor of Italy's president. (Man on left unidentified.) October, 1989.

Jim Baker and George Bush enjoy a hunting excursion in Beeville, Texas. December 1989.

Best friends Bush and Baker enjoy a successful fishing trip at Perry Bass Ranch, Corpus Christi, Texas. December 1989.

President Gorbachev and President Bush shake hands during their first bilateral meeting of the Malta Summit as Eduard Shevardnadze and Secretary Baker look on. December 1989.

James Baker in discussion with German chancellor Helmut Kohl in Bonn, West Germany. May 1990.

James Baker and Eduard Shevardnadze in Berlin during talks regarding German reunification. June 1990.

CHAPTER FIVE

48 Months

A S THE 1988 PRESIDENTIAL ELECTION CAMPAIGN CAME TO A close, both Bush and Baker were feeling confident in the election outcome. The double-digit Dukakis lead that early-summer polls had shown had completely evaporated, with Bush and running mate Dan Quayle now confidently in front — according to all pre-election poll numbers. Forty-eight hours before Election Day, Baker and Bush were relaxing at Number One Observatory Circle — the official residence of the vice president of the United States — when Bush made a comment that definitely caught Baker's attention.

As Baker recalled, Bush said, "I want you to be secretary of State if I win." Baker said he accepted on the spot. After all, it was a job that had been on his mind. After serving as chief of staff to two presidents as well as secretary of the Treasury under President Reagan, Baker had no interest in returning to Houston to practice law — not yet, at least — preferring the high-stakes political world that he'd become accustomed to.

With all the notable positions he'd held in Washington, Baker admitted it wasn't any big secret that he was highly interested in what some view as the most cherished of all Cabinet jobs. Yet it was also something that both men never spoke about during the 1988 campaign. According to Baker, his political future wasn't discussed when Bush asked him to leave his post as secretary of the Treasury under Reagan to run Bush's 1988 campaign. As Baker saw it, both men had enjoyed a thirty-year friendship and had come to know and understand each other quite well, and "like many things between the two of us, we were on the same wavelength."[217]

Baker was also confident he'd perform admirably as secretary of State, thanks in part to political and negotiating skills acquired not only during his years as a practicing lawyer, but also his thirteen years in the political bubble, starting off with what he jokingly calls his "low-level, bureaucratic job as undersecretary of Commerce" in August 1975. But in all seriousness, he had the credentials to excel as secretary of State for a number of fundamentally obvious reasons.

Baker was ultimately joined by three men in the foreign-policy arena — Dick Cheney [secretary of Defense], Brent Scowcroft [national security advisor] and Colin Powell [chairman of the Joint Chiefs of Staff] — all friends and political colleagues. He had also gained almost eight years of foreign-policy experience while serving as secretary of the Treasury and White House chief of staff. And Baker admits one luxury was "an unprecedented personal relationship with the president of the United States. . . . In politics and government service, our careers have been inextricably linked and, to a large degree, mutually reinforcing since 1970. Neither one of us has been very comfortable stretching out on the couch and talking about personal ties, but he's characterized it as a big brother – little brother relationship. I think that's a fairly accurate description, and one that I consider quite a compliment."[218]

President Bush made somewhat of a surprising choice for his chief of staff by selecting New Hampshire governor John Sununu. Though there were reports following the announcement that Baker wasn't overly enthusiastic about the choice, Baker said that was "quite contrary to the facts" and that Sununu's selection was appropriate. Years later, Baker confirmed that his name had come up even before they'd won the election, stating that he thought John would be excellent. "I happen to believe Sununu was a fine chief of staff for President Bush, until he got in trouble. Now, when I say fine, I mean he was smart. He was I think loyal. He was a little bit too inclined to appropriate unto himself all economic-policy power."[219]

Cheney recalled, "He [John Sununu] called and asked to come see me to talk about the job of being chief of staff. I'm then in Congress. So, I made an appointment, he came up, sat down in my office, and said, 'I'm here.' Then he leaned back in his chair and started twiddling his thumbs. Absolute signal. 'I don't have a care in the world about what you're saying to me. It's absolutely irrelevant to me. I'm here because somebody [President-elect Bush] told me I had to be here.'"[220]

Apparently, Sununu wasn't interested, nor did he care to hear any of the advice Cheney was willing to impart. Advice that he had passed on to other chiefs — lie low, stay out of the public eye, shun the media — fell on deaf ears with Sununu. The man's brashness ultimately got the best of him as embarrassing stories began to leak of him using government planes for personal use — stamp auctions, dentist appointments, and more. "A big embarrassment that he's flying around on nonofficial business on Air Force aircraft. He was arrogant and it showed, and he let it show," said Cheney.[221]

After two years in the position, Sununu was replaced by Sam Skinner, Bush's then secretary of Transportation who inherited one of Washington's most powerful and demanding jobs.

SECRETARY OF STATE

Between Bush's win in November 1988 and his inauguration in January 1989, Baker immersed himself in the study of international issues, spending time with many ranking State Department officials and having his transition staff prepare strategy papers on a wide range of issues from arms control to knowing the names of foreign leaders around the world. According to Baker, "There was no way I was going to let any senator [during Senate confirmation hearings] embarrass me . . ." He was not going to be caught not knowing the names of world leaders.[222]

Baker, clearly aware that the secretary of State position was a political appointment, established three core measurements by which to assess all issues presented to him. First: how plausible is it to build a domestic consensus for the issue? Second: what is the political reaction that will unfold from both our allies and our adversaries on such an issue? Third: what can the US expect in terms of changes in our political relationships on the international scale?[223]

The man who defeated Bush in 1970 for the US Senate — Lloyd Bentsen — was the man who introduced Baker to the Senate for his confirmation hearings. "He's a native of Houston, Texas. He combines an intellectual toughness with a personal friendliness that

I think that we all treasure. His family has given our state generations of leadership, and now Jim Baker is carrying on that tradition in Washington. . . . And through all of that [his previous professional accomplishments], he's had an impeccable reputation for integrity. . . . I believe that our foreign policy will be in firm hands and that our national interests will be strongly protected if Jim Baker is secretary of State. And I would hope that this committee would very speedily confirm him."[224]

Baker, in his commanding, yet soothing and reassuring Texas drawl, gave an impressive performance to the Senate Foreign Relations Committee, diving into details on many foreign-policy issues relating to democratic revolution, the spread of free enterprise, changes in the Communist world, technological progress, and new military trends. The native Houstonian also added, "Some have described my philosophy as pragmatic. I'd like to say that labels can sometimes be misleading. I am actually a Texas Republican, all of whom are conservative. I will admit to pragmatism, however, if by that you mean being realistic about the world and appreciating the importance of getting things done." Baker continued, "There is a second issue we must resolve. . . . It concerns the relationship between the executive and the Congress in the realm of foreign policy. Simply put, we must have bipartisanship to succeed. That is the verdict of history and that is the verdict of recent experience."[225]

Baker was confirmed as Bush's secretary of State unanimously, 99-0, on a roll-call vote. As prepared as he was to lead America's foreign-policy efforts throughout the globe, nobody could have predicted the turbulent — and consequential — events that played out during Bush's single term as president of the United States.

BUILDING THE REST OF THE TEAM

Elizabeth Dole became Bush's secretary of Labor, and Richard Darman became director of the Office of Management and Budget, both also approved on a 99-0 roll-call vote. But the Senate gave Bush the first setback of his presidency when they rejected John G. Tower's nomination for secretary of Defense. Tower, a close political friend and ally of Bush, was dogged by repeated allegations of conflict of interest and private misconduct. In the end, his nomination was defeated 47 to 53, making him the first Cabinet nominee to be rejected since 1959.

Tower had approached Baker during the 1988 presidential transition period, asking for his support to become Bush's secretary of Defense. The two men had been friends for many years, and though Baker was sorry that Tower had suffered the rejection of the Senate, he had privately worried that Tower may not have been the best fit for the job. As Baker explained, "I've never known many mandarins of the Senate who didn't have sharp elbows, and while Tower was an old friend and political ally, he was no slouch at the power game."[226] Tower had promised Baker that if appointed secretary of Defense, he'd play ball only on his turf, but Baker wasn't so sure. Baker envisioned Tower flexing his defense muscle and encroaching on foreign-policy issues, but that never happened, and it wouldn't happen with the man ultimately approved by the Senate as secretary of Defense.

After Tower's defeat, the president wasted no time finding a more than capable nominee to fill the Cabinet position. He chose Dick Cheney, a highly respected member of the Republican leadership during his five terms in Congress and also admired within many Democratic circles on Capitol Hill. At just forty-eight, Wyoming's lone member of Congress was hailed as "the best and proper choice," a man of principle and a trusted friend, according to President Bush.[227]

As Baker saw it, Cheney was not only a natural for the job, but the best candidate for what many in Washington consider one of the two most powerful Cabinet positions — the other being secretary of State. According to Baker, "I was sure that Dick Cheney would never try to be secretary of State, and he knew I wouldn't tread on his turf."[228]

The Senate moved swiftly on hearings for Cheney, voting without dissent, 92–0, confirming the Wyoming congressman as America's top man in the Pentagon. House Minority Leader Bob Michel, a close friend and mentor of Cheney, offered up his sentiment during the Senate confirmation hearings, stating, "If I had my way, I would keep Dick Cheney in the House. Only someone who has worked as close as I have with Dick knows the special kind of excellence he brings to every job. The incisive intelligence, the quiet persistence, the gentle, yet effective power of persuasion that he has. . . . And it was when he was President Ford's chief of staff that I first noticed what I would call the Cheney style of leadership, the ability to listen carefully, the capacity to act decisively, and the willingness to work as long and hard as it takes to get the job done right."[229]

Bush appointed Brent Scowcroft, a man for whom he had deep affection, as national security advisor, a post Scowcroft also held under President Ford. Slight in stature, Scowcroft nevertheless was a giant in terms of assessing the national security landscape and "wasn't hampered by a towering ego, and he never peddled a private agenda. Instead, he always bent over backward to be an honest broker for the president [Bush]," according to Baker.[230]

Baker noted how Scowcroft always extended an optimistic, welcome hand to him, unquestionably collegial. Scowcroft wasn't going to dominate the airwaves. He understood his role, but he also had strong opinions on various issues. According to Baker, Scowcroft held a 7:00 a.m. breakfast every Wednesday in his office with Baker and Dick Cheney to ensure they were all "singing from the same hymnal."[231] Scowcroft was a facilitator, a man who excelled at listening and assessing everyone's viewpoints. He often stayed silent in NSC meetings, but it was well-known by all that he had President Bush's eyes and ears when it mattered. Bush trusted Scowcroft immensely.

Scowcroft himself takes great pride when discussing his relationship with George H.W. Bush, calling him a "good friend, someone I knew well and admired enormously. We had met when I first came to the White House in 1972. . . . Since the early days of the Ford administration, we had frequent interaction. . . . It was during his days at the CIA that we developed a close relationship. He would frequently visit his family's summer home in Kennebunkport, Maine, for the weekend, and he would always call to inform me he was going."[232] Years later, after Bush's presidency, he and Scowcroft co-authored *A World Transformed*, behind-the-scenes accounts of immensely consequential events that took place during Bush's single term as president.

As to Baker, Scowcroft joked about how their relationship was more casual, "mostly a bantering one" that seemed to center on how the two of them had "tried to deal with President Ford's misstep in the 1976 campaign when, in the San Francisco debate with Carter, he declared that Poland was not dominated by the Soviet Union."[233] Scowcroft recalled his heart sinking into his shoes when he heard Ford say it, and it got worse as he and Baker were thrown to the wolves when asked in the press room how many actual Soviet divisions were stationed in Poland. About six, according to a rather grim-faced Scowcroft.

Once Bush was in the White House, with Baker at State, Cheney at Defense, and Scowcroft as national security advisor, the pieces were all falling into place for what became a legendary group of men tasked with immense challenges throughout the globe during Bush's presidency. In October 1989, Colin Powell became chairman of the Joint Chiefs of Staff, further bolstering an already star-studded cast of Washington power players within the Bush White House.

A sea of change engulfed the world during Bush's single term as president, testing his resolve like never before as a series of cascading events unfolded. The Berlin Wall — a symbol of human oppression — was torn down after thirty years. Saddam Hussein invaded tiny neighboring Kuwait, throwing the Middle East into turmoil and panic. Mikhail Gorbachev, the leader of the Soviet Union, was placed under house arrest in an attempted coup. And the Soviet Union ceased to exist on December 26, 1991. Events no historian or political operative could have accurately predicted, nevertheless, moments in history that placed George Herbert Walker Bush and James Addison Baker, III front and center on the world stage. America sought to lead and take charge during one of the most consequential eras of any modern presidency. Coalition forces, led by America's military, ousted Saddam Hussein from Iraq. Bush's foreign-policy experts — under the watchful eye of Secretary of State Baker — also played a critical role in a series of international events that forever changed the world.

From January 20, 1989, to Bush's exit from office four years later, America's 41st president saw a world transform like never before. Bush himself acknowledged, "Some of the most dramatic and epochal events of the twentieth century took place during the short period of 1989 to 1991, events grouped broadly under the umbrella of the conclusion of the last great confrontation of the century — the Cold War." And by Bush's side during those years was the man he often called "Bake," one of his very best friends . . . "a real fighter, and he goes the extra mile . . . a tough trader and a strong negotiator; I knew he would always tell me directly and forcefully how he felt on various matters."[234]

TENSIONS IN TIANANMEN SQUARE

Following the April 1989 death of Hu Yaobang, a former Communist Party leader who worked tirelessly to introduce democratic reforms into China, students descended on Tiananmen Square in Beijing, China. The peaceful demonstration grew to tens of thousands of people by the middle of May 1989. Frustrated with a one-party system and no real voice, the students' protests grew louder, more vocal, forcing Chinese party leaders to unleash the military on the protestors, firing live rounds into the unarmed crowd. The horrific scene ended in bloodshed with thousands injured and possibly as many as 2,600 deaths — that, according to the Chinese Red Cross. Though the Chinese government put the official figure at 241 dead and 7,000 wounded, regardless, it was a scene of cold-blooded murder.[235]

Who can forget the brave soul who stood firmly in front of a column of tanks as they advanced across the square, shifting his position each time the front tank tried to maneuver around him? The video was smuggled out of China and given to a worldwide audience for all to see. It delivered a simple, yet profoundly powerful message — the democratic tenets that promote freedom of speech, the ability to openly and without fear express your opinions, and the right to live, think, and move about freely without fear of retribution from authoritarian governments were taking root in China. The Tiananmen Square Massacre was impactful and consequential in many regards — ironically — probably even more so outside of China. Europe was watching and taking note.

Adding to the Tiananmen Square showdown between protestors and the Chinese government was the arrival in Beijing of Soviet Union leader Mikhail Gorbachev for the first Sino-Soviet summit since 1959. As Gorbachev tried to make his way through the city in his heavily guarded motorcade, he was blocked by protestors nearly everywhere he went. While the visit by a State leader turned embarrassing for Chinese officials, it was no doubt a stark reminder to Gorbachev of how his very own country was undergoing a radical transformation, and the protestors very well knew it.

President Bush recalled watching the events closely, with apprehension that turned to disgust, believing any military crackdown on peaceful protestors was simply unacceptable. Bush wanted a "measured response, one aimed at those who had pushed for and implemented the use of force. . . . It was important that the Chinese leaders know we could not continue business as usual and that the People's Liberation Army realize that we wanted to see restraint."[236]

Reflecting back, Baker acknowledges that the president had to strike a careful balance of safeguarding his country's geopolitical relationship with China, while also appealing to the cause of the peaceful protestors and those who were killed. Just two days after the massacre, Bush announced various penalties against the Chinese, including suspension of military sales and a stoppage of all visits between the leaders of both countries. Said Baker, "But even as Bush punished China, he strove to keep diplomatic relations between the two countries alive. While it was important that the Chinese understood that he considered their behavior abhorrent and not to be ignored, he took no joy in imposing sanctions and sought ways to ease the estrangement. Bush dispatched high-level officials to China to let its leaders know that while he would not accept what they had done, he wanted to preserve the relationship."[237]

Bush, writing in his diary, admitted that trying to send signals to China that the United States wanted to continue and stay intact was, no doubt, difficult when "they're executing people and we have to respond. We've got to stand for what this country believes in — human rights, right for peaceful protests . . ."[238] Baker concurred wholeheartedly with the president. "Beyond the political realities at home, the Chinese also needed to understand that we weren't paper tigers on the matter of human rights."[239]

Was there a price to pay for the president taking a firm stand on human rights with the Chinese government? Perhaps. As Baker acknowledges, for the remainder of Bush's presidency, the Chinese relationship "essentially treaded water. . . . Any real chance for forward motion died along with the demonstrators in the square [Tiananmen Square] that fateful June [1989] evening."[240]

TROUBLE DOWN SOUTH

Manuel Noriega, the strongman ruler of Panama from 1983 to 1989, had seen relations with the United States rapidly deteriorate during his iron grip on the country. Noriega began to busy himself with drug dealing and money laundering, along with jailing and sometimes murdering political opponents. Though Noriega had supported the Contras, his dangerous and corrupt rule was becoming a source of embarrassment for the United States. President Reagan even pressured Noriega with drug indictments, which Noriega ignored, continuing his dictatorial rule of Panama. The relationship between the United States and Noriega completely unraveled during the 1989 Panamanian national elections when the pro-Noriega candidate Carlos Duque was defeated, but Noriega himself declared the elections null and void. Guillermo Endara, the opposition candidate, and his running mate were attacked in front of the foreign press by Noriega supporters the next day.

President Bush called for calm in Panama, yet bluntly told reporters, "I call on all foreign leaders to urge General Noriega to honor the clear results of the election. . . . I would like to think he will heed the call of the people and that he would listen to the international outcry that is building and that he would step down from office, in which case the relations with the United States would improve dramatically and instantly."[241] Not surprisingly, Noriega ignored Bush's demand, continuing to hold on to power, even foiling a second coup attempt by members of the Panamanian military. In December 1989, US servicemen were fired upon by the Panamanian Defense Forces (PDF) during a stop at a roadblock. The gunfire resulted in the death of an American Marine.

On December 17, Bush "called an emergency meeting of his senior advisors . . . for principals only — no staff." In Baker's words, "The meeting itself was anticlimactic . . . very little if any debate over the merits of invading Panama." Everyone in the room agreed with the president's sentiment: This is just going on and on." As such, "Most of the discussion centered instead upon the myriad diplomatic and logistical details linked to military action."[242] Bush had simply had enough of Noriega, and on December 20, 1989, he ordered the invasion of Panama.

Bush's statement from the White House that morning was laced with aggressive language toward the brutal dictator, stating, "General Noriega's reckless threats and attacks upon Americans in Panama created an [imminent] danger to the 35,000 American citizens in Panama. As president, I have no higher obligation than to safeguard the lives of American citizens. And that is why I directed our armed forces to protect the lives of American citizens in Panama, and to bring General Noriega to justice in the United States."[243]

Baker felt that military action against Panama would one day come as Noriega's involvement with international drug dealing continued to grow year after year while he was in power. Attempts to work with Noriega during the Reagan administration had simply failed, which according to Baker, only served to embolden the dictator. On Bush's decision to invade Panama and oust Noriega, Baker notes: "The president's decision to strike a blow for democracy sent a powerful signal that, like his predecessor, George Bush was willing to commit the military might of our country to protect vital American interests and support democratic principles in the Americas."[244]

Operation Just Cause, the invasion of Panama, consisted of approximately 27,000 US soldiers and 300 aircraft, with an emphasis on Noriega's strongholds throughout the country. While the death toll was relatively low for American servicemen, considerable civilian deaths were noted, forcing the United Nations to condemn the invasion. Noriega surrendered on January 3, 1990, detained as a prisoner of war, then sent to the United States to be put on trial. He served seventeen years in prison, only to be extradited to France on a wide range of charges.

Reflecting on the Panama invasion and subsequent ouster of Noriega, Baker said, "I also believe that in breaking the mindset of the American people about the use of force in the post-Vietnam era, Panama established an emotional predicate that permitted us to build the public support so essential to the success of Operation Desert Storm thirteen months later." Additionally, "All this flowed from a single event: the president's determination that a naked assault on democracy wouldn't be tolerated. In dramatic fashion, the United States had demonstrated once more that it would stand up for democracy, and behind its friends in the hemisphere."[245]

FALL OF THE BERLIN WALL

On August 13, 1961, the Communist government of the German Democratic Republic (GDR, or East Germany) erected a barrier in hopes of stopping the flow of mass defections from East to West Germany. What began as a border of barbed-wire fence evolved into a highly fortified, miles-long concrete barrier with armed East German border guards, thousands of land mines, German shepherd and Doberman pinscher attack dogs, and guard towers.

While the GDR stated that the official purpose of the slabs of concrete and barbed wire was to stop Western "fascists" from entering East Germany, the Wall became a symbol of oppression for the German people, now further separated as the Cold War raged hotter than ever.

Three decades later, on November 9, 1989, an official of the

Socialist Unity Party of Germany, the ruling party during most of the existence of the GDR, announced that citizens of the GDR would be free to cross the border as they pleased, effective at midnight. On that very night, the Wall began to fall. Piece by piece. Thousands swarmed to the Wall, walking freely into West Berlin, an act once punishable by imprisonment or death.

Between 1961 and 1989, at least 171 people were killed or died at the Wall. Exactly two years after that historic night, the demolition of the Berlin Wall was complete, marking the end of decades of oppression by a Soviet-dominated regime. The GDR, which had been built on fear, oppression, and tyranny, eventually crumbled also, giving way to East–West German Reunification on October 3, 1990.

Yet as symbolic and transformational as the fall of the Berlin Wall was, President Bush admitted he had given little thought to German reunification in the early months of his administration in 1989. He wrote: "I was no expert on the country, but I did see West Germany as a critical friend and ally. I had a great deal of respect for the Federal Republic [West Germany] and for the long-standing and vital American–German ties, which I was determined to do my part to make better."[246]

The Bush White House had a tough sell to many European countries fearful of a reunified Germany. French president Francois Mitterrand was skeptical, to say the least, telling British prime minister Margaret Thatcher that "reunification would result in Germany gaining more European influence than Hitler ever did," forecasting a return of the "bad" Germans and that Europe would have to bear the consequences. Mitterrand warned Thatcher that a new Germany would be unstoppable, militarily.

Bush, ever mindful and respectful of the concerns of these leaders, felt differently. "I tried to help other leaders understand my view that this new Germany would be different. . . . However complicated or risky the process might be, the pursuit of reunification was something for the Germans themselves to decide."[247]

Thatcher herself was no proponent of German reunification, opposing it at almost every possible opportunity once the Berlin Wall began to fall. Privately, she admitted to her closest political associates that it was almost inevitable that the two Germanys would reunite, but she was extremely concerned about what it meant for the future of Europe. Fresh on Thatcher's mind — along with Francois Mitterrand's and other European leaders' — were the two bloody wars that had cost tens of millions of lives, and the Germans' role in both. One of Thatcher's more memorable lines regarding the fall of the Berlin Wall and German reunification: "We beat the Germans twice, and now they're back."[248]

Publicly, Thatcher spoke in ominous terms regarding Germany's appetite for power, even telling *Der Spiegel* on March 26, 1990, that then German chancellor Helmut Kohl had told her that he did not recognize the Oder-Neisse border with Poland, a frontier drawn up after World War II. Kohl was naturally incensed by her assertions and denied ever making such comments to Thatcher.[249] Ultimately, the Iron Lady recognized that the political winds of reunification for Germany were just too strong to oppose as the United States, France, and even the Soviet Union, supported it. She fell in step with the political mainstream of the time, yet privately, never gave up her suspicions of the Germans.

Two core challenges with German reunification — which in part fueled concern from Thatcher, Mitterrand, and other European leaders — were the sheer pace of change spreading throughout the continent (the Soviet Union was on the brink of collapse) and that West Germany's leader, Helmut Kohl, had not informed the Bush White House, or other European countries, about his vision for German reunification before submitting it to the West German Parliament on November 28, 1989.

Things were moving very rapidly, prompting Baker to state, "Our policy position is that there are certain responsibilities reserved under the Allied powers that have to be considered when you deal with the question of German reunification. These things have to be considered and dealt with. It seems to me that working together with all of our Allies — and that does include the Federal Republic of Germany, the United Kingdom, the French, and taking into consideration the concerns of Germany's neighbors — that we can have influence on the process."[250] To be clear, according to Baker, German reunification would not just be a German issue, rather, one to be decided in consultation with NATO, NATO's neighbors, and naturally, the Soviet Union.

Just prior to Baker's remarks, which were aimed at Chancellor Kohl, President Bush outlined the following conditions in Brussels on December 4, 1989, regarding German reunification:

» It must be accomplished on the basis of free elections in both East and West Germany.
» It must be in accord with the 1975 Helsinki Final Act, which stipulates that the postwar boundaries of Europe are fixed and can only be changed by peaceful

negotiation, meaning that German claims on certain Polish or Soviet territories would be virtually out of the question.

» A unified Germany must remain in the Western alliance, meaning that it would be a member of NATO and the European Community.

» Unification must come about gradually and peacefully.[251]

Well into 1990, Thatcher continued to express grave concerns about a unified Germany. As Bush wrote in his diary: "Thatcher now has much more concern about a unified Germany than about a Soviet threat. We're in this fascinating time of change and flux . . ."[252] Mindful and respectful of her concerns, Bush nevertheless knew — as did Thatcher — that a unified Germany was inevitable, but more than that, it was necessary for the broader good of the European Continent, and the world.

In 2009, Baker had this to say about the fall of the Berlin Wall:

"I'll never forget East and West Germans striking their blows for freedom, taking sledgehammers to the barrier that divided them for almost three decades. The twentieth anniversary of this moment provides an opportunity to reflect on an extraordinary event — and to draw lessons that might guide us today.

"It may seem now like the fall of the Berlin Wall was a histori-cal inevitability — after all, the same European nations that battled one another for most of the twentieth century cooperate today on economic, political, and military matters. Though tensions still exist between Washington and Moscow, and between Russia and some of the former Soviet republics, there is cooperation on a range of issues unimaginable in 1989. It's easy to take what happened that day for granted.

"We shouldn't. For most of my adult life, I lived with the reminder that civilization might perish in a fiery hail of atoms; my kids ran practice drills in their school hallways in case Russia dropped the bomb. American diplomacy wasn't very complex: if the Russians were for it, we were against it. Cold or not, the world was at war. And it could have gotten much worse.

"But everything changed in the twenty-six-month period symbolized by the fall of the Wall. Less than eleven months later, on October 3, 1990, East and West Germany reunited. The Warsaw Pact dissolved in March 1991, and later that year, on Christmas Day, the Soviet Union ceased to exist."[253]

And on the commemoration of the thirtieth anniversary of the fall of the Berlin Wall, Baker reflected, "Thirty years ago, on November 9, 1989, as crowds of East and West Germans were tearing down the Wall that symbolized division and totalitarianism, I was fortunate to watch firsthand as President George H.W. Bush eschewed high rhetoric in favor of clear-eyed statecraft."[254]

Recalling the epic collapse of concrete and steel that kept millions of Germans segregated from one another for almost three decades, he also reminded us of four critical factors that he and President Bush kept in mind as Europe was being swept up by what Baker called "seismic changes." First and foremost, according to Baker, the president understood that timing was critical in terms of foreign-policy success, so, "When the Wall fell, the president went into full gear to take the next and much more monumental step of reuniting East and West Germany." Second, Bush was well aware that he needed domestic support for his programs, and if he didn't have it — certain elements of his foreign policy would be doomed. "Bush wasn't afraid to go it alone. But he knew that he would be more successful with the broad backing of the American people, and he crafted a bipartisan foreign policy accordingly." Third, Bush knew he had to have international support at its fullest to ensure his goal of German reunification after the collapse of the Wall. "Bush overcame those international concerns because he understood the importance of the fourth factor in successful foreign policy: deft, sustained diplomacy. He had developed strong relations with Soviet leader Mikhail Gorbachev, British prime minister Margaret Thatcher, and French president Francois Mitterrand. Each of them trusted the president as a leader who kept his word."[255]

The fall of the Berlin Wall paved the way for two Germanys to come together as one, a process that began in earnest in 1990, culminating on October 3, 1990, what is now known as German Unity Day. Yet before that could happen, the United States, United Kingdom, France, and the Soviet Union agreed to meet in Moscow on September 12, 1990, and relinquish their post-World War II occupation rights of Germany. When Soviet foreign minister Eduard Shevardnadze signed the four-power pact, he stated, "We are going through emotional and historic events. . . . We have drawn a line under World War II and we have started keeping the time of a new age."[256] Baker called the event "truly a rendezvous with history," adding, "Let our legacy be that forty-five years after the end of World War II, we have finally got the political arithmetic right: two plus four adds up to one Germany in a Europe that's whole and free."[257]

Thatcher and Mitterrand voiced two concerns about a new unified Germany: the blending of two almost entirely different social cultures and the demise of the East German economy, what little there was. Both of these concerns, and more, were set aside, put to rest — temporarily — as the world watched two countries become one. At 9:56 a.m., President Bush placed a call to German chancellor Helmut Kohl. "Helmut!" a joyous Bush said, "I am sitting in a meeting with members of our Congress and am calling at the end of this historic day to wish you well." Kohl replied, "Things are going very, very well. I am in Berlin. There were one million people here last night at the very spot where the Wall used to stand — and where President Reagan called on Mr. Gorbachev to open this gate. Words can't describe the feeling. The weather is very nice and warm, fortunately. There were large crowds of young people. Eighty percent were under thirty. It was fantastic. . . . When the parliamentary declaration is made, it will say that all American presidents from Harry Truman all the way up to our friend George Bush made this possible. I would like to thank you again for all your support for us."[258]

The call was a mere three minutes long, yet it represented a transformation for the ages in terms of what Germany had accomplished and what was still to come for Eastern Europe and the Soviet Union. Germany was just the beginning of a massive tidal wave of change for the world to witness.

ASSESSING THE SOVIET SITUATION

Before Bush officially took office as America's 41st president, the president-elect — the sitting vice president — spent a few moments with Soviet leader Mikhail Gorbachev at Governors Island, New

York. Bush recalled that crisp day of December 7, 1988, and how he was looking forward to meeting with Gorbachev, who had just finished a major address to the United Nations General Assembly. Gorbachev agreed to a brief summit with President Reagan as part of his visit to the UN. As the first sitting vice president to actually be elected president since Martin Van Buren, Bush admitted to being "in the awkward position of having to weigh my present role against my future one. I was only the president-elect, a few weeks away from my own inauguration and not yet setting policy."[259] Yet Bush was fully aware that Gorbachev was very interested in learning more about the next president's direction with the Soviet Union, and Bush himself was determined to continue on with the now much-improved relationship between the two superpowers.

Bush remembers how "a broadly smiling Gorbachev emerged from the ferry, waving, dressed in a smartly tailored gray suit and a serious red tie. . . . At one point, Reagan asked me if I had anything I wanted to add. I said I hoped to build on what we had achieved in the US–Soviet relations. . . . I pledged general continuity with Reagan's policies toward the Soviet Union."[260] Bush had no intention of reinventing the wheel or reversing course on many of the accomplishments made, yet he developed his own national-security team, his own advisors, and he needed time before he could give Gorbachev any specifics. The Soviet leader more than understood Bush's position, telling the president-elect he hoped things would continue in terms of the progress made.

Bush first met Gorbachev in 1985 at the funeral of his predecessor, Konstantin Chernenko and, over time, developed what he called a good feel for the new Soviet leader. In December 1987, during a summit visit to Washington, they briefly discussed the upcoming presidential race, Bush telling Gorbachev not to worry about the "empty cannons of rhetoric" he would hear during the campaign.[261] While Bush and Gorbachev were well aware of the fundamental changes sweeping through the Soviet Union, both men found themselves witness to one of the most cataclysmic changes the world had seen — the eventual collapse of the Soviet Empire.

From Baker's perspective, the more he thought about his role during the 1988 presidential transition period — soon to be sworn-in as secretary of State — the more "I understood that the central focus of my job initially had to be US–Soviet relations."[262] Baker knew that all indicators were showing a Soviet state in demise in every conceivable category — economics/finances, military might, and more — so managing this decline, in his view, was crucial. If Baker could assist the Soviet Union in what he called a "soft landing," it would only help to spread democracy and ease the tensions of decades-old authoritarian rule. A complete cutoff from a socialist society to a democratically run, civilized rule-of-law culture was simply naïve, something Baker was well aware of, as was Bush. The transition would take time, patience, and discipline because if the "soft landing" and reforms stalled, America, according to Baker, "would have to contend with a very unstable international environment."[263]

Well before taking the presidential oath of office, Bush was acutely aware of the unrest slowly but surely rising in Central and Eastern Europe. The Soviet system of government was coming undone, unravelling in rapid fashion, and in doing so, creating a tidal wave of changes that spread throughout the Soviet "satellite nations." Bush recalled how Gorbachev planted the seeds for reform and change in his own country with what became known to the West as "Perestroi-ka" — the process of restructuring and reforming the economic and political system of the Soviet Union. This, according to Bush, allowed Central and Eastern European countries to start thinking inde-pendently, asserting more control over their own countries, ultimately breaking away from the centralized, authoritarian rule that had been the custom since the end of World War II. Bush saw Poland as the likely leader in terms of liberalization, with promise also in Hungary. Yet as much as Bush hoped for change, he wanted to be careful. "The traumatic uprisings in East Germany in 1953, Hungary in 1956, and Czechoslovakia in 1968 were constantly on my mind . . ." said Bush of the early period of his presidency, as he did not "want to encourage a course of events which might turn violent and get out of hand and which we then couldn't — or wouldn't — support, leaving people stranded at the barricades. . . . The problem was figuring out exactly where that line was and what was likely to be seen by the Soviets as provocative."[264]

As Baker recalled, in the early months of the Bush administration, there were two prevailing thoughts regarding Eastern Europe and the Soviet Union. First, the "status quo plus" school of thought that things were going the United States' way and that a weakened Soviet Union had no choice but to reform and make concessions, so why not just hold firm on our policies? Yet Baker and his senior advisors felt differently. According to Baker, the "activist" view was more in line with his thinking, and strategically, to the benefit of the United States. By engaging with the Soviet Union, embracing change and moving forward with it, the United States would not be sitting idle, giving Gorbachev the upper hand on the world stage. Baker firmly believed that the Bush White House needed to develop measures that Gorbachev would feel obligated to embrace. "Standing back and standing pat would limit our options over time and allow the political terrain to shift against us."[265]

Baker traveled to the Soviet Union in May 1989, landing in Moscow and stepping onto Soviet soil for the first time in his life. America's secretary of State initially met with Foreign Minister Eduard Shevardnadze — a relationship that would strengthen over the years to become both a close political and personal friendship. The following day, May 11, 1989, Baker met with Mikhail Gorbachev. As Baker recalled, "Gorbachev bounded into the room, beaming as always with energy and confidence. While he was neither a tall nor a large man, Gorbachev had an actor's gift to fill a stage with his presence. . . . Whenever we met, he exuded optimism, and in this regard, he reminded me time and again of Ronald Reagan. . . . Like Reagan, Gorbachev was invariably positive."[266]

Gorbachev's persona was a stark contrast to Shevardnadze's, who, according to Baker, seemed to carry the burden of reform on his shoulders. Coupled with his gray hair and dark circles under his eyes, it made him seem older than he was. And the more Baker worked with both men, the more he clearly saw the differences between them. Gorbachev would promote reforms in public and on the world stage, leaving the details and the consequences of such actions to his subordinates. Shevardnadze — ever the pragmatist — knew how difficult and challenging such measures would be to actually implement and execute.

The meeting was short, yet it clearly laid the groundwork for America's strategy in the near future — keep engaged with Central and Eastern Europe and don't give up the offensive on the world stage to Gorbachev.

Bush agreed. "You're right. We must take the offensive. We cannot be seen as just reacting to yet another Gorbachev move. We need to do it to keep public opinion behind the alliance. Maybe Eastern Europe is it — get in there in his end zone. Not to stir up revolution, but we're right on human rights, democracy, and freedom."[267]

Two months after Baker's visit with Gorbachev in Moscow, Bush took the initiative, trekking to Poland in July of 1989 to announce a comprehensive six-part program of American aid. It was Bush's first official visit to Eastern Europe as president, and he wasted no time at all capitalizing on what he called an "unprecedented opportunity" for America to engage with Poland as it began experimenting with reform.[268]

While in Poland, Bush met with Solidarity leader, Lech Walesa, a man of "infectious enthusiasm . . . I liked him . . . He has a twinkle in his eye, and smiles and laughs readily," said Bush. Walesa and his wife Danuta hosted lunch at their very modest home on the outskirts of Gdansk for George and Barbara Bush. Bush recalled the six-course exquisite feast, complete with fine wine. "At the end of the day, I had the heady sense that I was witnessing history being made. . . . I was convinced that the people's desire for freedom was powerful and irreversible, and that the country would not willingly revert to Soviet domination."[269]

Bush, standing in the country's Senate chamber, said "Poland is where the Cold War began, and now the people of Poland can help bring the division of Europe to an end." But he also cautioned them that economic reform and recovery "cannot occur without sacrifices" by every Pole.[270]

Bush, Baker, and National Security Advisor Brent Scowcroft were confident that the president's visit to Poland had met their objectives. Next stop was Hungary. Six years earlier, Bush had been the first US vice president of the United States to ever step foot into Hungary, now six years later, he was the first US president to do so. Hungary was not Poland in terms of how far along they were in reforms. Regardless, change was in the air, as Bush quickly came to realize during his visit.

A heavy thunderstorm delayed the arrival of Air Force One, but it never dampened the enthusiasm of the crowd that patiently waited for Bush at Kossuth Square in Budapest. Bush stepped up to the microphone to deliver a scripted speech, then suddenly tore it up in full view of the crowd, who went wild. Bush then delivered some extemporaneous remarks praising Hungary for its reform-minded leadership. Scowcroft described a moment that followed: "Noticing an elderly woman who was standing near the podium, soaked to the skin, the president took off his raincoat and put it around her shoulders. As the crowd roared its approval, he plunged into its midst, shaking hands and shouting good wishes. It was an incredible scene; one I will never forget."[271]

As hope and change were sweeping through Eastern Europe, the Soviet Union was falling into deeper economic and political instability throughout 1990 and 1991. Gorbachev, who had assumed power as general secretary of the Communist Party in 1985, had embarked on his restructuring initiatives — Perestroika — and his glasnost (meaning openness) policy reforms, which led to a complete transformation of the Soviet Union in all regards. His reforms — hailed by the West — also unleashed strong opposition against Gorbachev by many within the old Soviet guard.

The rapid decline of the Soviet Empire, coupled with Gorbachev's reforms, came to a head in August 1991. A coup was staged by Gorbachev's opposition, and he was placed under house arrest. As Baker recalled, he was fast asleep in Wyoming — a state he confesses he loves as much as Texas — when a watch officer from the State Department Operations Center told him of the news unfolding in Moscow. Vice President Gennady Yanayev had assumed power as president of the USSR "due to Gorbachev's inability to perform his duties for health reasons."[272]

Baker telephoned Bush, who was in Kennebunkport, and though there wasn't much information coming out of Moscow, they clearly understood the gravity of the situation. According to Baker, he knew very well that old forces were trying to stop the tumultuous changes coming to the Soviet Union, yet "I felt that it would be hard for reactionary forces in the Soviet Union to put the freedom genie back in the bottle now. Reform had gone too far now."[273]

Bush concurred with Baker's assessment. In his tape-recorded diary, the president spoke with obvious concern regarding the coup. "Will there be general strikes? Will there be resistance? Will the military use so much force and crack down so much that they won't permit any democratic moves to go forward?"[274]

Bush's immediate response was to keep allies informed of the coup, speaking with Prime Minister John Major of Britain, President Francois Mitterrand of France, Prime Minister Brian Mulroney of Canada, German leader Helmut Kohl, and others. They all came to the same conclusion — the initial information coming out of Moscow was limited, at best, and Yanayev seemed to be nothing more than a figurehead in the attempt to oust Gorbachev. With Gorbachev under house arrest, Boris Yeltsin took to the streets, demanding the coup be stopped. Recalled Bush, "Yeltsin is out there on top of a tank saying the coup must be reversed. . . . You have to give him credit for enormous guts."[275]

In Moscow, and around the Kremlin, the scene was chaotic at times in the days following the coup. Armored personnel carriers and tanks flooded the streets as hardliners in the Soviet Union sought to take control of the country, while a resolute Yeltsin called for Gorbachev to be restored to power. Bush wrote: "We [United States] must cast our support to the forces of reform. Gorbachev, Yeltsin, Shevardnadze, others all having told me quite recently that these changes are irreversible. The test is about to come."[276]

Yanayev's "official" explanation for the coup — outlined in a letter to the US leaders and delivered via Soviet ambassador Viktor Komplektov stated: "There has emerged a situation of uncontrollability with too many centers of power. All this cannot but cause widespread discontent of the population. There has also been a real threat of the country's disintegration, of a breakdown of the single economic space, and the single civil rights space, the single defense, and the single foreign policy." To Yanayev and other Soviet hardliners, their way of life as they knew it — decades of centralized, authoritarian rule — was being squashed and trampled on by Gorbachev's reforms, and enough was enough. According to Yanayev's letter, "Under these circumstances, we have no other choice but to take resolute measures in order to stop the slide towards catastrophe . . ."[277]

Bush was flush with worries, and understandably so. What about instability in the Baltics? Who would be safeguarding the Soviet nuclear arsenal? Was Gorbachev having health issues? Yeltsin was declaring himself in charge of functions of the government — what did that mean? Bush finally reached Yeltsin, who told the president, "The situation is very complex. President Gorbachev is located in Foros in the Crimea. . . . Yanayev is using the pretext that Gorbachev is ill, but this is not yet confirmed." Bush concluded that pretext was more than likely a cover. Yeltsin told Bush that large numbers of troops had been brought into Moscow by the hardliners. Said Yeltsin, "The group has exposed itself as no more than a right-wing junta. I appeared before the people and soldiers and I said that actions of the committee were unconstitutional, illegal and have no force on Russian territory."[278]

Yeltsin was drawing a line in the sand, rolling the dice and taking the biggest political gamble of his life. If the coup were to be successful, he would be banished to the likes of Siberia, charged with any number of crimes against the government. Yet if the coup failed, he would emerge victorious, possibly eclipsing Gorbachev and positioning himself as the country's next leader.

The coup unraveled as quickly as it had begun, thanks in large part to the unanimous declaration by the Supreme Soviet of Russia that the coup was illegal, as were the people's demonstrations, Yeltsin's actions, and the plotters' overall inability to actually follow through with meaningful action after placing Gorbachev under house arrest. According to Scowcroft, "The failed coup accelerated the decline of central Soviet authority, particularly of the Communist Party, which was further discredited, and ultimately of Gorbachev. It also signaled the rise of the republics on the cue of an ascendant Yeltsin." Bush recalled that while Yeltsin did properly call for Gorbachev's return to power, "he [Yeltsin] was heavy-handed in the aftermath of the coup. I knew the two men did not like each other, but at times, Yeltsin treated a politically weakened Gorbachev with sheer disdain. He had won the day and was riding high."[279]

Bush remembers the events of the week after the coup being unbelievable as a massive purge occurred within the Soviet government — not just of the coup plotters, but of Gorbachev's closest allies. Yeltsin took the reins of power, clamping down on opposition forces by closing the Soviet Central Committee headquarters, banning Party newspapers, and even suspending the Russian Communist Party. Soon thereafter, Gorbachev resigned as general secretary and the Soviet parliament banned Communist Party activities. The Soviet Union was disintegrating rapidly, giving the Baltic states momentum they desperately needed for breaking away — once and for all — from decades-long Soviet rule.

The Bush administration had to now grapple with the immense changes — and the aftermath — taking place throughout the Soviet Union and Eastern Europe. From the Soviet Union, Bush sensed a real air of cooperation. After all, the United States had stood by both Gorbachev and Yeltsin throughout the coup. But more than that, Bush made it known to both men that the United States wanted their country to succeed, hence, an era of genuine dialogue and collaboration began. Bush wrote: "We had seen some strong evidence of this when Jim Baker went to Moscow in September 1991. He spoke separately with both Yeltsin and Gorbachev, who were working together as best they could, and had engineered a deal for both the United States and the USSR to end all support to the combatants in Afghanistan. Mikhail had also agreed to remove Soviet forces from Cuba and announced it even before telling the Cubans. Both Gorbachev and Yeltsin backed central control of nuclear weapons — whatever became of the Union."[280]

Bush wrote in his diary: "The end came swiftly. On December 21, at Alma-Ata, all the republics except the Baltics and Georgia signed the Declaration of Adherence to the Commonwealth of Independent States. There was nothing left of the USSR.

"My friend Mikhail Gorbachev resigned as president of the Soviet Union on Christmas Day. . . . He wanted a 'final call' . . . 10:00 a.m. Washington time. I took the call at Camp David where I was spending the holiday with my family." Bush remembers it as an emotional call for Gorbachev, and how the soon-to-be ex-leader of the Soviet Union thanked him for all the United States had done, and for the personal relationship the two men had developed over the years. Bush said Gorbachev "was not bitter about the collapse of the Soviet Union . . . but he seemed drained and uncertain about the future of the country he loved."

Bush expressed the United States' commitment to continue to work with the new Russian Republic and was glad to hear that Gorbachev would stay active on the global political stage. "I hope that our paths will cross soon again," said Bush. "You will be most welcome here [at Camp David]. And, indeed, I would value your counsel after you have had a little time to sort things out. And perhaps we could do it right back up here at Camp David." On the topic of a new Russia, Bush told Gorbachev, "I will, of course, deal with respect — openly, forcefully, and hopefully progressively — with the leader of the Russian Republic . . ."[281]

Gorbachev resigned his presidency of the Soviet Union later that day in a televised address, saying:

"Today, I'd like to express my gratitude to all citizens who supported the policy of renovating the country, got involved in the implementation of the democratic reforms. I am grateful to statesmen, public and political figures, millions of people abroad, those who understood our concepts and supported them, turned to us, started sincere cooperation with us.

"I am leaving my post with apprehension, but also with hope, with faith in you, your wisdom and force of spirit. We are the heirs of a great civilization, and its rebirth into a new, modern and dignified life now depends on one and all.

"I wish to thank with all my heart all those who have stood together with me all these years for the fair and good cause. Some mistakes could surely have been avoided, many things could have been done better, but I am convinced that sooner or later, our common efforts will bear fruit, our nations will live in a prosperous and democratic society. I wish all the best to all of you."[282]

Less than thirty minutes after the conclusion of Gorbachev's speech — approximately 7:32 p.m. Moscow time, the Soviet hammer-and-sickle flag was lowered outside the Kremlin for the final time, replaced by the prerevolutionary white, blue, and red flag of Russia.

Russia took USSR's permanent seat on the United Nations Security Council, with all Soviet embassies becoming Russian embassies. The Soviet Union continued to exist in name only for a mere six days and formally dissolved at midnight, December 31, 1991.

WAR IN THE GULF

The summer of 1990 found the Bush administration grappling with yet another international crisis as Iraqi leader Saddam Hussein invaded his country's neighbor, Kuwait. Over a two-day period, Hussein's forces poured into the tiny oil-rich Kuwait, and they would not be leaving anytime soon. While intelligence reports clearly showed Saddam had been building up a massive military presence on the Iraq–Kuwait border, there was general consensus it was to frighten the Kuwaitis. According to Baker, "By sending his armored columns all the way to the Kuwait–Saudi border, Saddam showed both his appetite and his willingness to run risks." And even with the United States and the Soviet Union issuing joint statements condemning Saddam's actions, he continued to pour forces into Kuwait over the weekend following the initial invasion.

As Bush recalled, "By Sunday evening, I was worried that the Iraqi forces would indeed move across the border into Saudi Arabia. With so many tanks heading south, it seemed incontrovertible that Saddam had such plans. . . . In retrospect, if Saddam had wanted to make a go for Saudi Arabia, he probably made a mistake in that he did not do it in this brief window — before my announcement that we would send forces [to the Middle East]."[283]

To say that Bush and Baker were dismayed would be an understatement, indeed. In the early days of the Bush administration, Baker had had high hopes for improved relations with Iraq, recalling how his initial meetings with a number of Iraq's top operatives — including Nizar Hamdoon and Tariq Aziz — were cordial, even to the point that he was impressed with Aziz. Baker's primary reason for developing constructive dialogue with Iraq was to help solve the never-ending challenges of Middle East peace. Yet the Bush administration's hopes for enhanced relations with the country were strained by Aziz when he took a sharp turn and began accusing the United States of meddling with Iraq's internal affairs. According to Baker, "Despite our pursuit of a course of incentives, our relations with Iraq turned worse as we entered the new year [1990]. There's no question Saddam's behavior changed for the worse in early 1990. His rhetoric grew more inflammatory and threatening."[284]

On August 5, 1990, Bush took a hardline stance against the invasion, bluntly stating, "This will not stand, this aggression against Kuwait," just after stepping off Marine One on the South Lawn of the White House. It was Bush's most famous — and according to Baker, his most courageous — line of his entire presidency. Bush's daughter, Doro, recalled, "The midafternoon summer shadows had only started to streak across the hazy South Lawn on August 5th when Marine One hovered in at 3:00 p.m. . . . I could see the somberness in Dad's face as he approached the bank of microphones staged near the Rose Garden. I sensed no apprehension, but rather a smoldering intensity in the way he spoke."[285] Bush's famous statement, according to Baker, "reflected his [Bush's] instinctive sense, very early on, that this was no ordinary crisis, that it truly would become a hinge point in history. His statement also showed his determination to undo Iraq's aggression."[286]

In his diary entry for that August day, Bush wrote: "It has been the most hectic forty-eight hours since I have been president. . . . The enormity of Iraq is upon me now. I have been on the phone incessantly. . . . The bottom line is that the West is together. . . . It boils down to cutting off everything economically with Iraq."[287] Yet just a day later, on August 6, 1990, he wrote: "Big day regarding Iran and Iraq. Dick Cheney goes to see [Saudi Arabia's] King Fahd and calls back. Fahd accepts [our offer] and invites our troops to come. . . . I feel tension in the stomach and neck. I feel great pressure, but I also feel a certain calmness when we talk about these matters. I know I am doing the right thing."[288]

The Saudis had agreed to receive the American delegation, but they had many questions and big concerns. They wanted assurances of America's intentions, specifically, King Fahd wanted ample US troops to get the job done and then, their mission complete, to leave. The very idea of a Western nation occupying a Middle Eastern country would create political rifts throughout the region that would be hard to undo. Cheney was the main voice of the American delegation, speaking directly to the Saudis on what needed to be done, why, and how. It was typical Cheney straight-talk — thorough, measured, and persuasive — and after a two-hour meeting, King Fahd agreed.

The troops Bush referred to in his diary were part of a massive international effort of nations around the world descending upon the Middle East and into Saudi Arabia in what became known as Desert Shield. It started with the deployment of the 82nd Airborne Division, and within two months, the United States had over 120,000 troops in the Saudi desert, 700 tanks, 1,400 armored fighting vehicles, and 600 artillery pieces. The number of American troops used for both Desert Shield (the protection of Saudi Arabia) and Desert Storm (removing Saddam's forces out of Kuwait) swelled to over 700,000 between August 1990 and January 1991.

Moving such a massive number of forces in such a short time was a logistical challenge the likes of which the US military had not seen in decades. But a key factor in its success was President Bush's diplomatic skills, which brought together a unified coalition of countries willing to help the United States in both defending Saudi Arabia and kicking Iraqi forces out of neighboring Kuwait. As Bush worked with dozens of leaders throughout the world to coalesce support, he also had to justify to both the American people and Congress the deployment of US troops. And in the early stages of the conflict, Bush came to recognize a painful reality, that using force would very well be the final and only resolution. "I could not see how we were going to remove Saddam Hussein from Kuwait without using force. I was reluctant to speak publicly of using force. We were just beginning to get our warships in place and implement the blockade. I was not yet fully confident that we had the domestic or international backing to act."[289] And even as Iraq had one of the largest standing armies in the world at that time, Bush confessed, "I just didn't see the Iraqis as being so tough. They had been unable to defeat Iran; they had never fought over long supply lines. . . . Besides, some of our Arab coalition friends were telling me that Iraq's military was overrated."[290]

As Baker saw it, the United States had the right to legally act "unilaterally" under Article 51 of the United Nations Charter, which allows member states the right of self-defense to protect their national interests. While a number of key allies were in agreement with such a move, including — not surprisingly — Prime Minister Margaret Thatcher, Baker admits, "As a practical matter, the United States had no real choice initially but to try a coalition approach in dealing with the crisis. Otherwise, we'd never attract the breadth of support to convince Saddam he was confronting the entire civilized world, not just a single superpower he may be able to demonize."[291]

Agreeing to a coalition was one thing; building it was an entirely different task, one that required steady leadership from Bush and heavy lifting from Baker. Baker revealed a number of critical points regarding the coalition; first and foremost, keeping it intact was a bigger challenge than actually creating it, and the Soviet Union was critical to the coalition, as were many Middle Eastern countries.

Soviet leaders were undergoing massive changes within their own country, changes that ultimately led to the collapse of the country in 1991. In fact, Baker later said that he "viewed the Soviets as key. In every strategy coalition, I considered their support a prerequisite to a credible coalition. They had to be courted, nurtured, and included to a degree once unthinkable by American policymakers."[292] The strong bond that Baker and Shevardnadze developed over the previous two years surely helped when dealing with the Soviet's minister of foreign affairs, a key player in helping America and the Soviet Union agree on many terms of the coalition. The Soviet Union, a failing empire at this point, was nevertheless hypersensitive about their status on the world stage, something Baker was keenly aware of, thus requiring him to put forth his best diplomatic efforts in such contentious times.

Baker and Shevardnadze slowly dropped their respective diplomatic formalities to discuss their private worries and thoughts. In many of their open and frank discussions, Shevardnadze discussed the huge social impact that political reforms were having, yet also of the Soviet Union's slow economic growth and inability to change and modernize. Their friendship endured well after Baker's tenure as secretary of State. Shevardnadze eventually became president of Georgia, a former Soviet republic that had endured years of oppression and hardship under Communist rule.

Bush, Baker, and others in the White House spent the fall of 1990 continuing to build international support for the growing coalition, while also turning their attention domestically to both the American electorate and Congress to earn their trust. Not surprisingly, various Democratic members in Congress began to play partisan politics, putting party ahead of peace when it came to Kuwait, something that incensed Bush to the core. Though he was accepting and respectful of political differences, now was not the time to play politics. Ultimately, Bush decided to go to Congress to ask for authorization to use force to expel Iraq's forces from Kuwait. Some — one in particular — felt he didn't need to ask Congress. Secretary of Defense Dick Cheney. As Cheney saw it, "I was not enthusiastic about going to Congress to ask for an additional grant of authority. . . . Legally and from a constitutional standpoint, we had all the authority we needed. . . . If we'd lost the vote in Congress, I would certainly have recommended to the president we go forward anyway."[293]

"If I don't get the votes" in Congress for war, Bush said to then deputy national security advisor Robert Gates one day in the Oval Office, "I'm going to do it anyway. And if I get impeached, so be it." In his diary, Bush confided: "I'm convinced that they'll support us — the Congress — provided it's fast and surgical. . . . But if it's drawn out and long, well then, you'll have all the handwringers saying, 'They shouldn't have done it,' and they'll be after my neck on, perhaps, impeachment for violating the Constitution." Senator Daniel Inouye of Hawaii even warned Bush that an American military defeat without congressional authorization would be fatal to the president, politically. "If you're wrong about this," Inouye told Bush, "you are going to be impeached by the Congress."[294]

Bush won the vote in Congress: 250 to 183 in the House, and 52 to 47 in the Senate. On the evening of Saturday, January 12, the president wrote in his diary: "The big burden, lifted from my shoulders, is this Constitutional burden — the threat of impeachment. . . . All that cleared now by this very sound vote of the Congress."[295]

Was war inevitable? Perhaps, but Baker would try one last time to find an eleventh-hour resolution for ending the conflict. Baker headed to Switzerland for the Geneva Peace Conference, and Bush, having written a letter to Saddam Hussein, entrusted it to Baker, whom he instructed to hand-deliver it to Tariq Aziz in Geneva.

Baker and Aziz squared off for seven long hours in hopes of finding a solution. "The truth is," admitted Baker, "that I hoped Aziz would be swayed by what he heard from me, but I was under no illusions. I assumed the talks would be unsuccessful, and that in a matter of days, we would be at war. . . . There was simply little reason for optimism beyond mere hope."[296] While both sides opened up with formal statements, as is customary in the diplomatic world, Baker quickly saw that Aziz was simply filling in the air with nothing more than probing questions.

Baker gave Bush's letter to Aziz, who read it only to refuse to accept it, saying the language and tone were inappropriate for correspondence between two heads of state. The letter, thoughtfully written by President Bush, would not get the chance to sway the minds of the Iraqis.

After the unsuccessful meeting with Aziz, Baker recalled, "I went back upstairs to my suite, took off my jacket and shoes, and stretched out on the bed while my call to the president was patched through to the White House. "There's no give," I reported. "They didn't give an inch. They're not prepared to change their position. They offered not one new thing, no single idea, and I told them that."[297]

The letter to Saddam Hussein was released in its entirety by the White House days later on January 12, 1991. Excerpts from the letter are as follows:

Dear Mr. President:

We stand today at the brink of war between Iraq and the world. This is a war that began with your invasion of Kuwait; this is a war that can be ended only by Iraq's full and unconditional compliance with UN Security Council Resolution 678.

I am writing you now, directly, because what is at stake demands that no opportunity be lost to avoid what would be a certain calamity for the people of Iraq. I am writing as well because it is said by some that you do not understand just how isolated Iraq is and what Iraq faces as a result. I am not in a position to judge whether this impression is correct; what I can do, though, is try in this letter to reinforce what Secretary of State Baker told your foreign minister and eliminate any uncertainty or ambiguity that might exist in your mind about where we stand and what we are prepared to do.

We prefer a peaceful outcome. However, anything less than full compliance with UN Security Council Resolution 678 and its predecessors is unacceptable. There can be no reward for aggression. Nor will there be any negotiation. Principle cannot be compromised.

I write this letter not to threaten, but to inform. I do so with no sense of satisfaction, for the people of the United States have no quarrel with the people of Iraq. Mr. President, UN Security Council Resolution 678 establishes the period before Jan. 15 of this year as a "pause of good will" so that this crisis may end without further violence. Whether this pause is used as intended, or merely becomes a prelude to further violence, is in your hands, and yours alone. I hope you weigh your choice carefully and choose wisely, for much will depend upon it.[298]

Baker and Bush knew what to expect in the aftermath of the meeting with Aziz; the likelihood of avoiding a military conflict to force Saddam's army out of Kuwait was simply non-existent. The UN-imposed deadline of January 15, 1991, for Saddam to remove his forces from Kuwait was fast approaching, yet Bush and Baker still carried the slim hope that peace was possible.

Two days after meeting with Aziz in Geneva, Baker met with the exiled emir of Kuwait in Taif, Saudi Arabia, then shortly thereafter, paid a visit to the pilots and crew of the 48th Tactical Fighter Wing. Baker knew Saddam watched CNN; thus, he revised his prepared remarks for one last remaining shot at peace, telling the servicemen, "Time is running out, but the path to peace remains open. There is still time for Iraq to walk that path. . . . They can still choose peace and avert disaster. But the choice is theirs and theirs alone."[299] Baker called the reaction from the servicemen "nervous tension," but believed they were ready, prepared, and willing to go to war.

Bush's diary entry of January 15, 1991, the deadline for Saddam to leave Kuwait: "There is no way to describe the pressure. It's 9:45 the night of the 15th. Deadline runs out in two hours, 15 minutes. . . . The reports from Baghdad are defiant. People marching in the streets. Their faces smile and they chant. And I think, 'Oh God, save their lives.' There's a kid that comes on television, and I pray to God that [the bombs] will be accurate and we will not hit that child."[300]

Baker remembers receiving a call from President Bush on the morning of January 16, 1991. The president wanted to have lunch so he and Baker could discuss privately what was about to happen. America was going to war, and a somber president was seeking what Baker felt was reassurance that this was the right and just act. The president knew there would be casualties on both sides — regardless of the positive news he had received from Dick Cheney on the overall readiness of America's forces — and this weighed heavily on his mind, according to Baker. The loss of human life — even a single soul — was painful for the president to even think about as he worried immensely about casualty reports for not just American troops, but the coalition forces also, along with innocent Iraqi and Kuwaiti citizens caught in the crossfires of an unfortunate conflict.

After the January 15 deadline came and went, on January 16, 1991, at approximately 7:00 p.m. EST, Desert Shield became Desert Storm. Bush wrote: "We began bombing Baghdad. . . . Operation Desert Storm was finally underway. Like most people in America, I watched it on CNN, with Barbara and Billy Graham."[301]

America's military muscle was on display as Baghdad was inundated with a barrage of attacks from coalition forces that hit Saddam in ways he surely couldn't have anticipated. Saddam, and the world, witnessed the most advanced military in the world unleash a flurry of new weaponry that was simply astounding.

On the first night of the Gulf War, Bush received news from Defense Secretary Dick Cheney: fifty-six Navy planes had gone out, and fifty-six had returned. Additionally, more than two hundred airplanes were above the skies of Baghdad and surrounding areas, with none reported missing. Bush sensed a sigh of relief, yet still felt compelled to pray as he knew casualties would come. Bush's first few nights found him anxious, restless, often unable to sleep, yet as the days progressed, he began to witness the complete collapse of the Iraqi military as American and coalition forces unleashed a furious assault on Saddam's supposedly venerable forces. The first real test of the war came when reports surfaced of a Scud missile strike by the Iraqis on Israel. As

Scowcroft recalled, "The attack was a shrewd attempt to split the Arab allies from the coalition, either by directly provoking an Israeli military response or by gathering support among radical Arabs."[302]

To say the Israelis were livid was an understatement. Defense Minister Moshe Arens, whom Baker had known from Arens' days as Israel's foreign minister, was incensed and demanded that Israel strike back. He told Baker, "We don't have a choice. We have to go. They've hit us. We have to hit them back. Israel can't sit here and be hit with missiles and do nothing."[303] Baker was in a bind and had to talk Arens down or risk a potentially catastrophic situation playing out in the Middle East, something Saddam Hussein wanted. Baker finally reached Prime Minister Yitzhak Shamir, but the country's leader was in no mood to compromise — he was preparing plans to hit Iraq. Baker dispatched Deputy Secretary of State Lawrence Eagleburger to Israel to find a solution, but it wasn't easy. In the end, the Israelis did not retaliate for the barrage of Scud missiles that hit the country, and by standing down, helped avoid plunging the entire Middle East into a senseless, wider conflict. According to Baker, "Ultimately, the Scuds proved to be more of a political weapon than a military threat. In the end, strategic interest won out over visceral impulse."[304]

As successful as the air campaign was, the ground war proved to be astonishing in terms of its accomplishments. Launched in the predawn hours of February 24, 1991, the ground war completely routed the Iraqi forces from the onset as witnessed by a massive surrender within the first forty-eight hours. On the evening of February 27, 1991, after consulting with General "Stormin' Norman" Schwarzkopf, the 100-hour ground war came to an end. In just six weeks, Desert Storm was over. Kuwait had been liberated as Iraq's forces were driven out of the tiny Middle Eastern nation. That evening, President Bush confidently reported to the nation: "Kuwait is liberated. Iraq's army is defeated. Our military objectives are met. Kuwait is once more in the hands of Kuwaitis, in control of their own destiny."[305]

But why not march to Baghdad, topple Saddam, and install a new regime free of tyranny and suppression? America's forces were at Iraq's doorstep and could have easily decapitated their entire army, crushing any remaining forces. President Bush and Brent Scowcroft offered a detailed assessment to address this very topic.

As Scowcroft wrote: "We were disappointed that Saddam's defeat did not break his hold on power, as many of our Arab allies had predicted and we had come to expect. . . . President Bush repeatedly declared that the fate of Saddam Hussein was up to the Iraqi people. Occasionally, he indicated that removal of Saddam would be welcome, but for very practical reasons, there was never a promise to aid an uprising. While we hoped that popular revolt or coup would topple Saddam, neither the US nor the countries of the region wished to see the breakup of the Iraqi state. We were concerned about the long-term balance of power at the head of the Gulf. . . .

"Trying to eliminate Saddam, extending the ground war into an occupation of Iraq, would have violated our guideline about not changing objectives in midstream, engaging in 'mission creep,' and would have incurred incalculable human and political costs. Apprehending him was probably impossible. We had been unable to find Noriega in Panama, which we knew intimately. We would have been forced to occupy Baghdad and, in effect, rule Iraq. The coalition would instantly have collapsed, the Arabs deserting it in anger and other allies pulling out as well. Under those circumstances, there was no viable 'exit strategy' we could see, violating another of our principles. Furthermore, we had been self-consciously trying to set a pattern for handling aggression in the post-Cold War world. Going in and occupying Iraq, thus unilaterally exceeding the United Nations' mandate, would have destroyed the precedent of international response to aggression that we hoped to establish. Had we gone the invasion route, the United States could conceivably still be an occupying power in a bitterly hostile land. It would have been a dramatically different — and perhaps barren — outcome."[306]

President Bush did acknowledge he was concerned that Saddam Hussein would emerge from the war a "hero," somebody who withstood the onslaught of the world's strongest military but was still in charge. Said Bush, "We discussed again whether to go after him. None of us minded if he was killed in the course of an air attack. Yet it was extremely difficult to target Saddam, who was known to move frequently and under tight security. The best we could do was strike command and control points where he may have been. We later learned Saddam had been caught in one military convoy attacked by coalition aircraft but escaped unharmed."[307]

Baker provided his assessment in a 1996 op-ed he wrote for the *L.A. Times* that points to five core reasons why marching toward Baghdad would have been incredibly reckless:

1. Loss of life. Even with our massive military superiority, the odds of finding Hussein were extremely long. In Panama, a small nation compared with Iraq, it

took American troops 15 days to find and capture General Manuel Noriega, in 1989. Iraqi soldiers and civilians could be expected to resist an enemy seizure of their own country with a ferocity not previously demonstrated on the battlefield in Kuwait. The ensuing warfare would certainly have resulted in substantially greater casualties to American forces than the war itself. For this reason, our military and the president's senior advisors were properly dead-set against it.

2. Military Occupation. Even if Hussein were captured and his regime toppled, US forces would still have been confronted with the specter of a military occupation of indefinite duration to pacify the country and sustain a new government in power. Unlike Panama, however, where a democratically elected government was available to assume power, there was no organized opposition to Hussein. Removing him from power might well have plunged Iraq into civil war, sucking US forces in to preserve order. Had we elected to march on Baghdad, our forces might still be there.

3. Bolstering Iran. As much as Hussein's neighbors wanted to see him gone, they feared that Iraq might fragment in unpredictable ways, which would play into the hands of the mullahs in Iran. The mullahs could export their brand of Islamic fundamentalism with the help of Iraq's Shiites and quickly transform themselves into the dominant regional power. This was also a

concern of the Bush administration and many of our allies. As if to prove the point, Iran quickly moved to support the dissidents within Iraq. Iranian President Hashemi Rafsanjani called on the Iraqi citizenry to rise against its discredited leaders. The Lebanonization of Iraq was ultimately in nobody's interests.

4. Fracturing the coalition. Diplomatically, pressing on to Baghdad would have caused not just a rift but an earthquake within the coalition. Going beyond our mandate from the UN Security Council could have made an Arab nationalist hero out of Hussein. Suddenly, an international coalition's war to liberate Kuwait from a universally condemned invasion would have been transformed into a war of US imperialism in the view of the 'Arab Street' throughout the region.

As Baker saw it, "It was important that the coalition survive the war intact, for at least two reasons. One was the possibility of reviving the long-moribund Middle East peace process. The other was that, during the war, we had learned that Hussein's program to develop weapons of mass destruction was both more substantial and better concealed than we had believed at the outset. We were determined to use our victory in Desert Storm to put the Iraqi regime under the intense glare of the most intrusive international weapons-inspection regime ever developed."

5. Destroying the foundations for post-war peace. For all the devastation on the ground, it was clear that

the invasion of Kuwait and its liberation by a US-led
coalition established a dramatic new reality in the
Middle East. Arab radicalism was defeated, creating
a unique opportunity to pursue a lasting peace in the
Middle East among Arabs and Israelis.

Baker concluded, "In liberating Kuwait, and promptly withdrawing from Iraq as we had promised, the United States had earned the
respect and gratitude of all the Gulf Arab states. At the same time,
we had taken care of the gravest threat to Israel's security — Iraq. US
credibility in the region was at an all-time high. Moreover, the Soviet
Union, long a force for trouble in the Middle East, was now a partner
of US diplomacy."[308]

THE ROAD TO MADRID

America's stunning victory in the 1991 Gulf War showed the world
that there was only one true superpower. Coalition forces, led by the
United States, had unleashed a fury of firepower against Saddam Hussein's supposed elite army, expelling Iraq's military out of tiny Kuwait
in a matter of weeks. President Bush and Secretary of State Baker,
eager to capitalize on America's triumph in Desert Storm, decided that
1991 was the time to begin peacemaking efforts in the Middle East,
once again.

Bridging the divide between the Arabs and the Israelis was not
new to either Bush or Baker; the Reagan administration had tried,
but failed, to make inroads with an international peace convention.
In December 1987, Palestinians in the West Bank and the Gaza Strip
had rebelled against Israeli military rule, resulting in widespread

violence. Then secretary of State George Shultz, eager to stop the confrontation and use the measure as a prelude for a possible international peace convention, tried to make inroads between the Israelis, Jordanians, and local Palestinians. Unfortunately, Shultz's initiatives went nowhere — dead on arrival — as both Israel and Jordan rejected the Reagan administration's key proposals. The Israelis flatly said no to Shultz's proposals because they did not call for an end to the Palestinian uprising — the *intifada* — as a precondition to negotiations. King Hussein of Jordan deemed Shultz's plan not workable, renouncing his kingdom's links to the West Bank.[309]

Throughout 1989 and 1990, additional efforts were put forward by the Bush administration — and supported by Israeli prime minister Yitzhak Shamir — calling for self-governance for Palestinians of the West Bank and Gaza Strip. As with many hopeful peacemaking measures, the plan ultimately failed, with diplomatic relations between the Israelis and Arabs remaining at a low point, then cut off in June 1990 when PLO chairman Yasir Arafat flatly refused to condemn a terrorist attack undertaken by the Palestinian Liberation Front, a PLO faction.

Yet the Gulf War created a window that the Bush White House wanted to explore in terms of a Middle East peace process — and Baker was ready. It was without question an elusive goal, one that had not been accomplished by any statesman. Recalled Baker, "It seemed to me the time was right to make a major effort. Brent [Scowcroft] thought I'd be wasting my time. We talked about it, and finally, we went to the president, and the president said, 'Well, Brent, if he's willing to do it, don't you think we ought to let him try?'"[310]

According to Baker's wife Susan, "Jim just really believed it would be possible to get an agreement so that both sides would not be in a constant state of war, and that was his passion."[311]

Recounts Thomas Friedman, then a *New York Times* diplomatic correspondent, "Baker was trying to get a deal with Yitzhak Shamir, Yasser Arafat, and Hafez al-Assad. And you have to understand, Hafez hated Yasser, Yasser hated Hafez, Yitzhak hated Yasser, Yasser hated Yitzhak . . . . And there was no lost love between Yitzhak and Hafez." Additionally, Friedman said, "Baker played hardball with everybody. That's what you got to do. And frankly, he and Bush were the last two — I would argue . . . to really play hardball with the Israelis and Palestinians."[312]

On March 6, 1991, before a joint session of Congress, President Bush boldly stated, "We must do all that we can to close the gap between Israel and the Arab states and between Israelis and Palestinians. . . . The time has come to put an end to the Arab–Israeli conflict. . . . The war with Iraq is over. The quest for solutions to the problems in Lebanon, in the Arab–Israeli dispute, and in the Gulf must go forward with new vigor and determination. And I guarantee you no one will work harder for a stable peace in the region than we will."[313] Bush then told Congress, "I've asked Secretary of State Baker to go to the Middle East to begin the process. He will go to listen, to probe, to offer suggestions, to advance the search for peace and stability."[314]

It was a long and grueling road to get the various delegations together for the conference, yet it happened, with much credit going to Baker. In May 1991, Baker hit an initial roadblock as Israel rejected his proposal for coming to terms between the Israelis and Syrians on how an actual Middle East peace conference would work. It was the same proposal that days earlier had been rejected by President Hafez al-Assad of Syria when Baker met with him in Damascus. Undeterred, Baker marched forward, flying back and forth to the Middle East in hopes of doing what no other diplomat to date had ever done.

Al-Assad was a man Baker called a brutal tyrant, someone extremely hard to deal with, lecturing America's secretary of State for hours. Recalled Baker, "I would meet with him over a two- or three-day period, he agreed to something one day, I went back the next day, and he started welching on what he'd agreed to. . . . In fact, at one point, he said, 'Well, I didn't agree to that,' and I said, 'Oh really, well then, there's not much point in my staying here.'" Baker closed his folder in front of al-Assad, preparing to leave. "If you do that," Baker explained of his actions, "you better damn well be ready to leave, and I was. Al-Assad quickly backtracked and said, 'Yes, well, that's right, that is what I agreed to.'"[315]

Baker's perseverance began to pay off. In August 1991, the PLO announced it was now willing to compromise on a number of issues to help move closer to an actual peace conference. Spirited by the news, Baker noted, "I am encouraged that we might yet see an outbreak of peace for the region. . . . Obviously, there is more work that needs to be done. For its part, the United States will continue to work diligently for peace. . . . I think it's important to note that a number of governments have taken some very difficult and tough decisions in recent days. There is in our view, at least, a golden opportunity here, and that opportunity should be seized."[316]

The Madrid Peace Conference took place in October 1991. At the opening session of the conference, President Bush spoke, as did Mikhail Gorbachev and others. In his speech, Bush said, "Our objective must be clear and straightforward. It is not simply to end the state of war in the Middle East and replace it with a state of non-belligerency. This is not enough; this would not last. Rather, we seek peace, real peace. And by real peace I mean treaties. Security. Diplomatic relations. Economic relations. Trade. Investment. Cultural exchange. Even tourism. What we seek is a Middle East where vast resources are no longer devoted to armaments. A Middle East where young people no longer have to dedicate and, all too often, give their lives to combat. A Middle East no longer victimized by fear and terror. A Middle East where normal men and women lead normal lives. Let no one mistake the magnitude of this challenge."[317]

Soviet Leader Gorbachev, whose own country was on the brink of collapse, said, "Today, we have a unique opportunity, and it would be unforgivable to miss this opportunity. Success is in everybody's interests, not only because the rights of the peoples and nations and of the individual are increasingly recognized today as the universal foundation for our world order, but also for another reason of particular urgency and gravity, and that is the fact that the Middle East has become one of the most heavily armed regions in the world, where lethal weapons and nuclear technologies are building up and where other weapons of mass destruction are also to be found."[318]

While the Madrid Peace Conference didn't bring about a prescriptive set of accords to help diffuse decades of turmoil in the Middle East, it was what Baker called "a resounding triumph," adding, "Its enduring legacy was simply that it happened at all. After forty-three years of bloody conflict, the ancient taboo against Arabs talking with Israelis had in the space of one carefully choreographed hour been dramatically consigned to the back benches of history."

The peace conference was also significant in that it marked the first time in history that Israeli leaders negotiated face to face with Lebanese, Jordanian, and Syrian delegations, and — equally important — with the Palestinians. Following the conference, Baker bluntly gave reporters his assessment. "We have to crawl before we walk, and we have to walk before we run, and today, I think we all began to crawl." Three years later, having watched the peace process mature, Baker said, "I am hopeful that in my lifetime, we'll see a splendid sprint toward a lasting peace . . . and I'm proud to have contributed to a process which has begun to replace hatred with hope, and fear with friendship."[319]

Other notable outcomes from Madrid, as published in the September 2014 *Baker Institute Policy Report* (Number 61) were:

"All six GCC [Gulf Cooperation Council] states [Bahrain, Kuwait, Oman, Qatar, Saudi Arabia, and the United Arab Emirates] participated in the Madrid Peace Conference in 1991, and Saudi officials joined with their Egyptian counterparts to pressure Arafat and Syrian president Hafez al-Assad to attend. By doing so, they accepted the Madrid framework of direct and bilateral Arab negotiations with Israel. Moreover, Oman, Bahrain, and Qatar all hosted working group sessions of the multilateral committees established as a result of the Madrid conference. One year after the signing of the Oslo I Accord on September 13, 1993, the GCC ended its secondary and tertiary boycott of companies doing business with Israel, stating that Israel's peace agreements with Jordan and the Palestinians rendered the blacklist unnecessary."

Aaron David Miller, a distinguished scholar at the Wilson Center, who has advised both Republicans and Democrats on the Middle East, declared Baker to be ". . . without a doubt the best negotiator since Henry Kissinger — and, as George H.W. Bush told me, a real tough trader too."[320] As Miller saw it, as secretary of State, Baker successfully employed the following key rules as he brought together the historic Madrid Peace Conference, along with his other notable foreign policy achievements:

» Make sure the president has your back: Bush and Baker seemed to walk in sync on almost every aspect of foreign-policy matters from1989 to 1992. A significant element indeed.

» Threaten to walk away: Baker knew when to play it soft, but also when to play hardball, something he did many times in his efforts to bring together the various delegations to Madrid.

» The United States is not to be the fall guy: If things go awry in the world of diplomacy — and they do — make sure the US isn't the one to blame or fault for.[321]

A TEAM LIKE NO OTHER

It's fair to say that no president in modern times, certainly not since the end of World War II, has been confronted with the tidal wave of cataclysmic events that Bush faced. Events that reshaped the global geopolitical landscape. The invasion of Panama and the ouster of a brutal dictator. The slaughter of innocent demonstrators at Tiananmen Square in China. The fall of the Berlin Wall and subsequent reunification of Germany. The Gulf War and the removal of Saddam's forces from neighboring Kuwait. The collapse of the Soviet Union and her Eastern European "satellite nations." Riveting events — all caught on camera as America came front and center into a world of cable television and the dawn of a seemingly never-ending news cycle.

National Security Advisor Brent Scowcroft was Bush's "honest broker," an effective conduit who gathered and presented all the issues and viewpoints essential for the commander in chief to make informed decisions on national security and other essential matters. Scowcroft had held the position once before, serving in the same capacity for President Gerald Ford.

Dick Cheney's proven track record of policy expertise in virtually every conceivable area of government served Bush well. Well-schooled in many areas within the national security apparatus and intimately familiar with how the bureaucratic world of Washington worked, Cheney was well-liked and well-respected by both sides of the political aisle. By most accounts, Cheney's history will point to his being one of the most successful Defense secretaries of all time.

Colin Powell, the chairman of the Joint Chiefs of Staff, was the first-ever African American to hold the position. Well-liked and knowledgeable when it came to military affairs, some might say Powell's biggest asset was his ability to understand and adapt to his new position, one that was arguably more political than any post he'd held before. Handpicked by Cheney — who passed over numerous other generals — Powell became an instrumental figure in many of the Bush administration's foreign-policy achievements.

Vice President Quayle, a true conservative, proved to be highly effective in building a strong working relationship between the White House and the Senate, along with the House, where Quayle had served for two terms, from 1977 to 1981. As a senator, Quayle had reached across party lines on various policy issues, most notably with Senator

Edward Kennedy on the Job Training Partnership Act of 1982, which was approved by a vote of 94–0.

According to one notable Washington insider, Quayle has "a sophisticated grasp of complex issues and bureaucratic institutions that — unlike many of his congressional colleagues — encompasses an executive perspective."[322]

Baker — Bush's first and only choice for secretary of State — became a fixture in Washington politics, having arrived fifteen years earlier to serve as Rog Morton's deputy at US Commerce. Savvy, strategic, and a quick-learner, Baker served three US presidents all with a stellar record reflecting his value to those administrations and to his country.

By all measures, Bush's team was a star-studded cast of political heavyweights that were called upon time and again to confront a barrage of challenges presented to them from around the globe. They had all the core characteristics that are essential in men holding positions of power — experience, wisdom, character, patience, and a duty to serve their nation at almost any cost. But just as important, they worked extremely well together, a rarity in Washington where bickering and backstabbing is often the norm. They understood and respected each other's political turf, carefully avoiding conflict, instead, working through any disagreements they had in a constructive manner. They also worked for a president who disdained infighting within his administration. Bush chose these men for their formidable capabilities and the myriad of qualities they brought to the table, and they all performed admirably in their respective roles during the president's single term in office. According to Baker, "The most important thing for a secretary of State, in terms of whether he or she can be effective, is the relationship with their president. . . . Nobody was going to get between me and my president."[323]

Reflecting back, Cheney notes: "It was, in my opinion — and I'm probably biased — it was about the most successful national security, foreign affairs, and defense team that had been my experience to watch operate. . . . The president was obviously a key part of it."[324]

And as the years have passed, all of these men have written their own memoirs, where you'll find a common theme of respect and admiration as they speak about working with each other from 1989 to 1993. While events in later administrations — particularly George W. Bush's two terms as president — have altered the relationships between some of the key players — such as between Dick Cheney and Colin Powell — nevertheless, they were all part of a golden era in foreign policy, defense, and national security.

Unfortunately, in the end, the president did not win a second term, so this seasoned team of Scowcroft, Cheney, Powell, Quayle, and Baker found themselves out of office at 12:01 p.m., January 20, 1993.

UNFORESEEN EVENTS

Just months after America's victory in the Gulf War in early 1991, George H.W. Bush saw his approval ratings soar to stratospheric heights, making him the most popular president in more than four decades. A *Washington Post–ABC News* poll conducted in the first week of March 1991 had Bush just above a 90-percent approval rating, a ten-point jump from just two months earlier. Bush's support seemed to come from all corners of the country, including Republicans, Democrats, and Independents. Said one lifelong Democrat from Florida, "I didn't vote for him, but I would now. . . . He was always so positive. He wasn't going to take no for an answer. He was always very serious and determined, and always made you feel he was so full of confidence. . . . I wanted to wear red, white, and blue for the first time since the second World War. . . . I've never really felt strong about any politicians in a long time — not since Kennedy. . . . I do about Bush."[325]

Kenneth Duberstein, Ronald Reagan's chief of staff from '88 to '89, warned at the time, "The window of opportunity is not very long, because the stage is moving quickly toward the politics of the campaign and all its divisiveness. He has to decide if he wants to be revered for his domestic accomplishments — or just for what he's done abroad."[326]

Bush was riding high in the polls, but could he translate his foreign-policy success — and political capital — into effectively addressing pressing domestic issues? He'd already gone back on the pledge he made during the 1988 convention: "read my lips, no new taxes." But that wasn't the issue central to his re-election, according to Baker. Running campaigns is about making pledges and promises, some you can't fulfill and some you have to break — that's how Washington works. Baker knew this, and so did the American people. The bigger issue, as Baker saw it, was not moving forward aggressively with domestic legislation immediately after the Gulf War. The president had momentum — in a big way — but internal forces inside the White House thwarted any real efforts to produce constructive policy measures for the economy.

As the 1992 election approached, the unthinkable was beginning to play out. Could a war-time president who was at the helm for the triumphant end of Gulf War I, with a stratospheric approval rating in March 1991, possibly be headed for defeat in re-election? After more than a decade of economic prosperity under both Reagan and

Bush, the economy had begun to slow down and sputter, leaving Bush vulnerable to whomever the Democrats would nominate to challenge him. It seemed as if America's stunning victory in the Gulf War, coupled with all of the accomplishments by George H.W. Bush on the international stage, were being overshadowed by economic numbers that were slowly sinking his re-election efforts.

Bush's first hurdle was to fend off a fiery Pat Buchanan in the Republican primaries, which he did. But he faced a greater challenge in the general election when he found himself up against not only Bill Clinton, a little-known governor from Arkansas — and the Democrats' nominee for president — but also Texas billionaire H. Ross Perot, running as an Independent. Bush now had two opponents to tangle with, and both Clinton and Perot had measurable strengths that would prove incredibly daunting for the incumbent president.

Clinton was young, charismatic, engaging — somebody who truly connected with voters throughout the country. His relentless attack on the Bush economy began to make inroads in the Rust Belt and other traditionally Republican strongholds throughout the South. Perot was the fiery Texas businessman who jumped into the race hellbent on cleaning up Washington and the economic woes of America's growing debt problem.

Bush's chances of re-election were clearly slipping away. The commander in chief who had accomplished so much in his first three and half years in office was dangerously close to losing to a candidate — Governor Bill Clinton — who simply wasn't his equal in many regards, either politically or when it came to character.

By Memorial Day 1992, the campaign was adrift and confused, and with Skinner as Bush's chief of staff, the White House was being managed by someone who was challenged to adequately perform his job responsibilities. Bush needed help, and many of his closest political associates had already pressed Bush with a simple message: Remove Skinner and get Baker back as soon as possible.

In times of trouble and turmoil in our lives, we turn to our friends. Hearing the message from those around him, Bush turned to his longtime friend and ally with an urgent request: return to the White House as chief of staff and take command of a now-failing campaign.

On August 13, 1992, Baker gave one of the most difficult speeches of his life to the foreign-service officers at the State Department — his resignation as secretary of State. "I have decided to resign . . . effective August 23rd, to work with the president to help develop a second-term agenda that helps build on what has been achieved and that fully integrates our domestic, economic, and foreign policies."[327] Baker, struggling to maintain his composure, admitted he was less emotional when he gave the same speech to the American public, yet he also used the time to highlight the sharp differences between Bush and his main challenger, Bill Clinton. Baker was officially back in campaign mode, facing one of the biggest political challenges he'd ever accepted — help his good friend win re-election as president of the United States.

As Baker saw it, there were "too many cooks" in '92. "You did not have one central focus and point of control, which is what you're talking about, which is the reason I ended up resigning as secretary of State and going over there."[328] Bob Teeter, while a brilliant pollster, wasn't Baker when it came to running a campaign — something the president clearly knew when asking Baker to return to the White House. And Skinner made two crucial mistakes from the beginning, according to John Sununu. First, he tried to marginalize Bush's budget director Richard Darman, who was handpicked by Baker. Second, Skinner felt it was a good idea for Bush to address the economy head on, convincing Bush to talk about the "sluggish economy" between 1991 and 1992, when in fact, it was on the rebound. As Sununu writes, "Pretty soon, it was abundantly clear to everyone that my friend Sam Skinner was in over his head . . ."[329] And regarding the 1992 campaign team that was in place prior to Baker's return, Sununu recognized that they were good and competent, but nowhere near the caliber of the 1988 campaign operatives.

Yet to Skinner's credit, the embattled chief of staff recognized the importance of getting Baker back to the White House, admitting that he went to the president on numerous occasions to recommend Baker's return. According to Skinner, "We knew we were in a fight for our life" against Clinton and Perot, who had reentered the race in October 1992.[330]

Along with too many cooks in 1992, there was also a key figure missing from the campaign, Harvey LeRoy Atwater, simply known as Lee. In the world of political hired guns, Atwater reigned supreme — at least in 1988 as he played a central role in Bush's presidential race against Michael Dukakis. Shrewd, tough, and feared by his opponents who knew all too well his skill in carrying out political attacks, Atwater was named chairman of the Republican National Committee due largely to his efforts in the 1988 presidential campaign. Atwater was called many things in his political career — a rebel, mastermind, political hack, and some other not so kind words. But Atwater was effective; there's no debating that. He employed Nixon's "Southern Strategy" for the Republicans — which began with Reagan kicking off his 1980 campaign in the deepest of the deep South, Philadelphia, Mississippi. He employed the same tactics for Bush's 1988 campaign with a barrage of aggressive tactics. As Atwater, a product of South Carolina upbringing, saw it, "Republicans in the South could not win elections by talking about issues. . . . You had to make the case that the other guy, the other candidate, is a bad guy."

As noted by one of his adversaries: "Atwater was more than adept; he was an unrivaled master with a specialty in smear campaigns. He clearly saw politics as a game and played hardball to win."[331] His passion was politics — nothing else — and he wasn't an ideologue in terms of his true political views, rather, a man who wanted his candidate to win at almost any cost. As Atwater himself admitted in 1989, "My entire adult life, I've had exactly one job, which is managing campaigns."[332]

Bush wrote in his diary that August 6, 1990, was "one of the most traumatic days of my presidency. I went to see Lee Atwater and he looked terrible. He has the courage to fight on. Brain-swelling tumor may be under control, but who knows. . . . I am convinced they think he has [a] very, very short time to live. I am very, very worried about our friend who is fighting with such conviction."[333] Unfortunately, 1988 was Atwater's last presidential campaign. He died on March 29, 1991, from a brain tumor.

Baker would take charge of the White House and spearhead Bush's general-election campaign for the next ten weeks, while continuing to oversee key foreign-policy measures abroad. Those close to the president privately confessed Bush was relieved Baker was coming back to the White House, in effect asking his closest friend to help salvage re-election efforts that were now on shaky ground.

Democrats used this chance to criticize Bush, saying he was putting politics ahead of foreign policy by removing Baker as secretary of State. Governor Clinton took note of Baker's move from the State Department to the campaign trail: "He's [Baker] one of the best politicians, deal makers, and political handlers they've got."[334]

John Sununu, Bush's first chief of staff, noted that Baker brought many positives that simply couldn't be produced by anybody else. He was the president's closest confidant, he brought Robert Zoellick with him to the White House as his deputy chief of staff, and "wisely reestablished contact with some of the political strategists from the 1988 campaign, among them Roger Ailes, and was able to restore order in the White House."[335] Yet with the presidential election just a few months away, as brilliant a tactician as Baker was, there almost wasn't enough time to fix what Sununu called "all the failings of a broken and dispirited campaign."[336]

Both Clinton and Perot found their followers — and unfortunately for Bush — they were millions of Reagan Democrats, Independents, and even moderate Republicans, all who were jumping ship from the GOP to the new Democrats of Bill Clinton and Al Gore — or to Ross Perot. After three Republican landslides — all of which George Herbert Walker Bush was a part — he would go down in defeat to Bill Clinton in 1992. As election night unfolded, Clinton walked away with 370 electoral votes, with Bush garnering 168. Clinton also carried a hefty thirty-two states to Bush's eighteen. The young Arkansas governor — now president-elect — also bested Bush in the popular vote.

Bush's daughter, Doro Bush Koch, recalled, "We all gathered in Dad and Mom's suite to watch the returns. We were in the living room, and Mom was in the bedroom reading a romance novel. Things were not looking good at all, casting a pall over the room. Periodically, however, Mom would walk in the room and say, 'What's it like to drive a car?' And then walk back out. A few minutes later, she came in and asked, 'How do you buy an airplane ticket?'"[337]

Baker admits that the loss "was devastating. He [George H.W. Bush] was devastated by that loss." Baker is also quick to point out, "I read a lot . . . comments, pundits and so forth saying he lost because he broke his no-new-taxes pledge. That's not why he lost. . . . Everybody ought to get that straight. I ran that campaign, and I saw it every day in the polling. He lost because of a little guy from Dallas, Texas, called Ross Perot, who took nineteen percent of the vote. And we knew from our polling he [Perot] was taking two out of every three votes from us. We got 38, Clinton got 43. You add two-thirds of 19 to 38, and we get 51."[338]

More specifically, Baker said, "We lost for four reasons. . . . We lost, number one, because we'd been there for twelve years, and change is the only constant in politics. If you can't show that you're an agent for change, you start out way behind. . . . Secondly, we had Ross Perot taking two out of every three votes from us, and there's no doubt about that. . . . those two were not our fault . . . But another major reason . . . well, I didn't mention the economy, which was not really our fault either, I don't think. . . . The fourth reason was our fault, and that is we did not go up to Capitol Hill in January of '91 when George Bush was enjoying a 90-percent approval rating and propose a domestic economic program around which we could build a campaign."[339]

Yet Bush may have also been denied re-election due to the long and seemingly never-ending Iran–Contra saga that had begun years earlier while he was Ronald Reagan's vice president. On October 30,

1992, four days before the presidential election, special prosecutor Lawrence Walsh indicted Caspar Weinberger (Reagan's secretary of Defense from 1981–1987) for his role in the Iran–Contra scandal. Many in the GOP ranks felt the timing was planned so as to hurt Bush in the campaign. And while it was not a direct indictment of the president himself, it gave the campaign a big blow as Bush was closing hard and fast on Clinton in the last week. Fred Steeper, Bush's campaign pollster, showed the race dead even just four days prior to the election. Bush was trending up and Clinton was trending down, but the polling numbers turned in different directions that weekend, just after Walsh's announcement.[340]

The day before Walsh had even announced his indictment against Weinberger, Clinton very conveniently began to change his stump speech by talking about Bush's character and how the Reagan administration gave us Iran–Contra when Bush was vice president. A week after Bush's failed re-election efforts, Senator Bob Dole called the indictment "the straw that broke the camel's back" for Bush, calling Walsh's legal henchmen nothing more than a "hotbed of Democratic activist lawyers."[341] A month after Bush's loss to Clinton, a federal district judge threw out the one-count indictment against Casper Weinberger, and two weeks after that, Bush pardoned Weinberger and five other individuals implicated in the Iran–Contra affair.

Dick Cheney reflected on his time serving as Bush's secretary of Defense. "One of the great things that happened with 41 [George H.W. Bush] — in the closing days of his administration, he called Jim Baker and me one day and asked us to come over to the White House. . . . The question he had for us: should he pardon . . . those . . . who had been involved in Iran–Contra? And we said absolutely. We were very supportive of it, and in my mind, it was always a mess Reagan should have cleared up. Reagan left office without taking care of it, and Bush had the *cajones* to deal with it and solve that problem to the extent it was possible to rectify the difficulties there."[342]

And to the critics that say Bush didn't have the energy or enthusiasm during the 1992 campaign compared to his previous campaigns? Baker, well aware of this talking point that lingered for years after Bush's defeat to Clinton, provided his own assessment. Baker saw firsthand how competitive Bush was — at everything in life — business, on the tennis court, and in politics. "He didn't want to quit in '80 [GOP primary battle against eventual nominee and president, Ronald Reagan] . . . I saw him working his butt off in '92 . . . I did not see him slacking in '92," yet Baker was fully aware of the chatter that Bush was not "that much interested and committed to the campaign."[343]

Barbara Bush had been diagnosed with Graves' Disease in February of 1989. And though not a contagious disease, when Bush began showing signs of fatigue, it was reported that he, too, was suffering from the disease, which can have a noticeable effect on one's physical stamina. Bush wrote during that time period: "I don't have the energy that I've had before."[344] Bush at one point told Colin Powell, then chairman of the Joint Chiefs of Staff, that the medicine he was taking caused "a slowing down of the mental processes" for a time. Powell remembers that during the campaign, "I saw a passive, sometimes detached George Bush," and not the vigorous leader he had come to know.[345]

Privately, Bush's press secretary Marlin Fitzwater and others close to Bush believed the disease was having a direct impact on the president and on his campaign, though the White House never publicly acknowledged the issue. "They didn't want people to think that they were going to elect a damaged president," said John Sununu, then White House chief of staff.[346] Fitzwater said, "The campaign people were in mortal fear."[347]

According to Fred Malek, Bush's campaign chairman, "If they hadn't had Graves' Disease, he would have been re-elected, I think. Nobody at that point recognized the depths of what that caused." Malek said Bush "had the energy to get up in the morning and handle his in-box, but he didn't have the mental energy to initiate, to cause change." He found it difficult to respond aggressively to the country's economic challenges and to the political challenges presented by Clinton, whose campaign was emphasizing his youth, vigor, and empathy."[348]

On the subject of Perot, there's been much discussion over the years as to his real reason for jumping into the 1992 presidential race. A dislike of Bush? A vendetta against the White House? A feeling of inferiority against Bush? All of the above, and then some, according to political pundits of the time. "I think he was driven by a personal dislike, a personal resentment of me, you might say . . . " commented Bush.[349] According to both Bush and Baker, as vice president under Ronald Reagan, Bush became the unfortunate messenger to pass along the news from the president to Perot that Reagan had no further reason to believe there were any Americans — MIAs — left in Vietnam. What's more, the Reagan White House then asked Perot to turn in his access card. Said Baker, "I think that Ross got pissed off and shot the messenger. . . . He did have an animus toward Bush 41 because of that episode . . . though the two stop short of blaming the ordeal entirely for Perot's run."[350] Bush agreed, stating, "I think he took it very personally . . . got ugly and mean, and I didn't like it at all."[351]

Dig a little deeper, and you'll find a Texan in Dallas, Perot, who did not generally care for the Texas transplant in Houston, Bush — or his family. In 1994, as Bush's eldest son, George W. Bush, was seeking the Texas governorship, Perot publicly backed incumbent Democrat Ann Richards, about which one political analyst remarked, "I feel very certain that personal animus moved him more than any positive affection that he has for Ann Richards. He's magnificently inconsistent in his political loyalties . . ."[352]

Their differences were cultural, a core reason for the strained relationship between both men. Perot, the self-made billionaire, drove his own car, bought his suits at Men's Warehouse, and dined often with what he called "the regular people." He didn't have a home on the beautiful, rugged Maine shoreline of Kennebunkport (though he could have easily afforded such luxuries), and according to individuals close to him, he disdained the preppy, Ivy League, East Coast image that Bush — in Perot's view — tried to hide while also portraying himself as a Texan. Perot seemed to come unhinged at times during the contentious 1992 presidential campaign, accusing the Bush campaign of the wildest of acts, from trying to sabotage his daughter's wedding to infiltrating his campaign with ex-CIA spies, and more. "Preposterous," according to Marlin Fitzwater, the president's spokesman, in response to Perot's allegations. Margaret Tutwiler, the White House communications director, said, "It's all loony," while Bobby R. Burchfield, general counsel for the Bush campaign, said, "There is absolutely nothing to them," after investigating the charges.[353]

Reflecting back on 1992, John Sununu had this to say about Ross Perot: "He was known to be thin-skinned and was in the campaign just to spite George Bush. . . . Had [Lee] Atwater still been in the game, I feel certain he would have nailed Perot between the eyes with a two-by-four every time he opened his mouth. . . . The overarching liberal bias of the national press didn't help the president, either, and dogged him throughout the campaign."[354]

Bush's parting shot to Ross Perot came in the documentary *41*, produced by Jerry Weintraub. In it, Bush — known for speaking favorably about people, had this short statement on Perot: "No, can't talk about him. I think he cost me the election, and I don't like him. Other than that, I have nothing to say."[355]

Throughout it all, Baker has "always admired George Bush because he was willing to do things that were long shots. You know, you've got to really admire somebody who's willing to get out there and do what he did in '79 [decide to run for president]. There's an asterisk in the poll; nobody knew who the hell he was. I remember when we first started, and I wrote this in my book. He said, 'Do you think I'm crazy doing this?' We were flying out to see Reagan and Ford to tell them that George was going to run for president. Or he was thinking about it. And I said, 'No. Hell, I don't think so at all.'. . . People say, 'Oh, well, he comes from a privileged background. He's reserved, and he's too much of a gentleman for the hurly burly.' I don't buy all that stuff. He can get in there with the best of them."[356]

Baker believes that one of the biggest mistakes the administration made was not following up on Desert Storm — the kicking of Saddam Hussein and his forces out of Iraq — with what he called a "Domestic Storm" for the American economy.[357] But it didn't happen.

And why? Because a number of the president's advisors at the time — in the spring of 1991 — said the economy was fine, so no action was needed by the federal government. The economy, however, became the central theme of the election, effectively used by Clinton to hammer away at Bush as a president out of touch with American voters. Yes, there was a recession, the economic numbers clearly showed that, but it technically ended in 1991, and growth began to pick up again throughout 1992, but the damage had already been inflicted by the Clinton camp.

Former Clinton administration speechwriter Edward Luce gave his rationale, offering, "Their opponent was George H.W. Bush. He was one of the most decent figures ever to occupy the Oval Office. But he was unable to match the economic optimism of Mr. Clinton. Even then — in far gentler times — the US voter chose a serial adulterer over an uxorious grandfather. The moral of the story is hard to miss."[358]

Others in the administration agreed, including Dick Cheney, secretary of Defense at the time, and Dan Quayle, Bush's vice president. According to Cheney, "Perot cost us the election, that I strongly believe. . . . His nineteen percent of the vote was crucial, and it no doubt helped Bill Clinton." Quayle echoed similar sentiments, saying, "Bill Clinton won the presidency over Bush for the simple fact that Ross Perot pulled a huge number of our voters into his corner. Without Perot in the race, we would have beat Clinton." Yet Quayle also acknowledged another big reason for Bush's defeat — three key people were missing from the 1992 campaign. "We didn't have Roger Ailes, John Sununu, or Lee Atwater, and that was a big difference when comparing '88 to '92."[359]

And Bush's son, George W. Bush, now a former president himself, acknowledged, "I believed then, and I still believe today, that had Ross Perot not been on the ballot, George Bush would have won the 1992 election. I know that Dad felt the same way."[360]

Barbara Bush in her memoir asked herself the question, "Why did we lose?" According to the former first lady of the United States, "I think we lost because people really wanted a change. We had . . . twelve years of a Republican presidency. The Cold War was over, and now it was time to turn our attention toward the home front and the many problems that were and are facing our country. People were worried about jobs and the economy. There was an impression that George was more interested in foreign affairs and did not have a domestic program, which was not true. He had accomplished so much, and still had much he wanted to do. But that was the impression. For more than a year, George had been attacked by five Democrats, one Republican, and one Independent. I think people began to believe what they heard. And the press, I honestly believe that most of them wanted Bill Clinton to win. He was one of them — baby boomers."[361]

While her husband's defeat to Clinton in 1992 was hard to grasp, Mrs. Bush eventually warmed to Bill Clinton as the years passed. In a 2014 C-SPAN interview, Mrs. Bush said, "I love Bill Clinton. Maybe not his politics, but I love Bill Clinton. . . . My husband, Bill Clinton, and I have become friends, and Bill visits us every summer. We don't agree politically, but we don't talk politics."[362] Mrs. Bush also shared, "Bill's father wasn't around . . . and I think that he thinks of George a little bit like the father he didn't have, and he's very loving to him. And I really appreciate that."[363]

Bush felt the sting of his re-election defeat as reflected in his private diary. "I ache, and I now must think: how do you keep your chin up, keep your head up through a couple of difficult days ahead? I think of our country and the people that are hurting, and there is so much we didn't do. And yes, progress that we made, but no, the job is not finished and that kills me."[364] He did what all candidates do when they lose: thank supporters and give an uncomfortable, but necessary, concession speech, while also telephoning the winner and congratulating him on a hard-fought campaign.

Bush called Governor Clinton in Little Rock, Arkansas, conceding to the baby-boomer president-elect and assuring him of a smooth transition of power. Bush was a war veteran, a man who dedicated his entire life to public service yet found himself going down in defeat to a "draft dodger" who had engaged in antiwar demonstrations as a Rhodes Scholar in England. Bush, while admitting, "I like him," nevertheless confessed, "How do you be commander in chief when you duplicitously avoid service to your country? Maybe it's time for a new generation. He's George's [George W. Bush's] age, a generation more in touch, a background more in touch. . . . I've never felt 'out of touch,' but then I've always assumed there was duty, honor, country."[365]

And to the critics who felt Bush should have replaced Vice President Quayle on the re-election ticket? Not a chance, and perhaps for one single reason more than any other — loyalty. Quayle had come under constant assault from the media during his single term, yet he never wavered once when it came to his steadfast loyalty to the man who put him on the ticket in 1988. If anyone ever questioned Bush's firm stance on keeping Quayle on the ticket, all one had to do was listen to his concession speech to Governor Clinton. "Let me thank our great vice president, Dan Quayle. In the face of a tremendous pounding, he stood for what he believes in, and he will always have my profound gratitude, and certainly my respect." But even more compelling than the statement was its timing. It didn't come at the end of his concession speech or days later as some off-the-record comment. It came just three minutes into Bush's speech at the Houston Galleria on the evening of November 3, 1992.[366]

On January 20, 1993, George and Barbara Bush left the White House. It was time to go home, but not to Kennebunkport, Maine. They headed to Houston, Texas, his beloved adopted city where Bush's political career began. He and Barbara temporarily moved into a friend's vacant house near the Tanglewood community of Houston as they prepared to build a permanent retirement home in exclusive West Oaks. Bush opened his official post-presidency office in the Park Laureate Building at 10000 Memorial Drive.

On his last day as president of the United States, Bush tended to a laundry list of duties: extending US Secret Service protection for Vice President Quayle, appointing a faithful servant in the counsel's office to a United States–Panama commission for the environment, conversing with White House groundskeepers, posing for keepsake pictures, monitoring the American air raids on Iraq, even turning over the nuclear launch codes for the nation's ICBM arsenal.[367]

Yet just before exiting the Oval Office for the last time as America's 41st president, he left President-elect Bill Clinton a note. As Clinton recalled, "On January 20, 1993, I entered the Oval Office for the first time as president. As is the tradition, waiting for me was a note from my predecessor, George Herbert Walker Bush. It read:

Dear Bill,

When I walked into this office just now, I felt the same sense of wonder and respect that I felt four years ago. I know you will feel that, too.

I wish you great happiness here. I never felt the loneliness some presidents have described.

There will be very tough times, made even more difficult by criticism you may not think is fair. I'm not a very good one to give advice; but just don't let the critics discourage you or push you off course.

You will be our president when you read this note. I wish you well. I wish your family well.

Your success now is our country's success. I am rooting hard for you.

Good luck—

George [368]

THE OVAL

First established in 1909 by President William Howard Taft in the Old Executive Office Building, the Oval Office has been the president's official working office. The modern Oval Office, located on the White House's West Wing southeast corner, has been in place since 1934, thanks in part to President Roosevelt's dissatisfaction with the overall size and layout of the West Wing itself.

Bush shared his thoughts on the Oval Office both in his personal diary and in public. According to Bush, while the office itself is not that large — approximately 816 square feet — it is nonetheless an office that has "a special atmosphere about it. Even as I left the presidency, I had the same feeling of awe and reverence for the room as when I entered it in earlier administrations. It is a symbol of the institution of the presidency itself, with an almost overwhelming aura of history. I could feel the presence of the long line of presidents preceding me, a feeling reinforced by my own pleasure in reading American history and learning about events that had taken place in the room where I was sitting. . . . I enjoyed working in that room."[369]

Bush often found himself looking out the window and watching his grandchildren play. Other times, he'd find his dog Ranger at the door, dripping wet from the rain and begging to come in. Bush looked forward to the fireplace being lit in the fall and winter as it gave the room a feeling of warmth and cheerfulness.[370]

Baker, also having time to reflect back on his position as secretary of State, noted: "I'm struck by my good fortune in occupying that office during a time of revolution, war, and peace: a revolution of freedom that swept away communism; a war of liberation that reversed a dictator's aggression, and progress toward peace that established a foothold of reason in a region of enmity and conflict. . . . The world today is infinitely freer and safer than it has been during any other time in my life — and for that, I am grateful."[371]

CHAPTER SIX

Life After Office

LOSING HIS BID FOR RE-ELECTION WAS DIFFICULT FOR A competitive man like George H.W. Bush. The American people voiced their frustrations at the ballot box, and much like the young aviator who decades earlier had taken orders without pause, Bush respected the outcome and dutifully moved on with life. He joined Richard Nixon, Jerry Ford, Jimmy Carter, and Ronald Reagan — living former presidents — in perhaps the most exclusive club in the world, where membership is afforded only to those who have served as America's commander in chief.

Lucrative speaking engagements, book deals, endless requests for appearances, and a US Secret Service detail for life. Yes, life as a former president, while fundamentally different from serving, was a privilege indeed. Bush left office on January 20, 1993, at just sixty-eight years old, physically fit and healthy, yet curious — anxious — as to what would come next. In the time-honored tradition of respecting the new president, Bush steered clear of any public criticism of Bill Clinton throughout the early period of his presidency. After all, Bush knew the challenges of being commander in chief, and as he saw it, Clinton deserved his time to settle into the toughest job in the world.

Recalled Barbara Bush, "At 7:30 a.m. on January 21, [1993], George went to his new office on Memorial Drive to settle in and sort out, among other things, how in the world he was going to answer all his mail . . . with the seven hundred letters a day that poured in."[372]

Within months of leaving office, Bush became the target of an assassination attempt in Kuwait. On April 13, the day before Bush was scheduled to arrive for the three-day visit, accompanied by his wife, two of his sons, Baker, former chief of staff John Sununu, and former Treasury secretary Nicolas Brady, Kuwaiti authorities foiled a plan to assassinate him, arresting sixteen alleged perpetrators, including two of the plot's ringleaders, later identified as Iraqi nationals. The next day, Kuwaiti authorities found a Toyota Land Cruiser with a powerful car bomb hidden in it. The Land Cruiser had been driven across the Iraqi border into Kuwait City on the prior evening.[373]

On June 26, 1993, President Clinton ordered a cruise-missile attack against the facility housing the Iraqi Intelligence Service (IIS) in Baghdad as retaliation for the assassination attempt on Bush's life, citing "compelling evidence" of direct involvement by IIS operatives. According to news reports, the attack killed eight individuals. On June 27, 1993, Madeleine Albright, US ambassador to the United Nations, addressed an emergency session of the Security Council and provided evidence to support the attack on the IIS facility.[374]

Following the attack, Vice President Al Gore said it "was intended to be a proportionate response at the place where this plot [to assassinate Bush] was hatched and implemented."[375]

As Bush's post-presidency took shape, historians and political pundits spoke frequently about the "what if" march to Baghdad — the opportunity to remove Saddam Hussein from power.

The international coalition that Bush had assembled when Iraq was expelled from neighboring Kuwait in 1991 was, without question, one of his greatest achievements, yet many still wondered if he had done enough. Should he have marched to Baghdad and disposed of Iraq's brutal dictator, Saddam Hussein? No, said Bush, time and again. And in a speech in Cancun in 1994, he stated how history would prove him right for not forcing Saddam Hussein from power during the Gulf War. According to Bush, "The Mideast peace talks that offer hope to the world would never have started if we had done that. . . . The Arabs would never have talked to us."[376]

In fact, there was complete and unanimous consensus among all top Bush administrative officials — Baker, Cheney, Scowcroft, Powell, Quayle, and others — that the war in the Gulf effectively ended when Saddam was forced out of Iraq.

Five years after the Gulf War, Baker wrote in the *LA Times* in 1996: "In the aftermath of the US strikes against Iraqi military targets, some armchair generals and talking-head diplomats argue that, in 1991, the Gulf War coalition should have toppled Saddam Hussein's regime even if it meant marching to Baghdad or beyond in order to apprehend him. . . . Continuing the offensive to Baghdad would have been a dangerous mistake. For a host of reasons — strategic, political, military, and diplomatic — the marching-to-Baghdad canard is as nonsensical now as it was then. All our political and war aims, as enunciated by the Bush administration throughout the crisis, had been achieved."[377]

In a 1994 interview with the American Enterprise Institute,

former secretary of Defense Dick Cheney again reaffirmed his position on not marching to Baghdad, stating ". . . because if we'd gone to Baghdad, we would have been all alone, there wouldn't have been anybody else with us, there would have been a US occupation of Iraq, none of the Arab forces that were willing to fight with us in Kuwait were willing to invade Iraq. . . . Once you got into Iraq, took it over, and took down Saddam Hussein's government, then what are you going to put in place? That's a very volatile part of the world, and if you take down the central government of Iraq, you can easily see pieces of Iraq fly off, part of it the Syrians would like to have in the West, part of Eastern Iraq the Iranians would like to claim."[378]

According to Colin Powell, "We never had a plan that said we were going to go to Baghdad and actually remove this guy from power the way we removed Noriega from power in Panama. Because we had no international authority for that, we had no agreement within the coalition, especially the Arab members of the coalition, that we would do such a thing. They were anxious to see Iraq stay together, the Iraqi army out of Kuwait, Saddam gone preferably but the son of Saddam, figuratively, or another Sunni leader emerge to hold this country together and so that the country's not so prostrate that Iran could walk over it. . . . We had no objective that said go to Baghdad. We had no objective that said split apart Iraq."[379]

RISING STARS OF THE NEXT GENERATION

Just as the monumental political career of America's 41st president was coming to an end, two of the Bush boys were beginning to make their own way in Texas and Florida. George W. Bush, the president's eldest son, was set to challenge incumbent Texas governor Ann

Richards in 1994, while Jeb Bush was gearing up for a race against incumbent Florida governor Lawton Chiles. Richards had made many enemies — even with Democrats in her home state — when she childishly remarked at the 1988 Democratic National Convention, "Poor George, he can't help it — he was born with a silver foot in his mouth." George W. Bush, known for his fierce protection of the family name — and unwavering loyalty to his father — never forgot or forgave Richards for the cheap comment, making his gubernatorial victory over her in 1994 all the more memorable for the Bush family. Bush bested Richards by a sizable nine-point victory, 54 percent to 45 percent.

The flamboyant and frank-talking Richards fell victim to not only the changing political landscape of Texas — it was becoming increasingly Republican — but also to the campaign-savvy, highly personable and engaging candidacy of George W. Bush. At his victory celebration, Bush proudly proclaimed, "Texas is ready for a new generation of leadership. I have heard from Texas tonight, and I hear the call of constructive change — change of our juvenile justice system to save a generation of our young, change of our welfare system to end a dependency on government, and change of our education system."[380] Jeb, meanwhile, lost by a razor-thin margin to Chiles, yet came back to defeat Florida lieutenant governor Buddy MacKay soundly in 1998.

Referring to George W.'s victory in Texas and Jeb's defeat in Florida in 1994, Bush told *ABC News*: "I have very mixed emotions. Proud father is the way I would sum it all up."[381]

On election night, 1998, talk of a political dynasty flooded the airwaves as two Bushes won governorships in two of the most populous states in the nation. According to the *Chicago Tribune*, the

Bush gubernatorial wins "made the sons of the former president forces to be reckoned with and an important factor in Republican politics in two years and, perhaps, decades to come as the brothers took charge of two of the nation's most heavily Hispanic states."[382]

George W. Bush's victory over Texas land commissioner Gary Mauro was an absolute landslide, 68 percent to 31 percent, and talk immediately began of a possible presidential run in 2000 for George W. Suddenly, the born-again Christian who had given up beer for the Bible was seen as the front-runner for the GOP nomination, though he hadn't even officially announced his candidacy. Bush would ultimately throw his hat in the ring in 2000, and after a hard-fought, mudslinging campaign against his main opponent — Arizona senator John McCain — won the GOP nomination, and the right to challenge what many considered a formidable and likely unbeatable candidate — two-term vice president of the United States, Al Gore.

The economy was steamrolling along, and though the Clinton impeachment was an unpleasant scene for the entire country, voters generally found Gore to be trustworthy, a family man, but also someone with a rather stiff personality and hard to warm to. Bush was the more personable candidate, a man extremely comfortable with crowds, and highly engaging when it came to one-on-one dialogue with voters. Both candidates, and their respective running mates — Bush chose Dick Cheney for the second spot on the ticket, while Gore went with Connecticut senator Joe Lieberman — found themselves in a slugfest throughout the general election period, leading to a statistical dead heat, according to most polls, just days before the election. There were some memorable moments during the campaign — Gore's sighing and huffing and puffing during the first of three presidential debates, along with Cheney's masterful performance in the one and only vice-presidential debate — but the real memories for millions of Americans are of election night and the thirty-seven long and grueling days that followed until an ultimate winner was finally declared. Bush and Cheney were headed to the White House.

WHAT DOES A FORMER POLITICAL GIANT DO IN RETIREMENT?

The first time Bush bailed out of an airplane had not been by choice — his Navy torpedo bomber had been on fire during a raid on Japanese-occupied Chichi Jima in 1944. More than a half-century later, Bush once again found himself parachuting out of an airplane — but this time, it was perfectly planned and executed. On March 25, 1997, the six-foot-two, seventy-two-year-old former president took his planned jump at the Yuma Proving Ground, a parachute-training base and winter home of the Golden Knights, the Army's elite parachute squad. Glenn Bangs, the US Parachute Association's director of safety and training, was positioned securely on Bush's right side ready to hold his harness in free fall, while Andy Serrano, of the Golden Knights, was on his left. When the plane reached 12,500 feet, Bangs shouted, "Mr. President, are you ready?" Bush responded enthusiastically, "Yes!" At 4,500 feet, Bush pulled his ripcord; the canopy opened perfectly, and the president was on his own.[383] With the exception of the head bump Bush suffered when exiting the plane, the jump was perfect. And it wouldn't be his only jump.

In 1999, he again took to the skies to mark his seventy-fifth birthday, parachuting solo near his presidential library and museum in College Station, Texas. Retired Army general Hugh Shelton, who jumped with Bush that day, recalled how the former president could have possibly died, as he risked becoming entangled in his parachute. "He just kept right on tumbling and he went right through the — right through the level, the 5,000-foot level, and went right on down. Until finally, just short of when the activation device would go off, he'd stabilized."[384]

Five years later, in 2004, Bush marked his eightieth birthday with yet another skydive, and in 2007, he was again skydiving, this time marking the rededication of his presidential library and museum. For his eighty-fifth birthday, Bush skydived at their family compound in Kennebunkport, Maine. "Just because you're an old guy, you don't have to sit around drooling in the corner. . . . Get out and do something. Get out and enjoy life," said Bush.

As Bush's ninetieth birthday approached in 2014, age had taken its toll on America's 41st president, leaving him wheelchair-bound. Regardless, he still undertook a successful tandem skydive at Kennebunkport.

Bush's ninety-fifth birthday jump never happened. Yet after he passed away at age ninety-four, retired Golden Knight sergeant Mike Elliott, who had jumped with Bush previously, said the former president was still considering a jump in 2019, telling a North Carolina news channel, "I know he said he wanted to jump on his ninety-fifth birthday. I was hoping he'd live to jump on his ninety-fifth, but he's left a lot of great memories for me. He was just a great American icon, and, to me, a superman."[385]

Bush joined forces with former president Bill Clinton, spearheading fundraising and relief efforts for the victims of the December 2004 tsunami that hit Sumatra, Indonesia, killing more than 228,000 people. In January 2005, with former presidents Bush and Clinton by his side at the Roosevelt Room, President George W. Bush said, "I'm honored to be standing here with two former presidents, President Bush 41, President Clinton 42. We have come together to express our country's sympathy for the victims of a great tragedy. We're here to ask our fellow citizens to join in a broad humanitarian relief effort. . . . In the coming days, President[s] Clinton and Bush will ask Americans to donate directly to reliable charities already providing help to tsunami victims."[386]

As Clinton and Bush were preparing to travel thousands of miles away from home to see for themselves the devastation and destruction in Indonesia, they quickly realized there was only one bed on the plane. The younger Clinton immediately told Bush to take the bed, even digging his heels in to the point where Bush had no choice but to accept. According to Bush, "He was very considerate of the old guy. That's me. I mean, like the room on the plane. There was every reason in the world he should have had equal time if not priority, but he insisted. That's a tiny, little thing . . . that meant a lot to me."[387]

Their gentlemen's agreement over the bed seemed a far cry from the bitter 1992 presidential election that saw Bush lose to a younger, vastly inexperienced candidate hailing from the same generation as Bush's son, George W. Political enemies no more? Many people were surprised by the unlikely pairing of Bush and Clinton for the Tsunami relief efforts, but they were equally surprised when they learned how long both men had known each other, a relationship that had begun in the early 1980s when Bush was vice president and Clinton was governor of Arkansas.

Following the relief efforts, Bush found people asking him about his relationship with the very man who defeated him in 1992. Said

Bush, "What a lot of people don't realize is we've never really been hostile. You get into a campaign and there's understandable hostility. But I've always had a rather pleasant personal relationship with him, and he said yesterday he felt the same way about me. So, it's not surprising to us. But it is surprising to everybody else."[388] Bush, aware that Clinton lost his father in a car accident just before he was born, added, "Maybe I'm the father he never had."[389]

Clinton recalled his first-ever meeting with Bush in 1983 at the Bush compound in Kennebunkport. "My daughter was three years old, and I introduced her to George Bush. . . . I said, 'Chelsea, this is Vice President Bush, and this is his wonderful home.' She looked at him and she said, 'I have to go to the bathroom.' He took her by the hand and took her to the bathroom. It really impressed me. . . . I've always liked him."[390]

CHAPTER SEVEN

Back to Houston

A S THE BUSH ADMINISTRATION NEARED THE END OF ITS
single term in office, Baker found himself on the receiving end
of a myriad of job offers and other opportunities. "I got a lot of offers
from many of the leading corporations in the country. But I decided
two things. I was going to go back to Houston, to Baker Botts, and I
wasn't going to sit on a lot of boards. I can give one speech and make
more than what my retainer would be for a year on a board, with no
liability. So, I agreed to sit on two boards of Baker Botts's choosing
[EDS and Reliant Energy]."[391]

Shortly after returning home to Houston, Baker helped found and
became the honorary chair of the Baker Institute for Public Policy
at Rice University. Baker's desire for the institute, which has now
become one of the world's leading think tanks, was "to build a bridge
between the world of ideas and the world of action. . . . Scholars
should learn firsthand from statesmen of the practical imperatives
that impact policy, often times making the 'perfect' the enemy of the

'good.' Statesmen and policymakers should hear rigorous, logical — and always practical — scholarly analyses of how to improve the work they do. And students, the next generation of scholars and statesmen, should be enriched through participation in this dialogue and go on to be better scholars and statesmen as a result."[392]

The groundbreaking ceremony in 1994 was memorable indeed as four former US presidents — Gerald Ford, Jimmy Carter, Ronald Reagan, and George H.W. Bush — participated in the ceremony, creating what Baker had wanted all along: a bipartisan, forward-thinking, global public-policy institute focused on pressing issues facing the country and the world.

HOUSTON HEAVYWEIGHTS

The founding of the Baker Institute represented the culmination of a longstanding relationship between two of Houston's most cherished institutions — the Baker family and Rice University. It all began with Captain James A. Baker, a prominent attorney in the law firm of Baker, Botts & Baker, who represented William Marsh Rice, one of the richest men in Texas at the time. In 1891, Captain Baker was made a member and eventually board chairman of the William M. Rice Institute for the Advancement of Literature, Science and Art, which Rice wanted built in Houston after his death. Captain Baker alerted authorities to the possibility of foul play when Rice died in 1900. Because of Baker's efforts, authorities ultimately determined Rice had been murdered in his sleep by his servant. The murder case and subsequent litigation over the will, which left a trust fund for the Rice Institute, took seven years to resolve.

As chairman of the board, Captain Baker oversaw the establishment of Rice Institute [later University] in 1912 as an elite education-al institution, serving as chairman until his death on August 2, 1941. His son, James A. Baker Jr., continued to forge strong ties with the university.

In 1992, Dr. Richard J. Stoll, director for Rice University's Center for the Study of Institutions and Values, as well as a professor of Political Science, sent a memo to George Rupp, then Rice's president, suggesting that Rice contact then secretary of State Baker regarding an institute in Baker's name. The momentum for the institute picked up quickly, and on March 31, 1993, Baker gave a speech accepting the university's offer of an institute in his honor, explaining his vision, that the Baker Institute would "draw together statesmen, scholars and students . . . and . . . build a bridge between the world of ideas and the world of action . . ." These founding words were later incorporated into the iconography of Baker Hall's architecture. Baker also served on the Rice Board of Trustees from 1993 to the present day, currently acting as Trustee Emeritus.[393]

During its first ten years, the Baker Institute hauled in a staggering $65 million, while also hosting an impressive list of prominent world leaders — Vladimir Putin, Nelson Mandela, Yasir Arafat, Helmut Kohl, Mikhail Gorbachev, and others. For a think tank in its relative infancy, its success was yet another example of what so many people call the "Baker Magic." With the Baker Institute in place, the down-to-earth, straight-talking, smooth-operating Texan came back home to the very neighborhood he had grown up in decades earlier — a homecoming that simply couldn't be scripted any better for one of Houston's most beloved citizens.[394]

A true Houstonian, Baker showed Texas, the country, and the

entire world what a boy from the Bayou City (one of Houston's most recognized nicknames) can accomplish. Baker ran with the best of the East Coast gentry, the very Ivy Leaguers who dominated America's political landscape for decades. And he did it with a charm, charisma, and a sense of humor that only a Texan — or more appropriately — a Houstonian could. He's been called the Velvet Hammer due to his immensely capable negotiating skills that get him what he wants, when he wants it and how he wants it, all without inciting anger or animosity from his adversaries. It's a rare talent that only the best political operatives in the world have, and Baker, one of the most accomplished statesmen of the last fifty years, has that very gift.

To celebrate the tenth anniversary of the Baker Institute, 800 guests were invited to a black-tie dinner that raised $3.2 million for the Institute's programs. Guests were treated to a keynote speech by Dick Cheney, a close friend of Baker's for more than three decades. Cheney lavished praise on Baker. "There is a certain kind of man you only encounter a few times in life, what I call a 'hundred-percenter' — a person of ability, judgment, and absolute integrity. . . . This is a man who was chief of staff on day one of the Reagan years and chief of staff twelve years later on the last day of former president Bush's administration. In between, he led the Treasury Department, oversaw two landslide victories in presidential politics, and served as the 61st secretary of State during a period of truly momentous change. . . . Every person who sat at the Cabinet table during those years will tell you that Jim Baker commanded the utmost respect for the work he did, for the intellect he brought to bear on every issue, and for the example he set for all of us every day."[395]

It was a fitting tribute coming from America's most powerful vice president ever as he spoke glowingly about Baker's astonishing political career. Yet Cheney was just warming up the crowd that night as he launched into a blistering diatribe against terrorists who attacked America on September 11, 2001. Baker went on to co-chair the Iraq Study Group just three years later, issuing a report that Cheney was critical of. But it and any other mild political disagreements the two friends had over the course of their political careers were just that — differences that never affected their longstanding friendship.

At just ten years young, the Baker Institute was on a path to unquestioned prominence and notoriety, counting itself among the bluest of blue-chip think tanks in the country. Baker has given back to the town and the university that are both so dear to his heart, and as he looks out his office window of the institute that bears his name, he can see a massive piece of concrete and steel that was once a part of the Berlin Wall, the very wall he helped bring down as secretary of State.

Jim Baker and George Bush enjoy a game of horseshoes at the White House. May 1990.

Bush pitching a horseshoe at the White House as Baker looks on. May 1990.

The Camp David Summit participants enjoy some fresh air. From left to right: US interpreter Peter Afanasenko, Jim Baker, George Bush, Dan Quayle, Brent Scowcroft, Eduard Shevardnadze, Mikhail Gorbachev, and Sergey Akhromeyev (back to camera). June 2, 1990.

Secretary of State Baker, on a trip to Mongolia where he was the first Western statesman to address their Parliament. July 1991.

John Sununu, Jim Baker, President Bush, and Brent Scowcroft meet while in Moscow prior to Bush and Gorbachev signing the bilateral Strategic Arms Reduction Treaty. July 1991.

Jim Baker delivering information to President Bush at an unnamed event. October 1991.

Secretary of State Baker and Russian President Boris Yeltsin, following a meeting at the Kremlin in Moscow. December 1991.

President Bush in discussion with his chief of staff, Jim Baker (L), and then secretary of Defense, Dick Cheney (R). May 1992.

President Bush and Jim Baker have an informal discussion on the patio of the Bush family home, Walker's Point, in Kennebunkport, Maine. August 1992.

President Bush and his chief of staff, Jim Baker, meet with President-elect Bill Clinton in the Oval Office to discuss the transition of administrations. November 1992.

Ladybird Johnson, Jimmy and Rosalyn Carter, George and Barbara Bush, Bill and Hillary Clinton, Gerald and Betty Ford, Nancy Reagan at the Bush Library Dedication Ceremony. November 6, 1997.

George H.W. Bush celebrates his 75th birthday with the first of what became an every-five-years celebratory parachute jump. June 1999.

George H.W. Bush speaks with the press following his 80th birthday parachute jump at his presidential library. June 13, 2004.

Jim Baker chats with his good friend George H.W. Bush on the sidelines before an NFL game between the Houston Texans and the Buffalo Bills, where Bush served as honorary captain on Military Appreciation Day, November 4, 2012. (Getty Images/MCT)

CHAPTER EIGHT

Baker's Brilliance

W HATEVER HAPPENS, HE CANNOT GO OUT ON STAGE," senior Gore advisor Michael Feldman told David Morehouse. On election night, November 7, 2000, Vice President Al Gore had just placed a call to Texas governor George W. Bush to congratulate him on becoming the 43rd president of the United States, conceding to the son of the very man he had helped oust in 1992. It was now past 3:00 a.m. on November 8, with Gore's motorcade arriving at the War Memorial Auditorium in Nashville, Tennessee, after a short trip from the Lowe's Hotel. A man "born to be president," according to Gore's father, Al Gore Sr., was now walking briskly down a long hallway to address a demoralized crowd that had been hoping for a far different outcome.

With his Secret Service detail preceding him, and agents strategically positioned throughout the crowd, Gore was just moments away from entering the stage when Morehouse, his trip director, bluntly told him, "Mr. Vice President, we have to go to a hold [room]." Gore, in an almost defiant tone, shot back, "I'm not going to the hold. I called the governor [Bush]. The governor's waiting on me, and I'm going to the stage now."[396] Just at that moment, Morehouse realized that Gore wasn't taking his recommendation, and with just a few steps separating the vice president from the stage, the six-foot-one, solidly built Morehouse effectively blocked America's 45th vice president from taking another step. Gore, at six-foot-two and a regular weightlifter, was not amused, telling his trip director, "This better be good." For Gore, it was good.

The vote in the critical state of Florida was getting tighter and tighter, with only a few thousand votes separating the two candidates, a number that vanished in an instant, effectively bringing George W. Bush and Al Gore to an almost statistical tie. What came next was one of the most bizarre episodes of the election — in almost any presidential election in recent memory. In the early-morning hours of November 8, Gore called Bush, retracting his initial concession. Stunned, Bush said to Gore, "You mean to tell me, Mr. Vice President, you're retracting your concession?"[397] With his fist pumping and enthusiasm lifted, Gore told Bush, "You don't have to be so snippy about it."[398]

BAKER HELPS GEORGE W. GET IN THE WHITE HOUSE

For the first time in more than a century, there was no clear winner in the presidential election a full day after the polls had closed. No question about it, the 2000 presidential election was one for the history books. The popular vote margin was the closest since John F. Kennedy defeated Richard M. Nixon in 1960 by a scant 100,000 votes. As for the Electoral College margin, it was the tightest since

1876, when Rutherford B. Hayes beat Samuel J. Tilden by a single electoral vote. It was thirty-seven days of political chaos as Bush and Gore waited to hear who America's 43rd president would be.

Both camps moved swiftly to put in place veteran political power players to run the Florida recount operations. Gore went with former secretary of State Warren Christopher, while Bush chose none other than Jim Baker, not only his father's close friend, but the man who had helped lead two of the last three presidents to victory.

While George W. Bush had worked hard to distance himself from his father's administration — save for Cheney as his running mate — the Texas governor was a political novice on the national scene and needed a trusted advisor to turn to. According to Baker, "Where else was he [George W. Bush] going to find (a) a family friend, (b) a former secretary of State, (c) someone who has run five presidential election campaigns, and (d) someone who has been a lifetime lawyer? If the Democrats had not gone to Christopher, I don't know who the Republicans might have gone to. But Gore made a big thing out of it."[399]

According to Richard Bond, a former Republican national chairman, "To be able to post James Baker up against [Al Gore's legal point man] Warren Christopher is very helpful. . . . He is steady as you go. He is tough. He is politically savvy. . . . Baker's valued talents and valued advice was being sought privately. It wouldn't make any sense otherwise."[400]

For Baker, November 7, 2000, had begun with a board meeting for the Howard Hughes Medical Institute in Washington, DC, then off to Austin, Texas, to await the election results. As one of the GOP's most formidable campaign operatives of the last quarter century, election nights — especially presidential elections — were a special time for Baker; the Texan had run five consecutive Republican presidential campaigns between 1976 and 1992. Upon arriving in the capital of the Lone Star State, Baker headed to Dick and Lynne Cheney's suite at the Four Seasons Hotel to watch the results come in. Cheney eventually headed off to the Texas governor's mansion, and Baker remained in the suite, planning to write letters of congratulations on hotel stationery to the president-elect and vice president elect; letters he quickly retrieved from a staffer following Gore's retraction of his concession.

The next morning, with the election in turmoil, Baker's cellphone rang. Don Evans, one of George W. Bush's closest personal friends, and the governor's campaign chairman, was on the line. He informed Baker that Gore had just brought Warren Christopher to Florida, to help with the series of legal battles surely to come. Evans's request to Baker: Would you represent the governor in Florida? A question that didn't have to be asked twice, and an answer that all knew was coming. Baker was heading to Florida — and when Bush campaign manager Joe Allbaugh met with Baker, he asked him how it would all end. "It's going to be decided by the Supreme Court," Baker replied.

Baker arrived in Tallahassee, Florida, less than forty-eight hours after election night, taking the reins — and full charge — of the Bush–Cheney operations regarding the disputed election. Baker was initially dismayed to find that while the Gore camp had sent a cadre of lawyers and political operatives to Florida, Bush's team was meager — both in size and political muscle. This changed immediately as Baker called for a full assault, complete with lawyers and dozens of communications and PR personnel.

While Baker initially wanted former senator from Missouri John

Danforth to lead many of the legal efforts, it soon became clear he wasn't the man. Danforth felt Bush's chances to win his argument in a federal court were close to zero. Besides, said Danforth, "You could ruin Governor Bush's career. He's only fifty-four years old, and a decision to file a court case like this one would be a black mark that followed him forever. And it would destroy the reputation of everyone involved on the Bush side."[401] Baker quickly turned to a man he trusted and who believed in the cause — Theodore "Ted" Olson, a federal appellate attorney.

As Baker saw it, Gore's mantra of "count all the votes" was an easy sell, something he had to buttress with an effective message, and they had no time to waste. The situation for Bush was dire, indeed, but Baker's prescient thought that this entire fiasco would wind up in front of nine justices at the US Supreme Court — which it ultimately did — had him thinking and strategizing in a way few Democrats had predicted. As the Gore team called for recounts in select counties they were contesting — a big mistake according to Baker — then surely Baker would call for a recount in select counties to give Bush a hopefully larger vote tally. He didn't pursue that strategy. Instead, Baker labeled the Gore tactics as "selective" recounts, a political PR win that angered Christopher, who had been blindsided. Christopher's reasoning for choosing only four counties was to not subject the entire state to a massive, sixty-seven county recount, but it put the Democrats on the defensive from the very beginning as their tactics were looked upon as "cherry-picking" counties.

In one of his first briefings to the media, Baker made it very clear who the winner was, regardless of how close the vote was in Florida. "Governor George W. Bush won thirty-one states with a total of 271 electoral votes. The vote here in Florida was very close, but when it was counted, Governor Bush was the winner. Now, three days later, the vote in Florida has been recounted. At the end of this recount, Governor Bush is still the winner, subject only to counting the overseas ballots, which traditionally have favored the Republican candidates. No evidence of vote fraud, either in the original vote or in the recount, has been presented."[402]

Baker also drew parallels to previous presidential elections that he was a part of — as a Republican, on the losing side — stating ". . . because I've been involved in them, that it is frustrating to lose an election by a narrow margin, but it happens. And it happened to the Republican presidential candidates in 1960 and in 1976. Both Vice President Nixon and President Ford put the country's interests first. They accepted the vote for the good of the country."[403]

The wise, straight-talking Texan wanted to be very clear on who the winner was, and while also hoping for a quick resolution to the disputed election, one of America's most astute politicians knew all too well what was coming his way — a bitter fight to the end, so time to dig in and play hardball.

Baker continued to hammer away at the Gore camp for its endless requests for manual recounts of ballots, stating in yet another news conference on November 11, 2000, "Governor George W. Bush was the winner of the vote, and he was also the winner of the recount. Based on these results, we urge the Gore campaign to accept the finality of the election subject, of course, to the counting of the absentee, the overseas absentee ballots, in accordance with law."[404]

Baker became the voice and leading media spokesman for the entire Bush–Cheney Florida recount. With more than one hundred lawyers under his guidance, he executed a series of legal moves that gave him what he ultimately wanted: stopping the manual recounts wherever possible, and moving the battle to the federal courts and eventually the United States Supreme Court, out of the Florida courts that were largely controlled by the Democrats. According to Baker, "The first thing I concluded is that we had a very tough row to hoe if we couldn't get into federal court. . . . I knew their political leanings . . . and furthermore, Dexter Douglass, Gore's lead lawyer in Florida, had recommended the justices to Chiles [Lawton Chiles, the former governor of Florida, and a Democrat] for appointment."[405]

All things related to the Florida recount went through Baker. There was one voice, one vision, and one message, and Baker delivered to the media as he saw fit. He also had daily calls with the Bush camp back in Austin, Texas. Two calls — one with the larger campaign team, and a second call — "the call," as Baker put it — with just Governor Bush and Dick Cheney.

While scores of publications have examined and chronicled the contentious thirty-seven-day Florida recount and its almost endless barrage of accusations, legal filings, and court hearings that gave Bush the presidency, the real winner may very well have been Baker. In a masterful display of political checkmate, Baker time and again outmaneuvered, outflanked, and ultimately, outworked his worthy opponent.

Christopher was well-liked, congenial and — at first glance — a formidable opponent for Baker, but he quickly found out that Baker wasn't interested in rounds of negotiations and formalized protocols and procedures. If it wasn't clear to Christopher during his initial meeting with Baker at the Governors Inn, in Tallahassee, that Baker would be playing hardball, he found out quickly. While Christopher may have been looking for civility in what became political trench warfare in Florida, Baker was ready for a brawl, an all-out war on every possible front — the media, the courts, and even on the streets. Baker had come to Florida to win, nothing less. As the days and weeks wore on throughout the Florida recount, Baker systematically deflated and defeated many of Christopher's tactics, prompting Vice President Gore to dispatch additional operatives to fight what was becoming a losing battle against Baker.

On paper, both Baker and Christopher were former secretaries of State, but that's about all they had in common. Christopher was a corporate litigator with virtually no campaign experience. Baker, on the other hand, was the unquestioned GOP operative of his generation, a tough-talking Texan ready to engage in a political dogfight. Their personalities differed greatly also. Christopher was prudent, almost to the point of tentative; Baker was dogged, partisan, and ferocious, if necessary.

In his own memoirs, Christopher spoke about the well-known seventh floor of the State Department building, and its "large, graceful, rooms . . . furnished with museum-quality American antiques." He relished the luxuries of political office and the amenities afforded a wealthy corporate attorney — private jets, sumptuous dinners, and martinis. Tallahassee was far removed from his comfort zone — spartan accommodations and vacant retail space became Christopher's new ground zero — and he never seemed to fully adapt. According to one unidentified political observer: "Christopher brought a knife to a gunfight, if that, and nothing more."

Ron Klain, a key Gore operative during the Florida recount notes that, in his opinion, Bush did not have a stronger legal position than

Gore, but the Texas governor "did possess two practical advantages: certification of the outcome was in the hands of Florida's governor and secretary of State — who were our opponent's brother and state campaign co-chairwoman, respectively. And George Bush was ahead in the tally. We needed to change the count, while they needed only to run out the clock."[406]

Ted Olson, who ultimately — and successfully — argued before the Supreme Court for George W. Bush in *Bush vs. Gore*, recalled, "The recounts, protests and challenges in four Florida counties by the Gore–Lieberman legal forces were well underway, and our hurriedly assembled and rapidly expanding legal team had to work feverishly to catch up. . . . When that final decision came down, my wife and I were at our home with another couple — close friends. After I spoke by phone to my clients in the Bush–Cheney campaign, I went into the wine cellar, opened and poured the most expensive bottles of Champagne and Bordeaux I could find."[407]

In the end, Baker got what he ultimately came for in Florida — twenty-five electoral votes for George W. Bush, making the Texas governor the 43rd president of the United States. Baker delivered — big time — helping yet another Bush win the White House. And on the night of December 12, 2000, Baker, while still in Florida, placed a memorable call, telling Bush, "Congratulations, Mr. President-elect."[408] Baker placed a second call to his good friend, Dick Cheney, congratulating America's newly elected 46th vice president.

Reflecting back, Baker admits, "Florida will never happen again in American politics, in my opinion. It was a really unique situation. . . . A lot of people were saying this was terrible, the states should retain the rights to this issue. I knew if we did not make this a federal thing, we were toast. And they [Bush and Cheney] came right back and said go do it. We recruited Jack Danforth, and he said you shouldn't do this [filing a lawsuit], so went with Ted Olson, and we ended up winning."[409]

On January 20, 2001, George W. Bush was sworn in as America's 43rd president. On that day, Baker found himself with one of the best seats at the inauguration, the presidential reviewing stand with President George W. Bush, former president George H.W. Bush, and other close friends and political confidants of the Bush clan.

TROUBLE IN THE SAHARA

In March 1997, just four years removed as secretary of State, Baker found himself once again front and center on global affairs when United Nations secretary general Kofi Annan appointed him the special United Nations envoy for Western Sahara in an attempt to resolve the longstanding conflict in North Africa. Secretary General Annan said Mr. Baker was chosen because the United Nations needed a "most distinguished statesman" of "high international reputation" to secure the peace in the region and the longstanding dispute between Morocco and a rebel group known as the Polisario Front.[410] After years of failed attempts to resolve the issue, Annan asked Baker to become his personal envoy to help steer the parties toward a political solution, from the "winner-take-all" approach of the referendum.

The UN's involvement in Western Sahara started on December 16, 1965, when the General Assembly adopted its first resolution on what was then called Spanish Sahara, requesting Spain to "take all necessary measures" to decolonize the territory, while entering into negotiations on "problems relating to sovereignty."[411]

At the onset of Baker's mandates, the UN Security Council appeared extremely supportive of his efforts for resolving the conflict, however, doubt emerged when the Council was informed that the settlement plan no longer appeared a likely resolution, at which point the idea of finding a political solution, asking for compromises from both sides, was suggested. As difficult and trying as the situation was, "Throughout Baker's tenure, the Security Council expressed strong support and confidence in his ability to find an equitable solution to the conflict. However, when asked to make hard decisions and act on its professed support, especially with respect to the political solution, the Council did not act in a unified manner that would have sent a clear signal to both sides as to where it stood."[412]

Baker worked tirelessly to develop a resolution to an incredibly complex problem for which nobody had any real solutions, that is, until Baker presented his proposed solutions, generally known as Baker I and Baker II. As for Baker I, also known as the Framework Agreement, it offered the people of Western Sahara autonomy within the Moroccan state. And while Morocco accepted the plan, Algeria and the Polisario Front ultimately said no, with Algeria countering with their own proposal that called for the territory to be divided between the parties.[413]

Undeterred, Baker went back to the drawing board and developed a subsequent agreement, informally known as Baker II, which provided for Saharan self-rule under a Western Sahara Authority for a five-year period, followed up by a referendum for independence. The referendum allowed the entire present-day population of Western Sahara to participate, even people that had migrated from or been settled by Morocco after 1975, to which the Polisario Front had always said no.

In July 2003, the UN Security Council endorsed the plan, which had not occurred with Baker I, but Morocco ultimately rejected the plan, saying that it could not agree to a referendum that included independence as an option.[414]

Baker resigned his post in 2004 as frustration set in with the lack of progress by the UN Security Council to come to a unanimous agreement regarding Western Sahara. Algeria's ambassador to the United Nations Abdallah Baal stated, "We have been impressed by his strong personality, his patience, his perseverance, and his capability. He came up with very creative ideas, and his last plan received a favorable reception from the Security Council."[415] His resignation was deemed "a serious setback to the UN's efforts . . . to resolve in a fair and peaceful way the last decolonization issue in Africa."[416]

BAKER'S HALF DOZEN — RULES OF THUMB IN FOREIGN POLICY

During his years as secretary of State, Baker was at Bush's side as they navigated the multitude of cataclysmic changes taking place throughout the world, from China to Panama to the Middle East, not to mention Germany and the former Soviet Union. The consequential events that befell these countries all happened under the watchful eye of Baker, a brilliant negotiator and statesman who spearheaded key foreign-policy measures for the Bush White House from 1989 to 1992.

In May 2014, Baker was awarded the Ralph Bunche Award for Diplomatic Excellence for his many contributions to foreign policy. In his acceptance speech, he shared his foreign-policy rules of thumb — which he dubbed "a Baker's half dozen," six precepts of foreign policy to help guide US diplomacy. While Baker admits it's not a full and exhaustive list, nevertheless, it's what he considered "a useful starting point in assessing current and ongoing US foreign policy."

Below are excerpts of Baker's Half Dozen rules, as he presented in his speech that night:

1. Presidential commitment is critical.

A vast amount of our diplomacy is, frankly, fairly routine. And most of it can be handled at lower levels. That's why we have a secretary of State and a substantial bureaucracy to support the White House.

But there are certain times — notably during international crises and while pursuing important initiatives — when presidential involvement is indispensable. This is particularly true of situations where policies touch on domestic politics. Here the president must be prepared to weigh in if a policy is to succeed.

I experienced such a commitment firsthand in 1991 when I was secretary of State and began working on what, later that year, became the Madrid Peace Conference. Some members of our foreign-policy team argued that trying to negotiate Arab–Israeli peace was futile and thus, they said, a poor use of my time and our diplomatic assets.

But President George H.W. Bush wholeheartedly backed me, both during internal White House discussions and through his public statements and actions. His support was unequivocal.

The result of that support was that we broke a longstanding taboo, and Israel and all of her Arab neighbors eventually sat down at the negotiating table for the first time ever to discuss peace. None of that would have happened had President Bush not been willing to use his political capital to achieve that result.

2. Consistency matters in foreign policy.

Predictability reassures our allies and puts down clear markers for our potential adversaries. Let me be very clear here: I am not saying that the United States should continue unwise policies simply because we have supported them in the past. As circumstances change, we should be willing to reassess — and, if need be, reverse course.

But we should be very careful about making promises or threats without thinking through the consequences. This is especially the case when it comes to presidential declarations, which are authoritative statements of US foreign policy.

President Obama's famous "red line" on chemical-weapons use by the Syrian government is a cautionary example of the disarray that an injudicious statement — however off-hand — can cause. The awkward handling of the Syrian chemical-weapons issue last year — when US policy seemed to shift, at times, from day to day — clearly fostered unnecessary uncertainty among our friends in the Middle East and elsewhere.

There is room for "creative ambiguity" in foreign policy. But, as a general rule, we should say what we mean and mean what we say.

3. Effective foreign policy requires using all the tools at our disposal.
Our current approach to the crisis in Ukraine is an example. We should do far more to demonstrate both strength and resolve in opposing Moscow's aggression.

We should:

» Significantly expand economic sanctions, particularly financial.

» Reposition North Atlantic Treaty Organization military assets to Poland and the Baltic states. (We've done some of that.)

» Revive the missile defense program for Poland and the Czech Republic.

» Quickly approve all pending LNG [liquefied natural gas] applications. (The market impact of just the announcement of the action will increase Russian capital flight, further depreciate the ruble, and require Russia to pay more interest on its bonds.)

» And, we should encourage the development of shale gas in Poland, Spain, and Ukraine.

These are actions that the United States can take on its own. Our European allies are going to be far more reluctant to consider broad economic sanctions. But we shouldn't restrict ourselves to a lowest-common-denominator approach.

Let's be clear. Russia's actions in "rolling the tanks" is inconsistent with any concept of a stable world order.

Diplomacy is important, we would all agree. But I think we might also agree that diplomacy alone will not always settle all differences between nations. Competition between major nations is inevitable and therefore diplomacy is best conducted with a mailed fist.

4. Values matter, but so do interests.

Should the United States support democracy and human rights? Of course, we should! We have long espoused our values as part of our foreign policy. But those values must be weighed against our other interests.

In the Mideast, for instance, those interests include not only seeking to promote peace between Israel and its Arab neighbors, but also ensuring security of oil and gas supplies to world markets and encouraging joint action against terrorist threats to the United States or our allies.

As a practical matter, this means cooperation with regional governments that fall short — sometimes far short — of Jeffersonian ideals. And it further suggests that the United States should be very careful of "rhetorical overreach" when it comes to democracy and human rights.

Such language can both raise unwarranted expectations of support by Washington and subject us to inevitable charges of hypocrisy as we — correctly, in my opinion — take a case-by-case approach to the countries of the region.

5. Relationships are vital.

First and foremost, strong ties of trust and confidence between the president and secretary are critical to an administration's success in foreign affairs.

Let me share another anecdote, one that illustrates the importance of a seamless relationship between a president and his secretary of State.

After Iraqi troops invaded Kuwait in the summer of 1990, the UN Security Council imposed an arms embargo on Iraq. When two heavily laden Iraqi tankers bound for Yemen refused to be boarded, the secretary of Defense, the national security advisor, the chairman of the Joint Chiefs of Staff, and even Margaret Thatcher recommended using military force to halt them. We would look weak if it didn't act, they said.

I was at my ranch in Wyoming, but on the phone with Soviet

foreign minister Eduard Shevardnadze. Shevardnadze asked me to give the Soviets a couple of days to see if they could convince Iraq to turn the tankers back.

And so, I argued from afar that they should be given that time and not risk the Soviets abandoning their general posture of support for the US line regarding Iraq.

The president later wrote that he trusted me, and so he agreed with my isolated position. Ultimately, the Soviets convinced the Iraqis to turn their ships back.

Had President Bush not supported me, the Soviets would not have remained with us in the Security Council and we would never have been able to secure the Chapter 7 use-of-force resolution that we later got. (By the way, that was the only time — before or since — that the UN Security Council has invoked use-of-force against a member state, except Korea in the '50s when the Soviets walked out on the vote.)

Meanwhile, at an institutional level, close working relationships among all of the president's foreign-policy team promote consistency and avoid debilitating squabbles carried out through leaks to the press.

6. Always recall that our current role in world affairs depends upon our economic strength.

Our country's decisive advantage in military might is critical, surely. And so is the dense web of foreign alliances that permit us to leverage our influence.

But we cannot remain strong militarily or diplomatically unless we are strong economically. Our vibrant economy is the core reason we have been the world's preeminent power for so long. This is why defusing what I call our fiscal "debt bomb" is the number one challenge confronting our leaders and policymakers.

Our total public debt-to-GDP ratio at 100 percent is simply unsustainable. Unsustainable federal debt will inevitably squeeze our defense and diplomacy budgets. And it will also lower overall economic growth, making it ever harder to marshal public support for engagement abroad.

Let me end on a note of optimism. At times like today — as crisis brews in the Ukraine, the Syrian Civil War rages on, tensions rise in the Far East and terrorism grows stronger not weaker — it is easy to despair.

But we would be wise to recall that we still face a far more benign international environment than we did during the Cold War. And we should remember that, for all the current difficulties, we remain a country of unique economic, military, and diplomatic power.

Our task today is to sustain that power and use it wisely. We have met far greater challenges in the past.

And, if we have proper leadership, we can and will do so again.[417]

A SECOND TERM AND A NEW APPROACH

Just two years into George W. Bush's second term — and just three short years after the start of the Second Gulf War — Iraq was experiencing seismic challenges so big they would, if not addressed, ultimately jeopardize the initial American war efforts that had removed Saddam Hussein from power. Sectarian violence was out of control as thousands of Iraqis were being murdered each month. US and coalition forces were being killed at alarming numbers. Iraq's government seemed incapable and unwilling to respond. A change was needed.

Members of Congress — and millions of Americans — had grown tired of the escalating violence and instability within Iraq, and they wanted a change.

President Bush, aware of the growing criticism, agreed to a bipartisan commission to assess the dire situation in Iraq and provide a series of recommendations to the White House. Bush wanted Baker to lead those efforts, and Baker agreed to sign on. At the urging of Congress, the United States Institute of Peace, together with the Center for Strategic and International Studies (CSIS), the Center for the Study of the Presidency (CSP), and Rice University's Baker Institute for Public Policy formed the Iraq Study Group. This all-star, bipartisan team of political operatives — which included Baker, former Democratic congressman from Indiana Lee Hamilton, along with former deputy secretary of State Lawrence Eagleburger, attorney Vernon Jordan, former US attorney general Ed Meese, former US Supreme Court justice Sandra Day O'Connor, former White House chief of staff Leon Panetta, former secretary of Defense William Perry, former Virginia senator Chuck Robb, and former senator from Wyoming Alan Simpson — was asked to take a fresh, clean, and unbiased view on the many challenges facing Iraq. They conducted an independent assessment of the current and prospective situation on the ground in Iraq, its impact on the surrounding region, and consequences for US interests.

It had only been six years since Baker had jumped into the fray to help ensure Bush won Florida — and the presidency — both of which happened. Now, he was co-chairing a bipartisan panel to offer up recommendations and solutions for what many perceived as George W. Bush's failures in Iraq. In their opening remarks of the landmark study published in December 2006, Baker and co-chair Hamilton provided a rather ominous message:

"There is no magic formula to solve the problems of Iraq. However, there are actions that can be taken to improve the situation and protect American interests. Many Americans are dissatisfied, not just with the situation in Iraq but with the state of our political debate regarding Iraq. Our political leaders must build a bipartisan approach to bring a responsible conclusion to what is now a lengthy and costly war. Our country deserves a debate that prizes substance over rhetoric, and a policy that is adequately funded and sustainable. The president and Congress must work together. Our leaders must be candid and forthright with the American people in order to win their support.

"No one can guarantee that any course of action in Iraq at this point will stop sectarian warfare, growing violence, or a slide toward chaos. If current trends continue, the potential consequences are severe. Because of the role and responsibility of the United States in Iraq, and the commitments our government has made, the United States has special obligations. Our country must address as best it can Iraq's many problems."[418]

While not a stinging rebuke to the Iraq policies put forth by the very man Baker had helped win the presidency, it was a clear reminder to the president of the United States — George W. Bush — that conditions in Iraq were worsening, and change was needed.

The Iraq Study Group Report was comprehensive, discussing a plethora of topics critical to the success of the country, both short term and long term. Key elements within the study included building a strong international consensus, which ultimately called for a new diplomatic offensive, an "Iraq International Support Group," taking steps to appropriately deal with Iran and Syria, while also assessing Iraq's challenges from a wider regional context. The report made clear that "In order to foster such consensus, the United States should embark on a robust diplomatic effort to establish an international support structure intended to stabilize Iraq and ease tensions in other countries in the region. This support structure should include every country that has an interest in averting a chaotic Iraq, including all of Iraq's neighbors — Iran and Syria among them."[419]

True to the spirit of diplomacy that's unquestionably well-engrained into the mindset of the former secretary of State, the report was laced with heavy recommendations for improvements in diplomatic efforts for helping solve Iraq's mounting challenges. Baker said the report made very clear that "Our most important recommendations call for new and enhanced diplomatic and political efforts in Iraq and the region, and a change in the primary mission of US forces in Iraq that will enable the United States to begin to move its combat forces out of Iraq responsibly."

The report also provided a detailed assessment and list of recommendations for improving Iraq's internal challenges, which were many, indeed, noting: "The most important issues facing Iraq's future are now the responsibility of Iraq's elected leaders. Because of the security and assistance it provides, the United States has a significant role to play. Yet only the government and people of Iraq can make and sustain certain decisions critical to Iraq's future." The report covered almost every conceivable subject matter considered vital to Iraq's internal challenges, from performance milestones to national reconciliation, security and military forces, police and criminal justice, the oil sector, budget preparation, US personnel, intelligence, and more.

In the morning hours of December 6, 2006 — and after eight months of work — members of the Iraq Study Group met privately with President Bush in the Cabinet Room of the White House. Baker and Hamilton gave Bush their executive summary of the report, with other members each speaking briefly. Bush listened, nodded, keeping his comments very brief, and after all members had spoken, the press corps of reporters and photographers joined in.

In all, the Iraq Study Group members — ten Republicans and Democrats — put forth seventy-nine specific recommendations, to which President Bush told reporters: "This report will give us all an opportunity to find common ground, for the good of the country — not for the good of the Republican Party or the Democratic Party, but for the good of the country."[420]

At a news conference discussing the release of the report, Baker was forthright: "We do not recommend a stay-the-course solution. In our opinion, that is no longer viable."[421] On December 7, 2006, the day after the release of the report — which no doubt raised eyebrows in Washington — Baker stated that the White House must not treat the report "like a fruit salad."[422] President Bush then moved to distance himself from two key recommendations — reducing combat brigades in Iraq over the next fifteen months and opening up dialogue with Iran and Syria. While the report was against a massive troop buildup of American forces, it stated: "We could, however, support a short-term redeployment or surge of American combat forces to stabilize Baghdad, or to speed up the training and equipping mission, if the US commander in Iraq determines that such steps would be effective."[423] Ultimately, in 2007, Bush did order the troop surge, which proved effective.

BAKER FOR PRESIDENT?

One would think that, with such an accomplished résumé as Baker's, the idea of running for president of the United States would have been on his mind. And it was, Baker admitting, "We [he and his wife Susan] thought about running for president in '96. I had a high name ID in the country, maybe up in the eighties . . . and I had good approval/disapproval numbers, and I sure knew the job. I had worked for these presidents right at their right hand, but I was worn-out-tired. My wife and I, we talked about it, we looked at it carefully. But I had done five presidential campaigns. I'd done four years as White House chief of staff, four years as Treasury secretary, and four years as secretary of State, and I was absolutely worn-out and, you know, interspaced in between those were the political campaigns, and they take a lot out of you too."[424]

Baker admits to having been asked to return to the White House — this time for President George W. Bush — with a number of high-profile positions possibly on the table — director of CIA and secretary of Defense — jobs Baker privately declined to the president as his life was in Houston now, not the nation's capital.

CHAPTER NINE

Around the World
with James A. Baker, III

At a speech at the Asia Society Texas Center's annual Tiger Ball in Houston on March 29, 2011, Baker shared his thoughts on China and Japan at that time. Below are his comments from that day.[425]

ON CHINA

China's historic transformation, as far as economic transformation is concerned, is well-known here [the United States] and indeed around the world. And almost daily, it seems we hear some extraordinary statistic about Chinese economic growth, or Chinese trade, or Chinese investment. I happened to be visiting China periodically for thirty-four years . . . and I never cease to be astonished by the speed and the scale of China's transformation. Today, China is not just an immensely richer country than when I first visited, it is a much more dynamic, and a much more confident society. It is truly a great power, poised to take an increasingly important role on the world stage.

But allow me to be blunt. Some in the United States — not a

majority by any means, but certainly a vocal minority — see China's rise as a threat somehow to America's international status. They believe that conflict between our two countries is inevitable as Chinese ambitions clash with American position and power. Ladies and gentlemen, these observers are wrong. And they are not only wrong, they are dangerously wrong. And the reason is very simple — their analyses grossly underestimate the broad areas where Chinese and American interests converge. One such area, of course, is fostering global economic growth and cooperating wherever possible to address the financial crisis that has swept the world. Not only are America and China respectively the world's two largest economies now, they happen to be major trading partners. As major beneficiaries of more open trade and investment, each of them possesses a vital interest in the health of the broader world economic system.

These common interests are likely to expand and deepen with time as China's economy matures. Of course, the advantages to closer economic cooperation are two-fold. Importantly and obviously, first, it promises a greater economic well-being for the citizens of both countries. And secondly, that economic cooperation tends to dampen any chances of conflict. Another obvious area of common interest for the two countries is energy. Like the United States, China has a huge stake in the unimpeded flow of petroleum to global markets at a reasonable price. It would benefit neither country, for example . . . were the current political unrest in the Middle East to jeopardize the production of oil there.

Another threat to energy security is Iran's nuclear program, which could allow Tehran to blackmail its neighbors and set off a Middle Eastern nuclear arms race. Quite simply, China and America both, have a direct interest in avoiding such outcomes. A third area of common interest is regional stability in Asia. And of course, of particular concern there is North Korea's nuclear program. During the past year, North Korea has taken brinksmanship too far through unwarranted military attacks on South Korea. . . .

These challenges . . . are just a few of the areas of common interest between the United States and China. But there are many others. Combating terrorism, protecting sea lanes, stemming the proliferation of weapons of mass destruction are a few of those that immediately come to mind. In order to effectively tackle any of them, China and the United States are first going to have to manage their differences, and those differences exist, as they do between all countries, and particularly, all great powers. And those differences . . . are not going to go away. Over time in fact, larger differences may indeed emerge.

One potential flashpoint, Taiwan, remains an area of perennial concern, so does trade policy as witnessed the furor here in this country over our trade deficit with China. Human rights, Tibet, and proliferation are also areas of difference. Our task is to ensure that these differences do not escalate. At times of tension, we need to restrain the rhetoric on both sides of the Pacific, and we need to keep lines of communication open. We need to find compromises that allow us to meet halfway, and sometimes, we must simply agree to disagree.

The future is rich enough with opportunities to give both of our countries full rein for our ambitions and for our dreams, but if we slip into confrontation or conflict, then both sides will suffer, and make no mistake about it . . . the world will suffer with us.

One Cold War ended almost twenty years ago. We neither want nor need another one [Cold War]. I happen to be personally optimistic about our ability to avoid a tragic outcome, if we focus on the opportunities that the two countries have for cooperation. But even more important, perhaps, is the increasingly powerful network of interpersonal relationships that bind the two countries together.

ON JAPAN

The United States has never had a better or a closer ally than Japan in the last sixty-six years. We may have had some as close, but never any that's any better or any closer, and that relationship I saw firsthand when I was secretary of State, because that relationship was the basis of peace and security in the Pacific for all of those sixty-six years.

ON RUSSIA

In 1999, while serving as secretary of State, Baker spoke at the Kennan Institute's 25th Anniversary Dinner and presented his remarks on Russia. Below are excerpts from that speech.

Both countries must work hard to lay a positive groundwork for relations in the next century. We can only achieve a stronger relationship if our discourse and policies are based not on the heated debate of the moment, but on careful consideration of the broader importance of the relationship.

Here, obviously our relationship with Russia is important for many reasons. Russia's large nuclear arsenal and other advanced military technology could pose a major threat to us if it gets into the wrong hands, Russia's economy . . . has great potential. Russia has influence in areas of strategic importance to us, such as Central Asia and the Middle East. Russian organized crime networks stretch throughout the world and constitute a major problem to be reckoned with.

So, given Russia's importance, it clearly follows that engagement with Russia is the only sensible approach to dealing with the problems she faces and the strains in our relationship. A peaceful, democratic, and prosperous Russia is strongly in our national interest. And so, we should continue to work with Russia to help it reach this goal.

Yet we must have realistic expectations of Russia. We must not expect her to become a thriving market democracy that functions just like ours. We must recognize that Russia will develop on her own terms and in her own way. We must understand that major reforms may not be implemented for years, and that reform may not take place exactly as we would like.

We should also recognize that our involvement with Russia will not immediately produce great results. There will be further setbacks along the way. But we must be patient and persistent and seek to build bridges where possible.

We should voice our objections with Russia when appropriate, but we should seek always to turn our objections into a constructive dialogue.

The challenges facing Russia are immense, from security issues to economic reform to political strife. These problems are all exacerbated by the fact that Russia does not have an adequately functioning system of laws. Our efforts to help Russia meet her challenges can only have a modest impact on a country that vast and complex. But that impact in itself is well worth our time and resources.[426]

ON NUCLEAR ARMS REDUCTION

In November 2011, Baker wrote an op-ed for the New York Times *on reducing nuclear arms. The following is an excerpt from that article.*

I support the aspiration for a nuclear-weapons-free world that President Reagan envisioned. I disagree, however, with your Oct. 30 [2011] editorial "The Bloated Nuclear Weapons Budget," which endorses an American reduction to 1,000 nuclear weapons, even if other countries do not reduce at all.

As I outlined in a recent speech to Global Zero, an international movement to rid the world of all nuclear weapons, any effort to reach that goal must require reciprocal and proportional cuts so that all countries reduce their arsenals in concert. If you want to have any chance to achieve the goal, this condition cannot be negotiable. Without it, you will fail.

Three other conditions are equally important.

First, all countries must be parties to the effort, with no exceptions.

Second, frequent, rigorous, and intrusive inspections must be required. President Reagan was right: "Trust, but verify."

Third, the American president must personally take the lead and commit the required time, attention, assets, and political will. It will demand presidential leadership just as winning the Cold War required the concerted effort of nine consecutive presidents, Democrats and Republicans alike.

Even if these conditions are met, a nuclear-free world will take years to reach, if ever. But if accomplished, it would benefit every citizen of the world.[427]

In an interview with *Frontline*, Baker said, "The proliferation risk today is far greater. With the end of the Cold War, you had the collapse of Communism; the implosion of the Soviet Union; and you had the brain drain problem, particularly with respect to nuclear, but also with respect to chemical and biological. So [it's] probably easier today than it was in the past for terrorist groups to access, particularly, biological weapons of mass destruction or the technology."[428]

ON SAUDI ARABIA

In another op-ed to the New York Times, *on October 22, 2018, Baker wrote regarding his stance on Saudi Arabia. His comments included the following:*

In formulating and implementing United States foreign policy, there is often a tension between the promotion of America's values and the protection of our interests . . . But sometimes, effective foreign policy requires balancing our principles and values with our geopolitical interests. That balancing act can demand painful compromises. . . . Saudi Arabia has been an important strategic partner of the United States since President Franklin Roosevelt met with King Ibn Saud, the founder of the Saudi state, at the close of World War II. In recent years, the United States has worked closely with Saudi Arabia on issues critical to both countries. Stabilizing global oil markets, combating terrorism, and countering Iranian regional adventurism are just three. We also need to engage the Saudis in areas where we are not in 100 percent agreement, such as their debilitating war in Yemen and their conflict with Qatar.[429]

ON NORTH KOREA

In April 2015, Baker shared a few thoughts on North Korea in an interview with NBC's *Andrea Mitchell.*

China is the only country in the world that really has any influence, significant influence on North Korea. . . . We've seen the North

Koreans talk a lot but not do anything constructive by way of reducing their missiles and development of nuclear weapons.

If you fail here [with talks], then you better be prepared to know what your next step is going to be. And everybody knows the cataclysmic consequences of a war on the Korean Peninsula in terms of loss of life, primarily Korean loss of life.[430]

THE MIDDLE EAST

In 1994, Baker participated in a Middle East Forum, where he offered his views on various topics regarding the region.

ON ISLAM AND THE WEST

We're very quick to talk about Islamic fundamentalism, and I think that is the wrong way to speak of it. Saudi Arabia is an Islamic fundamentalist state, but it is a friend of the United States and very important to the United States. And the national interests that we have in the Gulf I think we've demonstrated in — in the aftermath of Kuwait. So, I always say, and I'm very careful to say whenever I speak of it, radical Islamic fundamentalism, because that really is what we're talking about. And it truly is antithetical to the West — to democratic values, free-market principles, and to the principles and values we believe in. So, we should oppose it to the extent that our national interests require.

I fear the current wave of radical Islamism is going to be a continuing problem as long as poverty and discontent exist in that part of the world. We must find a way to get beyond that and to achieve some economic development. I once made a proposal for a Middle East development bank. It was not picked up on, but it's still needed, for the Middle East is the only part of the world without a development bank.[431]

ON AN INDEPENDENT PALESTINIAN STATE

[In 1994] You find clear differences of position and view on the question of an independent Palestinian state. When this was the joint position of the Arab states in negotiations, they all were for it. But as unity disappeared in their pursuit of the peace process, you'll find each country looks at a Palestinian state from the standpoint of its own particular circumstances.[432]

ON THE RELATIONSHIP BETWEEN THE ARAB STATES AND ISRAEL

[In 1994] The Arabs no longer present as much of a unified front as they used to . . . At least with respect to the countries around Israel, you're not going to get real economic development until there's peace. And when you do get peace, boy, there's going to be tremendous development and economic activity in so many different ways in those countries — in Israel herself and in the countries bordering Israel. And I'm optimistic that you can get peace.[433]

PERCEPTIONS OF THE UNITED STATES IN THE MIDDLE EAST

[In 1994] The Middle East has a great number of conspiracy theories, some genuine, others manufactured for external purposes. Some Middle Easterners may genuinely believe in them, but I think in many other respects they're manufactured. A sense exists in the Middle East that our intelligence agencies are omniscient. Some also think that because of our status as a superpower, we possess capabilities that we really don't possess.

Some Middle Easterners understand the American system of government, in particular the division between the executive and legislative branches, others do not. It depends on the country. As time goes by, more and more of them understand the way the separation of powers works . . . It's more true the more rejectionist and radical the regime is. The more radical a state, the more it tends to view us in a conspiratorial way. Also, the more rejectionist the state, the more likely it uses Israel as a justification for policies and for maintaining itself in power.[434]

THE ART OF DIPLOMACY

In February 2020, during a Dallas Morning News *interview with William McKenzie, Baker shared his thoughts on the various skills needed to be successful in the world of politics.*

ON NEGOTIATING

An important aspect of successful negotiations is the ability to climb into the shoes of the other parties at the table and understand what motivates them personally, politically and professionally. After all, it's understandably hard to get something from someone if doing that will hurt that person more than it helps them.

A reason President George H.W. Bush was so successful in the practice of foreign policy was his uncanny ability to understand his adversaries. He understood the situation that Soviet president Mikhail Gorbachev faced as his nation was collapsing, and so he didn't try to squeeze him so hard that the hardliners in the USSR could take over from him.

As a result, negotiations don't always have to get down to the lick-log (as we say in Texas). But when they do, the best way to proceed is with candor and honesty. Let your adversaries know exactly where they stand and how their intransigence will affect the question at hand and, more importantly, how a bad decision might hurt them, as well.[435]

ON COMPROMISING

Compromise has become more difficult — and sometimes, it seems, impossible. But we should not despair. I am fundamentally optimistic about our country's future. I'm old enough to remember how we met challenges during the Great Depression, World War II and the Cold War — and triumphed.

While I would prefer a grand bargain addressing our alarming fiscal position, I would support any substantial initiative to begin tackling it. And, yes, both tax increases and budget cuts should be on the table. As President Reagan said: "If I can get 70 or 80 percent of what I want, I'll take that and then continue to try to get the rest in the future."[436]

HOW A CRISIS CAN PROMPT A GRAND BARGAIN OR BIG COMPROMISE

There is no doubt that a crisis or even a hard deadline can drastically improve the chances that a grand bargain can be struck. In 1981, for example, the Social Security trust funds were nearly empty and projected to run out of money within sixteen years if something wasn't done. Newspapers and television were filled with stories about the impending financial doom facing many aging Americans. The subsequent public pressure made it easier for President Reagan and Congress to reform Social Security in 1983 in a way that extended the solvency of Social Security payments for fifty-four years.[437]

LISTENING, TRUSTING, AND RELATING TO LEADERSHIP

In a December 2019 article written by William McKenzie for Inside Sources, *Baker shared some insights on values and leadership.*

On Values

You get your values in your upbringing and education. That's one problem today. Too many people are not being exposed to and trained in the principles and values that have made this country great. One of those is compromise, which is a dirty word today. Compromise is how the Founders arrived at agreements on things that were bitterly disputed. Sadly, we've lost that. The center is gone in politics. If you don't get (your values) from your upbringing, your education, or your study of history, I don't know how you're going to get them.[438]

On Great Leadership

I consistently go back to James MacGregor Burns, who defined it as "a commitment to values and the perseverance to fight for those values." I agree but would say it in a bit different terms: Leadership is knowing what to do and then doing it.

The tough part of leadership is the "doing it" part. A commitment to values is knowing what to do. The perseverance to fight for those values is doing it.[439]

WHAT'S HAPPENING RIGHT HERE, RIGHT NOW IN AMERICA?

In April 2019, Baker looked back on his time in Washington and the various positions he held for the leaders he served. "Washington worked back then. We sent people up there [Washington] with the will and the desire to do the people's business. We don't have that anymore."

He said it was a far different political climate from what we see today [in 2019].

"We are politically dysfunctional today in the United States and that's one of the biggest threats facing our country. The responsible center in American politics is disappearing. There's another factor though, that we ought to all be aware of, and that's the freedom of the press. Today, the press are not objective reporters of the facts, they are players. That's not good for our democracy. And we now have the Internet, which permits anybody anonymously to throw the wildest allegations and charges up there and see who salutes it."[440]

CHAPTER TEN

The Best of Friends

THERE HAVE BEEN MANY POLITICAL POWER PLAYERS IN
Washington over the years. Some are spouses, like Bill and
Hillary Clinton. Others are tenacious political ideologues, like Dick
Cheney and Donald Rumsfeld. Yet few, if any, can claim a bond
like the one shared by George Herbert Walker Bush and James A.
Baker, III.

Bush had been in Texas just over ten years — starting in Odessa
in 1948 before eventually moving to Houston in 1959 — before that
fateful day when he and Baker were paired to play men's doubles at
the same country club. Their families spent many weekends together,
hosting barbeques, playing touch football in their annual "Turkey
Bowl," and almost any other activity two growing families could
think of.

Bush and Baker were different in many regards, yet also the same
in some ways. Bush hailed from East Coast gentry. He left his family
and the comforts afforded him to venture out on his own to Texas

with hopes and dreams, coupled with a vernacular uncommon to residents of the Lone Star State. Cowboy boots and barbeque were foreign to Bush as he descended onto Texas.

As for Baker, he was as Texan as any Texan could be. He spoke with a distinct drawl, priding himself on his deep Houstonian roots and all things Texas. Cowboy boots and Red Man chewing tobacco were common elements of his early life, yet so were pinstriped suits and power meetings as Baker rapidly progressed up the corporate ladder, becoming one of Houston's most well-respected attorneys. As Bush's oil business endeavors were booming, Baker's law firm became his trusted counsel along the way. Their friendship grew into a lasting bond, leading both men to acknowledge that they were in fact the very best of friends.

"I LOVE YOU"

Baker reflected on the passing of his best friend, describing the final day on earth for George Herbert Walker Bush. "That last day was really a very, very gentle and peaceful passing for him. . . . When I showed up at seven o'clock in the morning, one of the aides who assisted him physically said, 'Mr. President, Secretary Baker is here.' And he opened both eyes, he looked at me, he said, 'Hey, Bake, where are we going today?' And I said, 'Well, Jefe,' I said, 'We're going to heaven.' He said, 'Good, that's where I want to go.' Little did I know, or did he know, of course, that by ten o'clock that night, he'd be in heaven."[441]

Baker said that Bush's last words to his son and former president George W. Bush were "I love you," to which George replied, "Dad, I love you, and I will see you on the other side."

Baker noted that after Barbara Bush's death earlier that same year, Bush had said that he wasn't ready to go. "I'm going to miss him," Baker added. "What a beautiful, beautiful human being. A friend of sixty years."[442]

Bush's passing also gave Baker — and others who served with Bush — an opportunity to speak about his remarkable political career and accomplishments. Both Baker and Dick Cheney, Bush's secretary of Defense, joined together with *FOX News Sunday* host Chris Wallace to remember George H.W. Bush. Cheney noted: "In terms of his leadership, the important thing to remember is what we put together during those years. . . . We'd all worked together back during the [President Gerald] Ford years."[443]

Baker agreed.

"He was a consequential leader," Cheney continued. "His knowledge of foreign leaders, people he'd worked with over the years, his understanding of the military, his willingness to support the military." Cheney then added: "We gave him a very long list of things we wanted to have in the Gulf [1991 Persian Gulf War] before we launched offensive weapons. He didn't turn us down on anything. He approved all of them and said humbly, 'Show me how you're going to do it.'"[444]

When asked by Wallace why Bush's legacy has been overlooked at times, Baker bluntly stated, "I'm not sure why they missed it, except perhaps he was not re-elected. He was a one-term president. In my view, and I would bet this is true with Dick Cheney as well, he was the very best one-term president this country has ever had and perhaps one of the very best presidents of all time."[445]

When asked by ABC News chief anchor George Stephanopoulos which single moment he will cherish the most about Bush, Baker replied, "Well, of course, I will cherish my friendship with him the most. He changed my life. There's no doubt about that. He was my best friend for many years. He gave me the opportunity and privilege of becoming involved in national politics and serving this great country of ours at a very high level."[446]

Baker paid final respects to his friend in his eulogy to George Herbert Walker Bush. Speaking with sadness, yet knowing full well his best friend had moved on to the heavens. Excerpts from his eulogy are below:

"My friends, we're here today in the house of the Lord to say goodbye to a man of great faith and great integrity, a truly beautiful human being, and to honor his noble character, his life of service, and the sweet memories he leaves for his friends, his family, and for our grateful nation. . . . I have always been proud that George Bush used to describe our relationship as one of big brother and little brother. He used to say that one of the things he liked best about me was that I would always tell him what I thought, even when I knew he didn't want to hear it. Then we would have a spirited discussion about that issue.

"But he had a very effective way of letting me know when the discussion was over," he continued. "He would look at me and say, 'Baker, if you're so smart, why am I president and you're not?'

"His deeds for his fellow man always spoke for him," Baker said. "'Give someone else a hand,' he would say, and he did. 'When a friend is hurting, show that you care,' he would say, and he did. 'Be kind to people,' he would say, and he was . . . My hope is that in remembering the life of George Herbert Walker Bush and in honoring his accomplishments, we will see that we are really praising what is best about our nation."

Baker concluded his eulogy, saying, "There is more to say than time permits, and anyway, when measured against the eloquence of George Bush's character and life, our words are very inadequate. And so, I conclude these remarks with his words, written some years ago to his old tennis buddy. 'We have known each other a long time,' he wrote to me. 'We have shared joy and sadness. And time has indeed gone swiftly by. Now it races on even faster, and that makes me treasure even more this line of William Butler Yates about where man's glory begins and ends, namely with friends. My glory is, I have you as such a friend.'"[447]

Following the funeral service in Houston, Texas, Bush's remains were taken by train, a Union Pacific custom locomotive numbered 4141 bearing the name "George Bush 41" on its side, to College Station where he was laid to rest next to his wife, Barbara, who passed away on April 17, 2018, and his daughter, Robin, who died of childhood leukemia at age three in 1953.[448]

As of this printing, James A. Baker, III is ninety years young and going strong. He works out daily — both core exercises and brisk walks in Memorial Park — and keeps busy with whatever he desires. His career — as he has publicly acknowledged — has been forever linked with that of George Bush's. They were in the trenches many times — both alone, yet more times than not, together — with countless victories on the political score board.

They struck out a few times in Texas, but those early defeats cannot tarnish their achievements once they reached the national stage. If politics was a game of baseball, they played their positions well, hitting singles, doubles, homeruns, and grand slams.

Even after losing his run against Reagan in the 1980 Republican presidential primary, there were smiles as wide as the state of Texas for both Bush and Baker when Bush accepted Reagan's invitation to become his running mate. Their landslide victory also propelled Baker to the unlikeliest of positions, chief of staff to President Ronald Reagan. Baker became known as arguably the most effective chief of staff ever to serve a president, carving out notable policy accomplishments for himself.

After Reagan and Bush won their second term in 1984, giving both men four more years to flex their political muscle, Bush began to look forward to 1988 for the ultimate political prize — the presidency.

As he did for Reagan in 1984, Baker ran Bush's 1988 presidential campaign, one that he executed almost flawlessly as Bush won in a landslide over Michael Dukakis. That Bush would ask Baker to be his secretary of State was all but a given. By that time, both men's political résumés were simply extraordinary, and — save for the political appointments Bush held during the 1970s — they were résumés built in a relatively short period of time. Two Texans — one born on Bissonnet Street in Houston, the other, a transplant who called Houston his home — became two of Washington's most consequential statesmen of modern times.

Following Bush's failed re-election bid against Bill Clinton and Ross Perot, both he and Baker returned to Texas, where their friendship had begun decades earlier — Houston. Baker was the bluest of blue-blooded Houstonians — a multi-generational legacy of Bakers who were unquestionably instrumental in shaping what's become America's 4th largest metropolitan area.

While Baker is known for having publicly doted on his good

friend. Bush doted equally on Baker, once saying, "Jim's legacy as one of the most decent and capable men to help guide our nation's foreign policy, and before that its economy, is secure. . . . No one knew their brief better; no one was a better advocate for American interests; no one was a more effective spokesman for the four presidents he served with class and distinction. On a personal note, it is highly unlikely I would ever have been president without his superb and wise counsel."[449]

Baker, somber and subdued at the passing of George Herbert Walker Bush, was nevertheless still doting on his big brother. "I've never had a better friend. . . . It's pretty neat to say you've had a best friend for sixty years."[450]

BAKER'S HOUSTON BECAME BUSH'S HOME

Texans take deep pride in their state. From El Paso to Beaumont, Perryton to Brownsville, the Lone Star State shines bright for all of those proud to call Texas home. And wherever one calls home in the 268,597 square miles of this former republic — regardless of size or location — all residents of the great state like to call their city the best, and no doubt, bragging rights come into play when the two behemoths of Houston and Dallas give it their best Texas two-step in terms of who's bigger and better than the other.

We'll leave that conversation to the sports fanatics, socialites, and other "experts" who like to battle it out every so often on the Houston vs. Dallas competition. One thing we do know, Houstonians are quick to claim — and rightfully so — George H.W. Bush and James A. Baker, III as "theirs." Make no mistake, they're Texans, but they're also Houstonians through and through, no question about it.

Baker was born and bred in Houston, one of the city's most revered citizens, an icon of modern times. His early-childhood home was at 1216 Bissonnet — and save for his beloved ranch in Wyoming — Houston was his only home, and he'd be the first to tell you that there's not another city he'd rather live in.

As for Bush, he came to Houston and —in reality — never left, calling it home since 1959. Shortly after arriving in the Bayou City, he took up residence at 5525 Briar Drive. Returning after his brief stint as CIA director, he moved to 5838 Indian Trail, yet another home in the coveted Tanglewood neighborhood. As vice president, Bush's "home" away from his official residence at Number One Observatory Circle was the John Staub-designed Manor House on the grounds of the Houstonian, only having to move out, and into Suite 271, while the home underwent much-needed renovation. When Bush became president, the Houstonian once again became his local residence of choice, even holding the 1990 G7 economic summit at the hotel.

Returning to Houston in 1993, the Bushes lived in a rental home while they awaited the completion of their new home at 9 S. West Oak Drive, a lot that Bush had purchased years earlier. "It's more like a good friend is back in town," said Betsy Parish, a longtime Houstonian.[451]

Bush fell in love with Houston, and by all accounts, the Bayou City reciprocated. The Bushes were regulars at many of Houston's sporting events, often sitting behind home plate at a Houston Astros game, attending a Texans football game, even cheering on the Houston Rockets. Bush made friends with the likes of Craig Biggio, Jeff Bagwell, Yao Ming, J.J. Watt, and others. He even found the strength to be present for the coin toss at Super Bowl 51. When the

World Series came to Houston in 2017, Bush took part in the ceremonial pitch in Game 5 against the Los Angeles Dodgers. Confined to a wheelchair, he nevertheless handed the ball off to another president — George W. Bush — who, donning a Houston Astros jacket, threw out the first pitch.

Bush and his wife were also regulars at many of Houston's restaurants during his post-White House years. But it wasn't the five-star, steak-and-lobster venues that they frequented, rather, places where regular Houstonians ate, making the Houston love affair with the Bushes all the more real. President Bush was a regular at Backstreet Café, Hugo's, Molina's, Otto's, and many other places.

"It was always a pleasure seeing President Bush at Backstreet Café," said Tracy Vaught of H-Town Restaurant Group, which owns and operates the restaurant, as well as Caracol, Third Coast, Xochi, and Hugo's. "He was always warm and gracious to all the guests that greeted him and asked for photos. He was dry-witted, friendly, and warm with guests, and he often saw a friend or two in the dining room — he knew so many people!" And Bush preferred dining outside on the patio. "He would put his hand on my shoulder for a bit of help navigating the steps out to his table . . . He came with his chief of staff and sometimes Barbara. We always had low-fat milk ready for his coffee or cappuccino. And he liked an occasional glass of wine 'even if it makes me sleepy,' he would say," said Vaught.[452]

President Bush sent a condolence letter to Raul Molina Jr. when his father and Molina's founder Raul Sr. died. Riccardo Molina remembered that Bush always ordered either tacos al carbon, cheese enchiladas, or beef fajitas with a Pacifico, Dos Equis Lager, or Modelo. According to Molina, "One memory that stood out was when these kids came up to the Bushes' table and asked if they could get a picture with them," said Riccardo. "Barbara responded, 'What, y'all want to get a picture with him?'"[453]

And then there was the time a young waiter was concerned about how to enforce state liquor laws when his guest was the former president of the United States of America. "There was one time that the Bushes snuck in early, before an Astros game when he was going to throw out the first pitch," said Riccardo. "Security came in and the place was suddenly super busy. A young college-aged waiter was serving their table. He came to me and said, 'I hope I didn't screw up.' I said, 'I hope you didn't screw up either, what happened?' He said, [Bush] ordered a beer and it was 11:45. He told him, 'I'm sorry, sir, you can't order a beer before noon on Sunday!'"[454]

"He was always a delight and very lighthearted to deal with and take care of. . . . We thought of him as part of our family," said Molina.[455]

Upon hearing that one of his favorite digs — Otto's on Memorial — was closing down, Bush stopped in for a final bite and to bid farewell to the iconic Houston restaurant. Said Bush, "We've been coming here for many years, [since] 1959 I think, and we knew Otto and we knew his widow, [and] just think the world of the people. They put on a good barbecue. I'll miss them. Our family will miss them."[456]

The former president's name can also be found throughout the greater Houston area with the George Bush Park located on the far west side of the city, George Bush High School in Mission Bend, George Bush Intercontinental Airport in North Houston, and the George Herbert Walker Bush Elementary School some 250 miles north in Addison, Texas.

"They were Houston's first family," said David Jones, chief executive of the George H.W. Bush Presidential Library Foundation. "They loved Houston and Houston loved them back. People embraced them wherever they went."[457]

"To me, to regular people, he was always one of us," said Judy Pierce, a Houstonian. "You would see him out and he would always talk to you. He did a lot of good things. Some things didn't turn out the way he wanted to, but that happens to all presidents. And he never did put on airs, you know?"[458]

Mark K. Updegrove of the LBJ Library, who authored a book *The Last Republicans* about Bush father and son, said, "There's a bumper sticker that said, 'I'm not from Texas, but I got here as soon as I could,' and the Bushes very much felt that way. . . . Texas was home, whether they were in Washington, New York, or China."[459]

HOUSTON REMEMBERS

Perched on a slight hill within Sesquicentennial Park in Houston stands an eight-foot-tall bronze statue of former president George Herbert Walker Bush. The monument, dedicated on December 1, 2004, and designed by Chas Fagan, having been funded by some of Houston's most well-known political power players, is yet just another in a long line of testaments to the close, almost inseparable bond between Houstonians and George H.W. Bush — the man who chose to call the City on the Bayou his forever home. The Bush statue has the former president standing with one hand in his pocket, gazing east toward the Houston skyline, with a semicircular wall behind him, featuring four bas-reliefs by Houston sculptor Wei-li "Willy" depicting Bush as a Navy pilot in World War II; as a Houston oilman and member of Congress; with Mikhail Gorbachev managing the peaceful end of the Cold War; and with wife Barbara at the inauguration of their oldest son as he became the 43rd president of the United States.[460] Bush, touched by how the city of Houston had honored him, joked, "All I can do now is hope that the pigeons will be kind and gentle."[461]

Charles Foster and David Jones, co-chairmen of the George Bush Statue Advisory Committee, penned an article in the *Houston Chronicle* just days after the ceremony, noting ". . . no president has ever been so closely identified with his home city before, during, and after his presidency. The location of the George Bush Monument, in Sesquicentennial Park, is also appropriate. By design, the monument ties the statue and its plaza into the park as well as our city's skyline in its foreground. . . . The statue was designed to be approachable to reflect the innate modesty of President Bush."[462] Reflecting back on the profound significance of the relationship between George H.W. Bush and the city of Houston, Foster points to two — among many — examples of just how special Houston was to Bush. "He brought the G7 Summit to Houston in 1990, and also the Republican Convention in 1992 . . ." Big events for the Bayou City.[463]

Years later, Chas Fagan designed yet another eight-foot-tall statue, this time, for none other than James A. Baker, III. At the dedication ceremony, held on October 26, 2010, Baker said, "It is heartwarming for me to know that the two of us will be looking across Buffalo Bayou at each other for a very long time. . . . And, of course, it is particularly fitting that the statue of President Bush is on higher ground. That is the way it should be, because I have always looked up to him and will continue to do so."[464] Bush, who attended the event, praised Baker as "one of the finest men I have ever known."[465] In addition to the statue of Baker, Baker Common — the name given to the section of the park — also includes three other plaques honoring three previous Baker family members, all of who played instrumental roles in shaping the city of Houston. Baker jokingly admitted, "It's a weird feeling to look at yourself cast in eight feet of bronze. . . . One thing it does is bring your own mortality home to you pretty vividly."[466]

CHAPTER ELEVEN

Honoring Two Great Men

IN DECEMBER 2018, UPON THE PASSING OF GEORGE HERBERT Walker Bush, the world heard words of praise and admiration from foreign dignitaries, former political rivals, and others. With their words, we remember and honor a great man, and a great American.

We also take time to reflect on Bush's closest friend of sixty years, James A. Baker, III, one of Washington's most accomplished and respected political figures in modern times, and a man whose sound insights continue to help our leaders navigate the ever-changing climate of government and politics.

AN AMERICAN PATRIOT: GEORGE HERBERT WALKER BUSH

Dan Quayle, 44th Vice President of the United States (1989 – 1993)
After the inauguration on Jan. 20, 1989, George Bush and I walked over to the east front of the Capitol to say goodbye to Ronald Reagan. A few moments later, as we watched the helicopter carry off the 40th

president, I heard the 41st say quietly: "There goes a man who was very good to me."

This was the end of Bush's eight-year partnership with Reagan and the beginning of his partnership with me. And though ours would last for just one term, it could hardly have been more collegial, uncomplicated, or free of tension. We were friends who quickly became close friends. We remained so through all the years since, right up until his passing.

In our conversations after the 1988 election, the new president's best advice for doing the job was: "Be prepared and be loyal." Even so, he didn't press me at all to handle my responsibilities exactly as he had done. He encouraged me to find my own approach to the office — a Quayle model. I told him the Bush model looked pretty good to me, and I would go with that.

I was only forty-one when we were sworn in, and naturally, I couldn't match my new boss's knowledge and wisdom. But I had been in Congress since I was twenty-nine. Any administration needs good contacts on Capitol Hill, direct lines of communication with members, and fresh reports on the legislative lay of the land. Contributing these became a big part of my portfolio.

One challenge in the vice presidency is that you're always on somebody else's turf. Even though you're one of only two constitutional officers in the West Wing, your involvement in this or that matter can draw resentment. Having seen this in his own tenure, Bush helped me avoid internal discord by assigning me well-defined tasks and, even more crucial, by generously expressing confidence.

Nothing was ever a big show with George Bush. The theatrics of politics ran against his nature and upbringing. He gave the job his best and expected people to notice, and he always did what he thought right. He could have paid more attention to his own speeches and would doubtless have fared better if he had written more of them himself — his letters reveal a lovely and insightful writer. Politics doesn't always reward modesty, however — one lesson of 1992.

The judgments of history are kinder, and a case could be made that George Bush gave America its most successful one-term presidency. That's not the distinction we were hoping for then, but looking back, it's remarkable to count his achievements. Even the economy, which withstood a brief recession that hurt us politically, was growing at a rate of more than 6 percent by the end of the term. That doesn't look bad in retrospect.

President Bush found a way to get things done with a Congress controlled by the other party. He respected the legislative branch, and lawmakers knew it. He never answered opposition with petulance or heavy-handedness. He worked faithfully with Congress; any president owes at least that much to the country.

For me, loyalty to President Bush was the easiest part. He was the kind of person who inspired loyal friendship even without the title, someone whose good opinion you wanted because of the kind of man he was. Our 41st president was the most honorable, decent and capable of gentlemen — as close to the ideal of the office as anyone in our lifetimes. If you're looking for a role model, I told my children when they were growing up, start with George Bush.

After he put me on the ticket in 1988, so many good things followed that I could never have expected in my own life. The finest of all was more than a quarter century of close friendship with someone I came to admire more with the years. When I heard the news from Houston, along with many others who knew and loved George Bush, I thought: There goes a man who was very good to me — and to his country.[467]

Donald J. Trump, 45th President of the United States

Excerpt from the Presidential Proclamation Announcing the Death of George H.W. Bush

It is my sorrowful duty to announce officially the death of George Herbert Walker Bush, the 41st president of the United States, on November 30, 2018.

President Bush led a great American life, one that combined and personified two of our nation's greatest virtues: an entrepreneurial spirit and a commitment to public service. Our country will greatly miss his inspiring example.

On the day he turned eighteen, six months after the attack on Pearl Harbor, George H.W. Bush volunteered for combat duty in the Second World War. The youngest aviator in United States naval history at the time, he flew fifty-eight combat missions, including one in which, after taking enemy fire, he parachuted from his burning plane into the Pacific Ocean. After the war, he returned home and started a business. In his words, "the big thing" he learned from this endeavor was "the satisfaction of creating jobs."

The same unselfish spirit that motivated his business pursuits later inspired him to resume the public service he began as a young man. First, as a member of Congress, then as ambassador to the United Nations, chief of the United States Liaison Office in China, director of Central Intelligence, vice president, and finally president of the United States, George H.W. Bush guided our nation through the Cold War, to its peaceful and victorious end, and into the decades of prosperity that have followed. Through sound judgment, practical wisdom, and steady leadership, President Bush made safer the second half of a tumultuous and dangerous century.

Even with all he accomplished in service to our nation, President Bush remained humble. He never believed that government — even when under his own leadership — could be the source of our nation's strength or its greatness. America, he rightly told us, is illuminated by "a thousand points of light," "ethnic, religious, social, business, labor union, neighborhood, regional, and other organizations, all of them varied, voluntary, and unique" in which Americans serve Americans to build and maintain the greatest nation on the face of the Earth. President Bush recognized that these communities of people are the true source of America's strength and vitality.[468]

Barack Obama, 44th President of the United States (2009 – 2017)
America has lost a patriot and humble servant in George Herbert Walker Bush. While our hearts are heavy today, they are also filled with gratitude. . . .

After seventy-three years of marriage, George and Barbara Bush are together again now, two points of light that never dimmed, two points of light that ignited countless others with their example. . . . Our thoughts are with the entire Bush family tonight — and all who were inspired by George and Barbara's example.[469]

George W. Bush, 43rd President of the United States (2001 – 2009)
Excerpts from the eulogy he gave for his father.
Dad taught us that public service is noble and necessary; that one can serve with integrity and hold true to the important values, like faith

and family. He strongly believed that it was important to give back to the community and country in which one lived. He recognized that serving others enriched the giver's soul. To us, his was the brightest of a thousand points of light.

In victory, he shared credit. When he lost, he shouldered the blame. He accepted that failure is part of living a full life, but taught us never to be defined by failure. He showed us how setbacks can strengthen.

None of his disappointments could compare with one of life's greatest tragedies, the loss of a young child. Jeb and I were too young to remember the pain and agony he and Mom felt when our three-year-old sister died. We only learned later that Dad, a man of quiet faith, prayed for her daily. He was sustained by the love of the Almighty and the real and enduring love of our mom. Dad always believed that one day he would hug his precious Robin again.

George Bush knew how to be a true and loyal friend. He honored and nurtured his many friendships with his generous and giving soul. There exist thousands of handwritten notes encouraging, or sympathizing, or thanking his friends and acquaintances.

He had an enormous capacity to give of himself. Many a person would tell you that Dad became a mentor and a father figure in their life. He listened and he consoled. He was their friend. I think of Don Rhodes, Taylor Blanton, Jim Nantz, Arnold Schwarzenegger, and perhaps the unlikeliest of all, the man who defeated him, Bill Clinton. My siblings and I refer to the guys in this group as "brothers from other mothers."

He taught us that a day was not meant to be wasted. He played golf at a legendary pace. I always wondered why he insisted on speed golf. He was a good golfer.

Well, here's my conclusion: He played fast so that he could move on to the next event, to enjoy the rest of the day, to expend his enormous energy, to live it all. He was born with just two settings: full throttle, then sleep.

He taught us what it means to be a wonderful father, grandfather, and great-grandfather. He was firm in his principles and supportive as we began to seek our own ways. He encouraged and comforted, but never steered. We tested his patience — I know I did — but he always responded with the great gift of unconditional love.

Last Friday, when I was told he had minutes to live, I called him. The guy who answered the phone said, "I think he can hear you, but hasn't said anything most of the day." I said, "Dad, I love you, and you've been a wonderful father." And the last words he would ever say on earth were, "I love you, too."[470]

Bill Clinton, 42nd President of the United States (1993 – 2001)

No words of mine or others can better reveal the heart of who he was than those he wrote himself. He was an honorable, gracious, and decent man who believed in the United States, our Constitution, our institutions, and our shared future. And he believed in his duty to defend and strengthen them, in victory and defeat. He also had a natural humanity, always hoping with all his heart that others' journeys would include some of the joy that his family, his service, and his adventures gave him. . . .

Many people were surprised at our relationship, considering we were once political adversaries. Despite our considerable differences, I had admired many of his accomplishments as president, especially his foreign-policy decisions in managing America's response to the end of the Cold War and his willingness to work with governors of both parties to establish national education goals. Even more important, though he could be tough in a political fight, he was in it for the right reasons: People always came before politics, patriotism before partisanship. To the end, we knew we would never agree on everything, and we agreed that was okay. Honest debate strengthens democracy. . . .

Given what politics looks like in America and around the world today, it's easy to sigh and say George H.W. Bush belonged to an era that is gone and never coming back — where our opponents are not our enemies, where we are open to different ideas and changing our minds, where facts matter and where our devotion to our children's future leads to honest compromise and shared progress. I know what he would say: "Nonsense. It's your duty to get that America back."

We should all give thanks for George H.W. Bush's long, good life and honor it by searching, as he always did, for the most American way forward.[471]

Jimmy Carter, 39th President of the United States (1977 – 1981)

His administration was marked by grace, civility, and social conscience. Through his Points of Light initiative and other projects, he espoused a uniquely American volunteer spirit, fostering bipartisan support for citizen service and inspiring millions to embrace community volunteerism as a cherished responsibility.

We again extend our heartfelt condolences to the Bush family.[472]

Dick Cheney, 46th Vice President of the United States (2001 – 2009)

George H.W. Bush was a phenomenal leader. . . . You couldn't find anybody better equipped when he arrived [to assume the presidency], those set of circumstances that we all experienced during that particular four-year period. . . . I mean, we had had seventy-some years of Cold War and so forth, but it was the time when everything came to a head, the Soviet Union went out of business — Germany was reunited, Eastern Europe was liberated. A bunch of things we worked [on] for years all of a sudden occurred on his watch, and he had to manage it and did a beautiful job of it.[473]

Al Gore, 45th Vice President of the United States (1993 – 2001)

President George H.W. Bush served our nation with extraordinary integrity and grace. I will remember him for his personal kindness and for his love of this country. He earned bipartisan respect for speaking up and taking action for what he believed was right, even when doing so was unpopular. He inspired countless Americans to volunteer and improve their communities through his Points of Light Foundation. President Bush leaves behind an American legacy of a lifetime of service that will be revered for generations.[474]

I remember when I gave my second and final concession speech in 2000, I was in the Secret Service car going back to the vice president's residence, and it was President George H.W. Bush calling me on the telephone, and he was overcome with emotion and he said the kindest things. It was really a touching call. . . . I remember his personal kindness. I was impressed by his intense love of our country.[475]

Mikhail Gorbachev, General Secretary of the Soviet Union (1985 – 1991)

I express my deep condolences to the family of George H.W. Bush and all Americans over of the death of the 41st president of the United States. I have a lot of memories associated with this person. We had a chance to work together during the years of tremendous changes. It was a dramatic time that demanded great responsibility from everyone. The result was an end to the Cold War and the nuclear arms race.[476]

John Major, Prime Minister, the United Kingdom (1990 – 1997)

Sometimes people think politics is tawdry. You could never have said that about the way George Bush behaved in politics. He had opponents but never enemies. He certainly was a man who made sure politics was a respectable profession and he understood its obligations to everyone, not just the powerful, not just the rich, not just the mighty, but to the people who were absolutely at the bottom of the heap as well.[477]

Brian Mulroney, Prime Minister, Canada (1984 – 1993)

Excerpts from the eulogy he gave for George H.W. Bush.

Do you remember where you were the summer you left your teenage years behind and turned twenty?

I was working as a laborer in my hometown in Northern Quebec, trying to make enough money to finance my years at law school.

It was a tough job, but I was safe and secure and had the added benefit of my mother's home cooking every night.

On September 2, 1944 . . . twenty-year-old Lieutenant George Bush was preparing to attack Japanese war installations in the Pacific.

He was part of a courageous generation of young Americans who led the charge — against overwhelming odds — in the historic and bloody battle for supremacy in the Pacific against the colossal military might of Imperial Japan.

That's what George Bush did the summer he turned twenty. . . .

Much has been written about the first Gulf War. Simply put, the coalition of twenty-nine disparate nations assembled under the aegis of the United Nations — including for the first time many influential Arab countries — and led by the United States will rank with the most spectacular and successful international initiatives ever undertaken in modern history, designed to punish an aggressor, defend the cause of freedom and ensure order in a region that had seen too much of the opposite for far too long. This was President Bush's initiative from beginning to end.

President Bush was also responsible for the North American Free Trade Agreement — recently modernized and improved by new administrations — which created the largest and richest free trade area in the history of the world, while also signing into law the Americans With Disabilities Act, which transformed the lives of millions of Americans forever.

President Bush's decision to go forward with strong environmental legislation, including the Clean Air Act that resulted in an Acid Rain Accord with Canada, is a splendid gift to future generations of Americans and Canadians to savor in the air they breathe, the water they drink, the forests they enjoy, and the lakes, rivers and streams they cherish.

There is a word for this: it is called "leadership" — and let me tell you that when George Bush was president of the United States of America, every single head of government in the world knew they were dealing with a true gentleman, a genuine leader — one who was distinguished, resolute, and brave.[478]

Brent Scowcroft, National Security Advisor to President Gerald R. Ford and President George H.W. Bush

The world has lost a great leader; this country has lost one of its best, and I have lost one of my dearest friends.

I am heartbroken.[479]

John H. Sununu, Chief of Staff to President George H.W. Bush
(1989 – 1991)

Bush, our 41st president of the United States and my friend, died on November 30 at age ninety-four. Although he would never be comfortable taking credit for the success of his life, most historians now agree that Bush was a great president who accomplished great things. He helped make America safer and the world more stable and more prosperous than ever before in history.

When Bush entered the White House in 1989, he faced many issues that had been lingering for decades: budget deficits, the struggle against communism, instability in Latin America, social inequality, threats to the environment, and struggling schools throughout the country. But he faced them as any former fighter pilot would, telling the American people: "I am a man who sees life in terms of missions — missions defined, and missions completed."

On the international stage, he not only orchestrated one of the largest and most effective military campaigns in history, to drive Saddam Hussein from Kuwait, but he also artfully led the world through the most dramatic and remarkable political transformations of the modern era: the fall of the Berlin Wall, the reunification of Germany, the restoration of democracy in Eastern Europe, and the collapse of the Soviet Union. Bush's quiet, skillful and steadfast guidance was exactly the kind of leadership America needed as it stepped onto the stage as the world's lone superpower. . . .

As president, George H.W. Bush laid a solid foundation for his successors to build on. Whether we have the fortitude and discipline to eventually do so remains to be seen.

In any case, the world will miss a great president. And I will miss a great friend.[480]

Colin Powell, Secretary of State (2001 – 2005)

He was a great man, a great American, and people loved him . . . because of who he was, the example he gave to the rest of us of character, of loyalty, of devotion, of humility, and humbleness. And I saw it every day I served with him. It was really six years — four years as chairman of the Joint Chiefs of Staff and then before that, for two years, I was deputy national security advisor and national security advisor to both he and President Reagan. And that's when I got to know him — when I was in the White House just down the hall from him. We had offices that were side by side for those two years. And it was always such a pleasure to be around him. He was a gentle gentleman, but he was also tough when he had to be tough, and that's what made him so great.[481]

Craig Fuller, Chief of Staff to Vice President George Bush (1985 – 1989)

I join with millions who reflect on the life of one of the nation's most remarkable individuals. His service to country has few parallels. The same can be said of his seventy-three years of marriage to Barbara Bush.

As I met him in 1981, it was clear that if the country sought to prepare an individual for the White House, the path George H.W. Bush followed provided the best possible experience. It was also clear the vast experience, when combined with his strong values, brought great judgment.

When he asked this Californian, who came to the White House with Ronald Reagan, to become his chief of staff for the second term of the Reagan–Bush administration, it was a bit of a surprise, but also a very high honor. We would travel to over sixty countries and every state in the nation multiple times as he served his second term as vice president and sought to win a presidential election.

Much will be said as people look back about all he accomplished and the significance of the positions he held. For me, the memories that stand out most are of the thousands who called him a trusted friend. It mattered not where we traveled, there were always people, be they world leaders or a person in a New Hampshire diner, who felt the warmth of true friendship.

While a sad time, my thoughts upon hearing the news were of how much he and Barbara Bush wished to end each day together and how on this day, that is exactly what will surely come to pass.[482]

Condoleezza Rice, Secretary of State (2005 – 2009)

President George Herbert Walker Bush was the epitome of a public servant. He loved America with all of his heart and served her as fully and completely as anyone ever has.

I am so grateful that I had the opportunity to work for him, to learn from him, and to experience his deep and abiding commitment to his fellow citizens. He was a mentor to me and a dear friend.

President Bush's legacy is deep and broad: the many people that he touched, the difference that he made in the life of the country, and the impact that he had beyond America's shores. We will never forget his steady and inspired leadership in guiding the world to the peaceful end of the Cold War.

Now he is in God's loving embrace with Mrs. Barbara Bush, his beloved wife of so many years. He has finished his race with honor and dignity. All who knew him and loved him — especially his remarkable family — will miss him. Yet, he lives on with us in spirit. Rest well, Mr. President.[483]

Margaret D. Tutwiler, longtime Baker aide and confidante

It would have been popular to sever relationships with China after Tiananmen Square. Popular at the time would have been to bomb Iraq into oblivion and take Saddam Hussein. Popular would have been to stick to Gorbachev and pop champagne on the Berlin Wall. Instead, he [George Bush] chose what was best for the country, not necessarily what was easy and popular — or what would have been great for George Bush.[484]

Arnold Schwarzenegger, Chairman of the President's Council on Physical Fitness and Sports (1990 – 1993), former Governor of California

George Bush was an inspiration to all Americans, and we will miss him dearly. From the day he first put on his US Navy flight suit and took off into the unknown, he always put his country first. He took on many jobs throughout his long career, and all shared one distinct trait: public service. His greatest legacy is that pure American spirit, that commitment to selflessness that drove him until the very end. . . .

I will always be grateful to him for his friendship, for embracing me and imparting just a fraction of his wisdom during our time together. Some of my fondest memories are of sledding with him at Camp David and inspiring America to join our fitness crusade by hosting the Great American Workout with him on the White House lawn and listening to his speech advice as we flew between campaign rallies. I will never forget the pride I felt the day he appointed me chairman of the President's Council on Physical Fitness and Sports.

I loved to hear him surprise people with his wild side — explaining the pure joy he felt as he flew and jumped out of planes. I also loved to hear him explain his passion for this country — it was a true love that knew no petty boundaries or party lines. He taught me so much, but most of all, he taught me the power of serving a cause greater than yourself. I count myself lucky for many reasons; but for the opportunity to call George Bush a mentor, I can't help but think I'm the luckiest man in America.

President Bush has left us for one last flight, but his destination isn't unknown. He's flying into the arms of the love of his life, Barbara. This evening, each of us should take a minute to look up and offer him a silent thanks.[485]

Washington Post Editorial Board

What Mr. Bush did was handle a series of historic crises with competence and restraint, while dealing with the everyday conflicts and compromises of legislating and budgeting in a responsible and reasonable way. Mr. Bush did well while holding office. His most unattractive acts came in the seeking of it.

The end of the Cold War and of the Soviet Union, momentous events, occurred on Mr. Bush's watch. There were missteps, but overall, his handling was skillful; Mr. Bush saw the importance of giving Soviet reformers tacit support while not provoking their opponents to act against them. His decisions in 1990 – 1991 to protect Arab allies and drive Iraqi forces from Kuwait were bold and well-taken. Less defensible were the call on Iraqis to rise up against Saddam Hussein after the war, and the failure to respond when Hussein proceeded to slaughter those who did.[486]

THE VELVET HAMMER: REFLECTIONS ON JAMES A. BAKER, III

George W. Bush, 43rd President of the United States (2001 – 2009)
Regarding the contested Florida votes in November 2000, and the need to get people on the ground immediately, "There was no time to develop a list or conduct interviews. . . . Baker was the perfect choice — a statesman, a savvy lawyer, and a magnet for talented people. I called Jim and asked if he would take on the mission. Shortly thereafter, he was bound for Tallahassee.[487]

Bill Clinton, 42nd President of the United States (1993 – 2001)
He staged-managed it [the 2000 Florida recount] in a way that just trumped what the Gore campaign could do. . . . He had a strong hand going in, but he played it very well, and like I said, I hated it, but he whipped us, he was good at it.[488]

Gerald R. Ford, 38th President of the United States (1974 – 1977)
Baker had little or no political experience — originally, he'd come to Washington to be Rog Morton's deputy at the department of Commerce — but he possessed a superb mind, he was an excellent organizer who got along with everybody and worked around the clock.[489]

Jimmy Carter, 39th President of the United States (1977 – 1981)

It was an eye-opener to me how courageous he was politically.[490]

Dick Cheney, 46th Vice President of the United States (2001 – 2009)

He's smooth, cool, competent, with an aura of confidence.[491]

Colin Powell, Secretary of State (2001 – 2005)

I learned from Jim how to put your cards on the table, but only as many as you really have to put on the table.[492]

Peggy Noonan, Republican Speechwriter

They're [George H.W. Bush and James A. Baker, III] these big, tall, lanky, hot-as-a-pistol guys with ambition so strong it's a like steel rod sticking out of their heads . . . but they always make a point not to show it. Steel with an overlay of tennis.[493]

Jeffrey Toobin, CNN Legal Analyst

Baker understood [that] in a complex controversy [the 2000 Florida recount], simplicity mattered.[494]

Aleksandre Chikvaidze, Georgian Statesman and Diplomat

I first encountered James A. Baker, III and his team right after the 1988 US presidential election. . . . The friendships that emerged with his core team from our work together in those early days continued throughout the Bush administration, first in Washington and later when I moved to Kremlin protocol. All that time, watching this extraordinary man in action, I could not help thinking — without disloyalty toward my side — how I would love to work for this guy. . . .

Secretary Baker's professionalism and meticulous approach to diplomacy, coupled with his "straight shooter" nature, was most evident in the run-up to Desert Storm. . . .

I often wonder how the post-Cold War world would have developed had the American electorate given George H.W. Bush a second term and had Baker continued as secretary of State.[495]

Edmund Hull, American Diplomat, and United States Ambassador to Yemen (2001 – 2004)

Baker was a brilliant negotiator. He had clearly in mind what he wanted to accomplish, but he had a human touch and was appreciated by Arabs for his willingness to take the time and make the effort to establish personal relations.[496]

Tom Brokaw, Journalist

In 1975, a Houston lawyer takes a job with President Gerald Ford, and politics in America is about to change. . . . In a time before compromise was a dirty word, when political parties worked together, he was a master of negotiation, always able to find common ground.[497]

Jon Meacham, Pulitzer Prize Winner and Presidential Historian

There are very few men in the history of the United States that have been as good at politics as Jim Baker.[498]

David Gergen, White House Director of Communications (1981 – 1984)

He's regarded as one of the best secretaries of State we've had in the 20th century.[499]

S.C. Gwynne, Author and Award-winning Journalist

To Houstonians . . . he is everything that the old, raw-knuckled, oil-and-real-estate boomtown has always wanted to be: smart, sophisticated, urbane, and still able to flat outdo and outhustle the pointy-headed swells from the Northeast. . . . What makes Baker different is how public his achievement has been; the Houston boy who was nothing at all like the loudmouthed, backslapping Texas pols of Eastern stereotype became a dominant force in American politics.[500]

Acknowledgments

A special thank you to all who participated in helping
review the content of *Texas Titans* : Vice President Dan Quayle,
Vice President Dick Cheney, Ambassador Chase Untermeyer,
Jean Becker, Jim McGrath, David Jones, John Williams,
Craig Fuller, Charles Foster, Sarah Eaton, David Valdez,
and many others.

Additionally, a successful book also requires a great team —
which I was lucky to have. Special thanks, again, to
Shelley Holloway of HollowayHouse.me, and
Michael Kellner of KellnerBookDesign.com.

Notes

1. "Miracle Man Given Credit for Ford Drive," *New York Times,* August 19, 1976, https://nyti.ms/3cuj6sG, accessed February 29, 2020.
2. "George H.W. Bush Concession Speech," November 3, 1992, C-span, https://cs.pn/37kBOR8, accessed August 5, 2019.
3. Mike Ward, "James Baker: 'the man who made Washington work,'" *Chron,* September 19, 2016, http://bit.ly/39VQNRx, accessed February 20, 2020.
4. "George H.W. Bush Remembered at Andover Prep School," CBS Boston, December 1, 2018, https://cbsloc.al/2rlGKVu, accessed December 21, 2019.
5. Ibid.
6. "George H.W. Bush," Miller Center of Public Affairs, University of Virginia, http://millercenter.org/president/bush, accessed December 21, 2019.
7. "History's Youngest Naval Aviator: George H.W. Bush," article extracted from *APPROACH* magazine, the Naval Aviation Safety Review, May 1990 in a special edition entitled "Reflections — Outstanding Naval Aviators Look Back," accessed December 21, 2019.
8. "George H.W. Bush, USN," YouTube video, 1:32, US Naval Institute interview with Bush about being shot down in WWII, posted by Americans at War, August 21, 2007, accessed December 21, 2019.
9. David Barron, "George H.W. Bush, A Quintessential Baseball Man," *Houston Chronicle*, December 1, 2018, https://bit.ly/3he3Dzj, accessed December 21, 2019.

10. George H.W. Bush, *All the Best: My Life in Letters and Other Writings*, (Scribner, Revised edition, 2013) 62.

11. Bush, 63.

12. Bush, 62.

13. Bush, 63.

14. Bush, 70.

15. Bush, 77.

16. Bush, 77.

17. Bush, 82.

18. Bush, 84.

19. Bush, 85.

20. Judy Woodruff, "James Baker on George H.W. Bush's 'extremely consequential' presidency," PBS, December 4, 2018, https://to.pbs.org/2Nz3tnV, accessed January 10, 2020.

21. James A. Baker, III, *Work Hard, Study. . . and Keep out of Politics!* (G.P Putnam's Sons, 2006), 8.

22. Baker, 9.

23. Baker, 12.

24. Baker, 15.

25. Robert Gearty, "James Baker said George H.W. Bush 'turned me around,' was a huge part of his life," *Fox News*, December 3, 2018, https://fxn.ws/2vldCiz, accessed February 8, 2020.

26. Baker, *Work Hard, Study. . . and Keep out of Politics!*, 158.

27. Baker, 18.

28. Baker, 18.

29. Baker, 17.

30. Baker, 15.

31. Jon Meacham, *Destiny and Power, the American Odyssey of George Herbert Walker Bush*, (Random House, 2015), 144.

32. Brian D. Sweany, "The Fixer," *Texas Monthly*, April 2015, http://bit.ly/37UMe9Z, accessed November 30, 2019.

33. Gearty, "James Baker said George H.W. Bush 'turned me around,' was a huge part of his life," https://fxn.ws/2vldCiz.

34. Martin Waldron, "Bentsen defeats Bush in Texas Despite Massive Effort by Nixon," *New York Times*, November 4, 1970, https://nyti.ms/2P3I72O, accessed December 1, 2019.

35. Bush, *All the Best*, 129.

36. Bush, 129.

37. Bush, 129.

38. Adam Wambold, "Nixon: Congressman Bush to Be US Representative to United Nations," Richard Nixon Foundation, December 11, 2014, http://bit.ly/2Li5LHH, accessed December 3, 2019.

39. Bush, *All the Best*, 138.

40. Bush, 144.

41. Bush, 164.

42. Bush, 167–168.

43. Bush, 185.

44. Gerald Ford, *A Time to Heal*, (Harper & Collins, 1979), 144.

45. George W. Bush, *41: A Portrait of My Father*, (Crown Publishers, 2014), 145.

46. Bush, *All the Best*, 197.

47. Bush, 202.

48. Bush, 208.

49. Bush, 211–212.

50. Bush, 217.

51. Bush, 217.

52. Bush, 217.

53. Bush, 225.

54. Meacham, *Destiny and Power*, 190.

55. Bush, *All the Best*, 234.

56. Bush, 235.

57. "The Family Jewels," CIA, Library, http://bit.ly/2LSX1bk, accessed December 13, 2019.

58. Bush, *All the Best*, 243.

59. Bush, 244.

60. Bush, 242.

61. Ford, *A Time to Heal*, 410.

62. Ford, 409.

63. Ford, 411.

64. Ford, 408.

65. James Baker, Interview by Richard Norton Smith, Gerald Ford Foundation, November 2, 2010, http://bit.ly/35Xfkn5, accessed January 17, 2020.

66. Ford, *A Time to Heal*, 412.

67. James Baker Interview, http://bit.ly/35Xfkn5, accessed January 18, 2020.

68. Ford, *A Time to Heal*, 414.

69. Baker Interview, http://bit.ly/35Xfkn5.

70. Baker Interview, http://bit.ly/35Xfkn5.

71. Meacham, *Destiny and Power*, 192.

72. Baker, *Work Hard, Study. . . and Keep out of Politics!*, 53.

73. Meacham, *Destiny and Power*, 192–193.

74. Bush, *All the Best*, 250.

75. Bush, 251.

76. Bush, 252.

77. Bush, 258.

78. Bush, *258*.

79. Bush, *258*.

80. Bush, 259.

81. Bush, 260.

82. Bush, 261.

83. Bush, 264.

84. Bush, 266.

85. Bush, 271.

86. Bush, 271.

87. Barbara Bush, *Barbara Bush: A Memoir*, (Scribner, 1994), 141.

88. Bush, *All the Best*, 273.

89. Patricia Hart, "Not So Great in '78," *Texas Monthly*, June 1999, http://bit.ly/2RXq55x, accessed December 16, 2019.

90. Hart, http://bit.ly/2RXq55x.

91. "TX Attorney General Race," Our Campaigns, http://bit.ly/34nAWZ7, accessed December 16, 2019.

92. Taylor Branch, "Baker's Washington," *Texas Monthly*, May 1982.

93. Branch, "Baker's Washington."

94. Branch, "Baker's Washington."

95. James A. Baker, III, *The Politics of Diplomacy*, (Putnam Adult; First Edition, 1995), 19.

96. Branch, "Baker's Washington."

97. Baker, *The Politics of Diplomacy*, 20.

98. Bush, George W., *41: A Portrait of My Father*, 132.

99. Dorothy Koch, *My Father, My President*, (Warner Books, 2006), 149.

100. Koch, 149.

101. Bush, *All the Best*, 283.

102. Bush, 283.

103. "Iowa Caucus History: George Bush Beats Expectations Against Ronald Reagan in 1980," Excerpt from "Caucus Iowa: Journey to the Presidency," Iowa PBS, 2016, http://bit.ly/34bPZpp, accessed November 22, 2019.

104. Bush, *All the Best*, 287.

105. "Reagan's Nashua Moment," YouTube video, 1:04, from the Nashua, New Hampshire, presidential campaign debate on February 23, 1980, posted by "theMacallan223," February 22, 2008, http://bit.ly/3478pYl, accessed November 22, 2019.

106. Baker, *Work Hard, Study. . . and Keep out of Politics!*, 91.

107. Koch, *My Father, My President*, 151.

108. Koch, 155.

109. Koch, 155.

110. Meacham, *Destiny and Power*, 236.

111. Meacham, 237.

112. Bush, *All the Best*, 297.

113. Michael Kramer, "Playing for the Edge," *Time*, February 13, 1989, http://bit.ly/3atdcaa, accessed January 20, 2020.

114. Baker, *Work Hard, Study. . . and Keep out of Politics!*, 103.

115. Meacham, *Destiny and Power*, 248.

116. Bush, George W. *41: A Portrait of My Father*, 117.

117. Bush, Barbara, *Barbara Bush: A Memoir*, 154.

118. Charles Denyer, *Our Nation's No. 2: The Rising Influence of America's Modern Vice Presidency*, (CambridgeKlein, 2019), 112.

119. Denyer, 112.

120. Baker, *Work Hard, Study. . . and Keep out of Politics!*, 99.

121. Denyer, *Our Nation's No. 2*, 103.

122. Woodruff, PBS, https://to.pbs.org/2Nz3tnV.

123. Ford, *A Time to Heal*, 393–394.

124. Presidential Debate in Cleveland, Transcript, The American Presidency Project, UC Santa Barbara, October 28, 1980, http://bit.ly/33sZL5e, accessed November 28, 2019.

125. M.J. Stephey, "No-Show, No-Go," Excerpt from the Top 10 Veep Debate Moments, *Time*, http://bit.ly/2RiUlY9, accessed December 4, 2019.

126. Baker, *Work Hard, Study. . . and Keep out of Politics!*, 30.

127. Alan Peppard, "Command and Control: Tested Under Fire," *Dallas Morning News*, May 13, 2015, http://bit.ly/2kIHH1I, accessed October 17, 2019.

128. Peppard, http://bit.ly/2kIHH1I.

129. Peppard, http://bit.ly/2kIHH1I.

130. Peppard, http://bit.ly/2kIHH1I.

131. Peppard, http://bit.ly/2kIHH1I.

132. Baker, *Work Hard, Study. . . and Keep out of Politics!*, 142.

133. Baker, 144.

134. Twenty-fifth Amendment, Cornell Law School, Legal Information Institute, http://bit.ly/2gqrPPA, accessed November 12, 2019.

135. Peppard, "Command and Control, Tested Under Fire," http://bit.ly/2kIHH1I.

136. Peppard, http://bit.ly/2kIHH1I.

137. Woodruff, PBS, https://to.pbs.org/2Nz3tnV.

138. Sweany, "The Fixer," http://bit.ly/37UMe9Z.

139. Sweany, http://bit.ly/37UMe9Z.

140. Dale Russakoff, "Bush Boasts of Kicking 'A Little Ass' at Debate," *Washington Post*, October 13, 1984, https://wapo.st/2k0mNMD, accessed February 15, 2018.

141. Woodruff, PBS, https://to.pbs.org/2Nz3tnV.

142. Baker, *Work Hard, Study. . . and Keep out of Politics!*, 240.

143. "James A. Baker, III, Oral History (2000)," UVA | Miller Center, January 29, 2000, http://bit.ly/32Teeb5, accessed October 27, 2019.

144. James A. Baker, III, http://bit.ly/32Teeb5.

145. Baker, *Work Hard, Study. . . and Keep out of Politics!*, 238.

146. Baker, 246.

147. James A. Baker, III, http://bit.ly/32Teeb5.

148. Craig Fuller, former chief of staff to Vice President Bush, Personal interview with the author Charles Denyer, Easton, Maryland, January 19, 2017.

149. Craig Fuller, Personal interview, January 19, 2017.

150. Baker, *Work Hard, Study. . . and Keep out of Politics!*, 245.

151. Baker, 255.

152. James A. Baker, III, http://bit.ly/32Teeb5.

153. James A. Baker, III, http://bit.ly/32Teeb5.

154. Josh King, "Dukakis and the Tank," *Politico Magazine*, November 17, 2016, https://politi.co/33SxhmA, accessed January 14, 2020.

155. King, https://politi.co/33SxhmA.

156. King, https://politi.co/33SxhmA.

157. King, https://politi.co/33SxhmA.

158. "James A. Baker, III Oral History (2000)," http://bit.ly/32Teeb5.

159. "1988 Presidential Campaign TV Ads–Bush Ads–Part 1," YouTube video, 9:39, posted by "danieljbmitchell," September 28, 2008, http://bit.ly/30nQuM8, accessed January 14, 2020.

160. Kramer, "Playing for the Edge," *Time Magazine*, http://bit.ly/3atdcaa.

161. Kramer, http://bit.ly/3atdcaa.

162. Kramer, http://bit.ly/3atdcaa.

163. Kramer, http://bit.ly/3atdcaa.

164. Kramer, http://bit.ly/3atdcaa.

165. "H.W. Bush Victory Speech," C-SPAN, November 8, 1988, https://cs.pn/2KtRMON, accessed November 17, 2019.

166. Baker, *Work Hard, Study. . . and Keep out of Politics!*, 266.

167. Baker, 258.

168. Baker, 123.

169. "James A. Baker, III Oral History (2000)," http://bit.ly/32Teeb5.

170. "James Baker, The Man Who Made Washington Work," Narrated by Tom Brokaw, PBS Documentary, John Hesse Productions, 2014, DVD.

171. Tony Kornheiser, "Cutting Chaff and Shooting Straight with Jim Baker," *Washington Post*, January 18, 1981, https://wapo.st/37V4hw0, accessed January 10, 2020.

172. "James Baker, The Man Who Made Washington Work," PBS Documentary, 2014, DVD.

173. Baker, *Work Hard, Study. . . and Keep out of Politics!*, 125.

174. Chris Whipple, *The Gatekeepers*, (BDWY, 2018), 107.

175. Whipple, 111.

176. Whipple., 114.

177. Baker, *Work Hard, Study. . . and Keep out of Politics!*, 126.

178. Richard Bruce Cheney Oral Interview at George H.W. Bush Library, June 9, 2014.

179. Kornheiser, "Cutting Chaff and Shooting Straight with Jim Baker," https://wapo.st/37V4hw0.

180. "James Baker, The Man Who Made Washington Work," PBS Documentary, 2014, DVD.

181. Baker, PBS DVD.

182. Cheney Oral Interview, June 9, 2014.

183. "James Baker, The Man Who Made Washington Work," PBS Documentary, 2014, DVD.

184. Baker, *Work Hard, Study. . . and Keep out of Politics!*, 133.

185. Kornheiser, "Cutting Chaff and Shooting Straight with Jim Baker," *Washington Post*, https://wapo.st/37V4hw0.

186. "James Baker, The Man Who Made Washington Work," PBS Documentary, 2014, DVD.

187. Baker, *Work Hard, Study. . . and Keep out of Politics!*, 135.

188. Baker, *The Politics of Diplomacy*, 22.

189. "James Baker," Gerald Ford Foundation, http://bit.ly/35Xfkn5, accessed January 15, 2020.

190. Baker, *The Politics of Diplomacy*, 21–22.

191. Donald Rumsfeld, "Rumsfeld's Rules," http://bit.ly/34pUA6T, accessed November 1, 2019.

192. Baker, *Work Hard, Study. . . and Keep out of Politics!*, 139.

193. Baker Daily Schedule while chief of ctaff under Reagan, retrieved from https://www.reaganlibrary.gov/digital-library/bakerjames, accessed April 10, 2020.

194. Baker, 158.

195. "James Baker, The Man Who Made Washington Work," PBS Documentary, 2014, DVD.

196. Sweany, "The Fixer," *Texas Monthly*, http://bit.ly/37UMe9Z.

197. Fox News, "Former Reagan Aide: 'He Taught us How to Love,'" Fox News, February 6, 2011, https://fxn.ws/3akAFd8, accessed March 25, 2020.

198. Patrick Gavin, "On TV: The real power brokers," *Politico*, September 9, 2013, https://politi.co/3bGphbG, accessed March 31, 2020.

199. Gavin, https://politi.co/3bGphbG.

200. Robert Siegel, "Book Examines 17 'Gatekeepers' into the White House's Inner Workings," NPR, April 4, 2017, https://n.pr/2yoA2Bf, accessed March 31, 2020.

201. "James Baker, The Man Who Made Washington Work," PBS Documentary, 2014, DVD.

202. Whipple, *The Gatekeepers*, 118.

203. Whipple, 130.

204. "James Baker, The Man Who Made Washington Work," PBS Documentary, 2014, DVD.

205. Whipple, *The Gatekeepers*, 126.

206. "James Baker, The Man Who Made Washington Work," PBS Documentary, 2014, DVD.

207. Reagan Library and Museum, https://bit.ly/3aKZG18, accessed April 4, 2020.

208. Dan Balz, Reagan, Baker to Trade Places in Major Shift, https://wapo.st/2JAxa6s, accessed April 2, 2020.

209. Balz, , https://wapo.st/2JAxa6s.

210. Baker, *Work Hard, Study. . . and Keep out of Politics!*, 204.

211. Finance Ministers' Meetings, https://bit.ly/2UGL2Ct, accessed April 4, 2020.

212. Takatoshi Ito, PHD, "The Plaza Agreement and Japan: Reflection on the 30th year anniversary," James A Baker, III Institute for Public Policy, 2015, accessed April 3, 2020.

213. David Mulford, A personal account of the Plaza Accord of September 22, 1985, 2015, accessed April 3, 2020.

214. Ronald Reagan, "Address Before a Joint Session of Congress on the State of the Union," The American Presidency Project, January 25, 1984, https://bit.ly/34dk2h5, accessed April 5, 2020.

215. "James Baker's Just Doin' the Tax Law Shuffle," *Chicago Tribune*, September 17, 1986, https://bit.ly/2Vh5o4u, accessed April 11, 2020.

216. Baker, *Work Hard, Study. . . and Keep out of Politics!*, 233.

217. Baker, *The Politics of Diplomacy*, 18.

218. Baker, 18–19.

219. "James A. Baker, III Oral History (2000)," http://bit.ly/32Teeb5.

220. Cheney Oral Interview, June 9, 2014.

221. Cheney Oral Interview, June 9, 2014.

222. Baker, *The Politics of Diplomacy*, 38.

223. Baker, 19.

224. "Secretary of State Confirmation Hearing, Day 1," C-SPAN, January 17, 1989, https://cs.pn/36v6wGt, accessed November 4, 2019.

225. C-SPAN, https://cs.pn/36v6wGt.

226. Baker, *The Politics of Diplomacy*, 23.

227. Gerald M. Boyd, "President Selects a Leader in House for Defense Post, *New York Times,* Marcy 11, 1989, https://nyti.ms/2vYyeuv, accessed August 20, 2018.

228. Baker, *The Politics of Diplomacy*, 23.

229. "Defense Secretary Confirmation Hearing," C-SPAN, March 14, 1989, https://cs.pn/2xLC5Lt, accessed September 23, 2018.

230. Baker, *The Politics of Diplomacy*, 23.

231. Baker, 26.

232. George H.W. Bush and Brent Scowcroft, *A World Transformed*, (Knopf, 1998), page 20.

233. Bush and Scowcroft, *A World Transformed*, 20.

234. Bush and Scowcroft, 19.

235. "Timeline: What Led to the Tiananmen Square Massacre," Frontline, June 5, 2019, https://to.pbs.org/2Uj0ipC, accessed February 2, 2020.

236. Bush and Scowcroft, *A World Transformed*, 89.

237. James A. Baker, III, "James Baker: Bush's response to China after Tiananmen Square is Model for Trump and Saudi Arabia," *Dallas News,* October 24, 2018, http://bit.ly/2ubjvPa, accessed February 2, 2020.

238. Bush and Scowcroft, *A World Transformed*, 102.

239. Baker, *The Politics of Diplomacy*, 104.

240. Baker, 112.

241. Bernard Weinraub, "Bush Urges Effort to Press Noriega to Quit as *Leader,"* *New York Times,* May 10, 1989, https://nyti.ms/38TKP3q, accessed January 30, 2020.

242. Baker, *The Politics of Diplomacy*, 189.

243. "Fighting in Panama: The President; A Transcript of Bush's Address on the Decision to Use Force in Panama," *New York Times*, December 21, 1989, https://nyti.ms/37HkMw3, accessed January 30, 2020.

244. Baker, *The Politics of Diplomacy*, 179.

245. Baker, 194.

246. Bush and Scowcroft, *A World Transformed*, 187.

247. Bush and Scowcroft, 187.

248. Von Carsten Volkery, "The Germans Are Back," http://bit.ly/2tK8owD, *Spiegel International,* November 9, 2009, accessed February 9, 2020.

249. Volkery, http://bit.ly/2tK8owD.

250. Thomas L. Friedman, "Upheaval in the East; Baker Said Unification Isn't Just a German Issue, *New York Times,* December 12, 1989, https://nyti.ms/2vnNe7J, accessed February 9, 2020.

251. Friedman, https://nyti.ms/2vnNe7J.

252. Bush, *All the Best*, 460.

253. Newsweek Staff, "James Baker: 20 Years After the Berlin Wall," *Newsweek,* November 4, 2009, http://bit.ly/37Yr8XZ, accessed February 3, 2020.

254. James A. Baker, III, "All presidents should follow George H.W. Bush's model of presidential diplomacy," *Washington Post*, November 7, 2019, https://wapo.st/2G7Lceb, accessed January 20, 2020.

255. Baker, https://wapo.st/2G7Lceb.

256. Andrew Glass, "Pact Clears way for German reunification, Sept. 12, 1990," *Politico*, September 12, 2017, https://politi.co/39Js4jF, accessed February 13, 2020.

257. Deseret News, "WWII Allies Sign Accord Approving a United Germany," *Deseret News*, September 12, 1990, http://bit.ly/2whn47h, accessed February 13, 2020.

258. "Bush-Kohl Telephone Conversation on the Situation in Germany," October 03, 1990, History and Public Policy Program Digital Archive, George H. W. Bush Presidential Library https://digitalarchive.wilsoncenter.org/document/116233, accessed February 13, 2020.

259. Bush and Scowcroft, *A World Transformed*, 3.

260. Bush and Scowcroft, 6.

261. Bush and Scowcroft, 5.

262. Baker, *The Politics of Diplomacy*, 41.

263. Baker, 41.

264. Bush and Scowcroft, *A World Transformed*, 39.

265. Baker, *The Politics of Diplomacy*, 70.

266. Baker, 79.

267. Baker, 87.

268. R.W. Apple Jr., "Bush, In Warsaw, Unveils Proposal for Aid to Poland," *New York Times*, July 11, 1989, https://nyti.ms/31MiRnQ, accessed February 12, 2020.

269. Bush and Scowcroft, *A World Transformed*, 122.

270. Apple Jr., https://nyti.ms/31MiRnQ.

271. Bush and Scowcroft, *A World Transformed*, 124.

272. Baker, *The Politics of Diplomacy*, 515.

273. Baker, 516.

274. Bush and Scowcroft, *A World Transformed*, Kindle Edition, location 10510.

275. Bush and Scowcroft, 523.

276. Bush and Scowcroft, 523.

277. Bush and Scowcroft, 524.

278. Bush and Scowcroft, 527.

279. Bush and Scowcroft, 536.

280. Bush and Scowcroft, Kindle Edition, location 11032.

281. Bush and Scowcroft, page 560.

282. Text of Gorbachev's Resignation Speech, *AP News*, December 26, 1991, http://bit.ly/2T6BdvB, accessed February 21, 2020.

283. Bush and Scowcroft, *A World Transformed*, 335.

284. Baker, *The Politics of Diplomacy*, 267.

285. Koch, *My Father, My President*, 338.

286. Baker, *The Politics of Diplomacy*, 276.

287. Bush, *All the Best*, 476.

288. Bush, 477.

289. Bush and Scowcroft, *A World Transformed*, 353.

290. Bush and Scowcroft, 353.

291. Baker, *The Politics of Diplomacy*, 279.

292. Baker, 281.

293. Kate Keller, "An Unlikely Hardliner, George H.W. Bush Was Ready to Push Presidential Powers," Smithsonianmag.com, May 14, 2018, http://bit.ly/2x2RVBg, accessed January 25, 2020.

294. Jon Meacham, "The Hidden Hard-Line Side of George H.W. Bush," *Politico*, November 12, 2015, https://politi.co/2uvn1nq, accessed January 25, 2020.

295. Meacham, https://politi.co/2uvn1nq.

296. Baker, *The Politics of Diplomacy*, 477.

297. Baker, 363–364.

298. "Confrontation in the Gulf; Text of Letter from Bush to Hussein," *New York Times*, January 13, 1991, https://nyti.ms/2K9TX9s, accessed April 16, 2020.

299. Baker, *The Politics of Diplomacy*, 367.

300. Bush, *All the Best*, 503.

301. Bush, 505.

302. Bush and Scowcroft, *A World Transformed*, 452.

303. Baker, *The Politics of Diplomacy*, 387.

304. Baker, 390.

305. Bush and Scowcroft, *A World Transformed*, 486.

306. Bush and Scowcroft, 488–489.

307. Bush and Scowcroft, 463–464.

308. James A. Baker, III, "Why the US Didn't March to Baghdad," *Los Angeles Times*, September 8, 1996, https://lat.ms/2YKDiPP, accessed January 5, 2020.

309. "The Madrid Conference, 1991," Office of the Historian, http://bit.ly/3dbCJ9g, accessed March 15, 2020.

310. "James Baker, The Man Who Made Washington Work," PBS Documentary, 2014, DVD.

311. Baker, PBS DVD.

312. Baker, PBS DVD.

313. "After the War: The President; Transcript of President Bush's Address on End of the Gulf War," *New York Times*, March 7, 1991, https://nyti.ms/3aTyb5a, accessed March 15, 2020.

314. *New York Times*, https://nyti.ms/3aTyb5a.

315. "James Baker, The Man Who Made Washington Work," PBS Documentary, 2014, DVD.

316. Doyle McManus, "Baker Encouraged on Mideast Peace Process," *Los Angeles Times*, August 6, 1992, https://lat.ms/2IW8QvI, accessed March 19, 2020.

317. "The Middle East Peace Talks; Excerpts From Speeches in Madrid: 'Long and Painful History' of Struggle," *New York Times* Archives, October 31, 1991, https://nyti.ms/2IRMoDS, accessed March 17, 2020.

318. "The Middle East Peace Talks, https://nyti.ms/2IRMoDS.

319. Baker, *The Politics of Diplomacy*, 512–513.

320. Aaron David Miller, "Five Lessons That Could Save John Kerry's Peace-Process Efforts," *New Republic*, April 7, 2014, http://bit.ly/2QmJXNC, accessed March 17, 2020.

321. Miller, http://bit.ly/2QmJXNC.

322. Richard N. Perle, "Dan Quayle's go the Right Stuff," *New York Times*, October 25, 1988, https://nyti.ms/2uLzPGM, accessed February 14, 2020.

323. American Secretaries of State Interviews, James A. Baker, III, Harvard Kennedy School | Belfer Center, https://bit.ly/3a95bWw, accessed April 16, 2020.

324. Kelsey Tamborrino, "James Baker: Bush's last words were 'I love you,'" *Politico*, December 2, 2018, https://politi.co/2GXHAvX, accessed April 16, 2020.

325. David S. Broder and Richard Morin, "Bush Popularity Surges with Gulf Victory," *Washington Post*, March 6, 1991, https://wapo.st/2uGCoKn, accessed February 16, 2020.

326. Broder and Morin, https://wapo.st/2uGCoKn.

327. Baker, *Work Hard, Study. . . and Keep out of Politics!*, 319.

328. "James A. Baker, III Oral History (2000)," http://bit.ly/32Teeb5.

329. John H. Sununu, *The Quiet Man The Indispensable Presidency of George H.W. Bush*, (Broadside Books, 2015), 377.

330. Andrew Rosenthal, "The 1992 Campaign: Baker Leaving State Dept. to Head White House Staff and Guide Bush's Campaign," *New York Times*, August 14, 1992, https://nyti.ms/2RuFZ5t, accessed January 18, 2020.

331. Antonio D'Ambrosio, "Lee Atwater's Legacy" *The Nation*, October 8, 2008, http://bit.ly/3arA4a2, accessed January 20, 2020.

332. Michael Oreskes, "Lee Atwater, Master of Tactics for Bush and G.O.P., Dies at 40," *New York Times*, March 30, 1991, https://nyti.ms/38p34xa, accessed January 20, 2020.

333. Bush, *All the Best*, 476.

334. Rosenthal, *New York Times*, https://nyti.ms/2RuFZ5t.

335. Sununu, *The Quiet Man*, 374.

336. Sununu, 374.

337. Susan Page, "How a Medical Mystery Tilted the 1992 Election in Bill Clinton's Favor," *Politico*, April 1, 2019, https://politi.co/3aiLmfA, accessed March 30, 2020.

338. Woodruff, PBS, https://to.pbs.org/2Nz3tnV.

339. "James A. Baker, III Oral History (2000)," http://bit.ly/32Teeb5.

340. Sununu, *The Quiet Man*, 379.

341. Bill Whalen, "Before Anyone Whines About Comey and Clinton, Try Revisiting Weinberger and Walsh," *Forbes*, October 29, 2016, http://bit.ly/3anFwuB, accessed January 20, 2020.

342. Cheney Oral Interview, June 9, 2014.

343. "James A. Baker, III Oral History (2000)," http://bit.ly/32Teeb5.

344. "James A. Baker, III Oral History (2000)," http://bit.ly/32Teeb5.

345. Page, *Politico*, https://politi.co/3aiLmfA.

346. Page, *Politico*, https://politi.co/3aiLmfA.

347. Page, *Politico*, https://politi.co/3aiLmfA.

348. Page, *Politico*, https://politi.co/3aiLmfA.

349. Tierney Sneed, "Exclusive Clip: Perot Driven by 'Personal Dislike,' Bush 41 Says," U.S. News, September 10, 2013, http://bit.ly/2ugt66V, accessed January 18, 2020.

350. Sneed, http://bit.ly/2ugt66V.

351. Sneed, http://bit.ly/2ugt66V.

352. Sneed, http://bit.ly/2ugt66V.

353. Paul Richter and Sara Fritz, "Perot Charges Plot forced him out," *Los Angeles Times*, October 26, 1992, https://lat.ms/3aoOV52, accessed January 18, 2020.

354. Sununu, *The Quiet Man*, 377.

355. Alessandra Stanley, "The Man of Kennebunkport, Sentimental Journeying," *New York Times*, June 13, 2012, https://nyti.ms/2wnF2VJ, accessed February 16, 2020.

356. "James A. Baker, III Oral History (2000)," http://bit.ly/32Teeb5.

357. Baker, *Work Hard, Study. . . and Keep out of Politics!*, 321.

358. Edward Luce, "US Democrats should remember, 'It's the economy, stupid,'" *Financial Times*, March 27, 2019, https://on.ft.com/2FFNb9p, accessed January 11, 2020.

359. Interview with Vice President Dan Quayle, Scottsdale, Arizona, February 13, 2020.

360. Bush, George W., *41. A Portrait of My Father*, 244.

361. Bush, Barbara, *Barbara Bush, A Memoir*, 498.

362. Brent Budowsky, "When Barbara Bush Praised Bill Clinton, and Clinton Praised the Man She Loved," *The Hill*, April 20, 2018, https://bit.ly/2WUXpN6, accessed March 30, 2020.

363. Catalina Camia, "Who loves Bill Clinton? Barbara Bush does," *USA Today*, January 21, 2014, https://bit.ly/2JrEstq, accessed March 30, 2020.

364. Meacham, *Destiny and Power*, prologue xvi.

365. Meacham, xvi.

366. Denyer, *Our Nation's No. 2*, 142.

367. Apple Jr., "The New Presidency, Last Day in the White House, 'Over and out,' Bush Says, Then Goes to Walk the Dog," *New York Times*, January 20, 1993, https://nyti.ms/2QJ9aRI, accessed January 2, 2020.

368. Faith Karimi, "The Letter George H.W. Bush Left for Clinton is a Lesson in Grace," CNN Politics, December 1, 2018,https://cnn.it/3bgHQTQ, accessed March 21, 2020.

369. Bush and Scowcroft, *A World Transformed*, 29.

370. Bush and Scowcroft, 29.

371. Baker, *The Politics of Diplomacy*, 672.

372. Bush, Barbara, *Barbara Bush, A Memoir*, Scribner, 516.

373. Andrew Glass, "Clinton orders attack on Iraq, June 26, 1993," Politico, June 26, 1993, https://politi.co/2MUrOoP, accessed January 3, 2020.

374. Office of Inspector General (OIG), "The Bush Assassination Attempt," http://bit.ly/2ZLNLvA, accessed January 3, 2020.

375. "The Long Road to War," *Frontline*, https://to.pbs.org/39GJ3nw, accessed January 3, 2020.

376. Reuters, "Bush on Iraq," *New York Times*, October 23, 1994, https://nyti.ms/2KhcT6k, accessed January 3, 2020.

377. James A. Baker, III, "Why the US Didn't March to Baghdad," *Los Angeles Times*, September 8, 1996, https://lat.ms/2YKDiPP, accessed April 17, 2020.

378. "Cheney '94: Invading Baghdad would create a quagmire," YouTube video, 1:22, from April 15, 1994 Interview: Dick Cheney with American Enterprise Institute, posted by "grandtheftcountry," August 10, 2007, http://bit.ly/2O9Sm8c, accessed October 6, 2018.

379. "Oral History — Colin Powell," *Frontline*, https://to.pbs.org/3056Cle, accessed January 9, 2020.

380. Sue Anne Pressley, "Bush Defeats Richards for Texas Governorship," *Washington Post*, November 9, 1994, https://wapo.st/35PDTTO, accessed December 23, 2019.

381. Sam Hove Verhovek, "THE 1994 ELECTIONS: THE NATION THE BUSHES; Texas Elects George W. While Florida Rejects Jeb," *New York Times*, November 9, 1994, https://nyti.ms/2MY60rX, accessed January 3, 2020.

382. Ellen Warren, "Ex-President's Sons Win Easily in Texas, Florida," *Chicago Tribune*, November 4, 1998, http://bit.ly/2ENIwBR, accessed December 23, 2019.

383. Karina Bland, "The Time President George H.W. Bush Jumped out of a Plane In Arizona," *AZ Central* |Part of *USA Today*, December 5, 2018, http://bit.ly/37w5ABi, accessed January 2, 2020.

384. Tom Porter, "George HW Bush would have been 95 today. He used to celebrate every fifth birthday by going skydiving," *Business Insider*, June 12, 2019, https://bit.ly/3e2Q7wf , accessed April 17, 2020.

385. Porter, http://bit.ly/2QgS3rE.

386. "Former Presidents Bush, Clinton Tapped to Help in Securing Tsunami Disaster Relief," InsuranceJournal.com, January 3, 2005, http://bit.ly/2QoECpM, accessed January 3, 2020.

387. Tony Freemantle, "Bush, Clinton form unlikely bond on tsunami tour," Chron.com, March 7, 2005, http://bit.ly/2QoaI4E, accessed April 17, 2020.

388. Freemantle, http://bit.ly/2QoaI4E.

389. Freemantle, http://bit.ly/2QoaI4E.

390. Freemantle, http://bit.ly/2QoaI4E.

391. S. C. Gwynne, "James Baker Forever," *Texas Monthly*, December 2003, http://bit.ly/379jFo9, accessed January 11, 2020.

392. "The History of the Baker Institute," Baker Institute, http://bit.ly/307oWKx, accessed January 9, 2020.

393. Guide to the Baker Family Papers, 1853–1971 MS 040, http://bit.ly/2FCsVWb, accessed January 10, 2020.

394. Gwynne, *Texas Monthly*, http://bit.ly/379jFo9.

395. Baker Institute Report, Number 21, April 2004, https://bit.ly/3fnPAFp, accessed January 12, 2020.

396. Denyer, *Our Nation's No. 2*, 171.

397. William Safire, "Snippy," *New York Times*, https://nyti.ms/2SrvDp1, accessed December 24, 2019.

398. Safire, https://nyti.ms/2SrvDp1.

399. Gwynne, *Texas Monthly*, http://bit.ly/379jFo9.

400. Susan Baer, "Baker returns from 'exile' to aid Bush in Fla.," *Baltimore Sun*, November 15, 2000, http://bit.ly/2Sc6Api, accessed February 8, 2020.

401. Jeffrey Toobin, *Too Close to Call: The Thirty-Six-Day Battle to Decide the 2000 Election*, (Random House, 2001), 49.

402. Eric Alterman, *What Liberal Media?: The Truth about Bias and the News*, (Basic Books, 2003), 179.

403. "James Baker Holds News Conference in Tallahassee, Florida," CNN Transcript, November 10, 2000, http://transcripts.cnn.com/TRANSCRIPTS/0011/10/se.03.html, accessed December 25, 2019.

404. James Baker, "James Baker: Accept the recount, Al!," *Salon*, November 11, 2000, https://bit.ly/2RMqkPY, accessed April 17, 2020.

405. Gwynne, *Texas Monthly*, http://bit.ly/379jFo9.

406. Ron Klain, "My Florida Recount Memory," op-ed *New York Times*, November 20, 2010, https://nyti.ms/2CZC0qW, accessed April 5, 2019.

407. Theodore Olson, "My Florida Recount Memory," op-ed, https://nyti.ms/2CZC0qW, accessed April 5, 2019.

408. Toobin, *Too Close to Call*, 278.

409. Interview with James A. Baker, III, August 27, 2018.

410. AP, "UN Names James Baker to Western Sahara Post," *New York Times*, March 18, 1997, https://nyti.ms/2Qvnkay, accessed January 6, 2020.

411. Bernard Miyet, "Autonomy: The Optimal Political Solution," Middle East Institute, May 22, 2012, https://bit.ly/3cujcQi, accessed April 17, 2020.

412. Anna Theofilopoulou, "The United Nations and Western Sahara: A Never-ending Affair," US Institute of Peace, July 1, 2006, http://bit.ly/37EwUNV, accessed January 6, 2020.

413. Baker Plan, http://bit.ly/2T8JjWh, accessed January 9, 2020.

414. Baker Plan, http://bit.ly/2T8JjWh.

415. AP, "Baker Quits Western Sahara as UN Envoy," *New York Times*, June 13, 2004, https://nyti.ms/36tJC1H, accessed January 6, 2020.

416. "Baker Resigns as UN Mediator After Seven Years," *New Humanitarian*, June 14, 2004, http://bit.ly/37KJbAC, accessed January 6, 2020.

417. "Baker's Half Dozen – Six Precepts of Foreign Policy," Association for Diplomatic Studies and Training, May 2014, https://bit.ly/3hrG8Tg, accessed May 8, 2020.

418. The Iraq Study Group, *The Iraq Study Group Report: The Way Forward – A New Approach*, (Random House, 2006), ix.

419. The Iraq Study Group, 43.

420. Bob Woodward, *The War Within*, (Simon & Schuster, 2006), 263.

421. David Sanger, "Panel Calls for New Approach to Iraq," New York Times, December 6, 2006, https://nyti.ms/39vwQ4L, accessed January 1, 2020.

422. Sheryl Gay Stolberg and Kate Zernike, "Bush Backs Away from 2 Key Ideas of Panel on Iraq," *New York Times*, December 8, 2006, https://nyti.ms/37qc84p, accessed January 1, 2020.

423. The Iraq Study Group, Kindle Edition, location 1026.

424. Sweany, *Texas Monthly*, http://bit.ly/37UMe9Z.

425. James A. Baker, III, "China's Rise No Threat," Asia Society Texas Center's 2011 Tiger Ball on March 24, 2011, Baker's speech, YouTube, 12:24, posted by "Asia Society," March 31, 2011, https://bit.ly/3c7rv45, accessed April 10, 2020.

426. James A. Baker, III, "Remarks by James Baker, III, former US Secretary of State, given at the Kennan Institute's 25th Anniversary Dinner, October 4, 1999," Wilson Center, December 15, 1999, https://bit.ly/3bgVS8k, accessed April 16, 2020.

427. James A. Baker, III, "James. A. Baker, on Reducing Nuclear Arms," *New York Times*, November 6, 2011, https://nyti.ms/2Xh7qEp, accessed April 8, 2020.

428. Interview with James. A. Baker, III, *Frontline*, https://to.pbs.org/2RCzjmT, accessed April 8, 2020.

429. James A. Baker, III, "The Trump Administration's Hard Choices on Saudi Arabia," *New York Times*, October 22, 2018, https://nyti.ms/2yQu8Jp, accessed April 9, 2020.

430. Adam Edelman and Andrea Mitchell, "James Baker: China holds key to denuclearization of North Korea," *NBC News*, March 28, 2018, https://nbcnews.to/39OOkId, accessed April 8, 2020.

431. James A. Baker, III, "Looking Back on the Middle East: James A. Baker, III," Middle East Forum, September 1994, https://bit.ly/3e0UNDt, accessed April 6, 2020.

432. James A. Baker, III, https://bit.ly/3e0UNDt.

433. James A. Baker, III, https://bit.ly/3e0UNDt.

434. James A. Baker, III, https://bit.ly/3e0UNDt.

435. William McKenzie, "James Baker is optimistic that America's politicians can return to the negotiating table," *Dallas News*, February 9, 2020, https://bit.ly/2VcrXXQ, accessed April 7, 2020.

436. McKenzie, https://bit.ly/2VcrXXQ.

437. McKenzie, https://bit.ly/2VcrXXQ.

438. William McKenzie, "James A Baker III on the Role of Listening, Trusting and Relating to Leadership," Inside Sources, December 6, 2019, https://bit.ly/3aBdzjc, accessed April 7, 2020.

439. McKenzie, https://bit.ly/3aBdzjc.

440. "The Extraordinary Life of James Baker," ABC News, April 9, 2019, https://abc13.co/2xunjwb, accessed March 25, 2020.

441. Eli Watkins, "James Baker, Bush's last day was 'very gentle,'" Channel 3000, December 3, 2018, https://bit.ly/2VineVX, accessed February 1, 2020.

442. Tamborrino, Politico, https://politi.co/2GXHAvX.

443. Aryssa Damron, "Dick Cheney and James Baker Remember George H.W. Bush: 'Perhaps One of the Very Best Presidents of All Time,'" *The Washington Free Beacon*, December 2, 2018, http://bit.ly/37QN0Ve, accessed February 1, 2020.

444. Damron, http://bit.ly/37QN0Ve.

445. Damron, http://bit.ly/37QN0Ve.

446. Roey Hadar, "Colin Powell, James Baker remember former President George H.W. Bush," *ABC News*, December 2, 2018, https://abcn.ws/2OriqK4, accessed February 5, 2020.

447. Caroline Hallemann, Transcript of James A. Baker, III Eulogy of George Herbert Walker Bush, *Town & Country*, December 6, 2018, http://bit.ly/2ulr4mB, accessed February 5, 2020.

448. Loren Elliot, "Former President George H.W. Bush laid to rest in Texas," Reuters, December 6, 2018, https://reut.rs/37x7zou, accessed February 15, 2020.

449. Ward, "James Baker: 'the man who made Washington work,'" Chron, September 19, 2016, http://bit.ly/39VQNRx.

450. Jack Highberger, "Family, friends Look Back the Legacy of George H.W. Bush," NBC|DFW, February 19, 2019, http://bit.ly/37PnChz, accessed February 20, 2020.

451. Sam Howe Verhovek, "No More Mr. President, Just a Texas Nice Guy," *New York Times*, January 5, 1994, https://nyti.ms/2uoXIDO, accessed February 24, 2020.

452. Holly Beretto, "George & Barbara Bush's Deep Ties to Houston Included Favorite Restaurants & Dishes — Updated, http://bit.ly/2v3w5Rg, accessed February 24, 2020.

453. Holly Beretto, George & Barbara Bush's Deep Ties to Houston Included Favorite Restaurants & Dishes — Updated," HoustonFoodFinder.com, December 7, 2018, http://bit.ly/2v3w5Rg, accessed February 24, 2020.

454. Beretto, http://bit.ly/2v3w5Rg.

455. Beretto, http://bit.ly/2v3w5Rg.

456. Sarah Rutica, "Bush said good-bye to Otto's BBQ," CultureMapHouston.com, January 20, 2010, http://bit.ly/2ve8blT, accessed February 24, 2020.

457. Annie Gowen, "'Always one of us': President George H.W. Bush comes home to Texas for the last time," Washington Post, December 5, 2018, https://wapo.st/2Pkc5QZ, accessed February 24, 2020.

458. Gowen, https://wapo.st/2Pkc5QZ.

459. Gowen, https://wapo.st/2Pkc5QZ.

460. Wally Gobetz, "Houston – Downtown: Sesquicentennial Park – George H.W. Bush Monument," Flicker, June 3, 2018, http://bit.ly/2IOowkA, accessed March 14, 2020.

461. Manny Fernandez, "Two Old Friends, in Bronze," New York Times, August 24, 2011, https://nyti.ms/33jlcqY, accessed March 14, 2020.

462. Charles Foster and David Jones, "Clip and save: A Baedker to new Bush Monument," Chron.com, December 4, 2004, https://bit.ly/2RPIP6d, accessed April 11, 2020 (news clipping provided in hard copy by Charles Foster).

463. Interview with Charles Foster, Houston, Texas, April 9, 2020.

464. Shelby Hodge, "An 8-foot-tall James A. Baker, III looks up to George H.W. Bush on the banks of the Bayou," HoustonCultureMap.com, October 27, 2010, http://bit.ly/2TPxPXA, accessed March 14, 2020.

465. Hodge, http://bit.ly/2TPxPXA.

466. Fernandez, *New York Times*, https://nyti.ms/33jlcqY.

467. Dan Quayle, "George Bush: 'Be Prepared and Be Loyal,'" *Washington Post*, December 1, 2018, https://on.wsj.com/2Y81wpa, Accessed May 12, 2020.

468. "Presidential Proclamation Announcing the Death of George H.W. Bush," The White House, December 1, 2018, https://bit.ly/3bh03R1, accessed March 22, 2020.

469. Javier E. David and Kevin Breuninger, "Tributes pour in for former president George HW Bush as state funeral preparations begin," *CNBC Politics*, December 1, 2018, https://cnb.cx/2QDnT1p, accessed March 22, 2020.

470. Video and Full Transcript of George W. Bush's Eulogy for His Father, *New York Times*, December 5, 2018, https://nyti.ms/2wkTsXb, accessed March 22, 2020.

471. Bill Clinton, "Bill Clinton: George H.W. Bush's Oval Office note to me revealed the heart of who he was," *Washington Post*, December 1, 2018, https://wapo.st/33sdX02, accessed March 22, 2020.

472. Chris Mills Rodrigo, "Jimmy Carter: George H.W. Bush's administration was marked by 'grace, civility and social conscience,'" *The Hill*, December 1, 2018, https://bit.ly/3dkcJbH, Access on March 22, 2020.

473. "Dick Cheney: George H.W. Bush was a 'phenomenal leader,'" CNN.com, December 3, 2018, https://cnn.it/3aekiyI, accessed January 14, 2020.

474. "Political World remembers George H.W. Bush," Fox43, December 1, 2018 https://bit.ly/2UafLrk, accessed March 22, 2020.

475. Michael Burke, "Al Gore remembers George HW Bush call after 2000 concession speech: 'It was really a touching call,'" *The Hill*, December 5, 2018, https://bit.ly/396Cf0M, accessed March 22, 2020.

476. "Political World remembers George H.W. Bush," Fox43, https://bit.ly/2UafLrk.

477. The Newsroom, "Sir John Major leads tributes to George H.W. Bush," *The Scotsman*, December 1, 2018, http://bit.ly/3a0otOp, access on March 22, 2020.

478. "Read the full eulogy Brian Mulroney delivered at George H.W. Bush funeral," CTV News, December 5, 2018, http://bit.ly/2Wr7T6j, accessed March 22, 2020.

479. Brent Scowcroft, "Brent Scowcroft Mourns President George H.W. Bush's Passing," The Scowcroft Group, December 3, 2018, https://bit.ly/2MTK80R, accessed May 2, 2020.

480. John H. Sununu, "Goodbye, George H.W. Bush. The world will miss a great president – and I will miss a friend," *Washington Post*, December 1, 2018, https://wapo.st/2TWLn3C, accessed March 22, 2020.

481. Michel Martin, "Colin Powell Remembers George H.W. Bush," NPR, December 1, 2018, https://n.pr/2UsMM11, accessed March 22, 2020.

482. Craig Fuller, "George H.W. Bush: A Lifetime of Commitment to Family and Country by Craig Fuller," *Talbot Spy*, December 1, 2018, https://bit.ly/2yKHVB1, accessed April 11, 2020.

483. "Political World remembers George H.W. Bush," Fox43, https://bit.ly/2UafLrk.

484. Koch, *My Father, My President*, 416.

485. "Arnold Schwarzenegger Pays Tribute to George Bush," *Daily Mail*, December 6, 2018, http://dailym.ai/2XTOBHl, accessed March 21, 2020.

486. Editorial Board, "George H.W. Bush had no grand dreams. His competence and restraint were enough," December 1, 2018, https://wapo.st/2IVgBSt, accessed March 12, 2020.

487. George W. Bush, *Decision Points*, (Crown, 2010), 79.

488. "James Baker: The Man Who Made Washington Work," PBS Documentary, 2014, DVD.

489. Ford, *A Time to Heal*, 393–394.

490. "James Baker: The Man Who Made Washington Work," PBS Documentary, 2014, DVD.

491. Louise Sweeney, "Reagan's — velvet hammer," *Christian Science Monitor*, January 2, 1981, https://bit.ly/3738eiU, accessed June 5, 2020.

492. "James Baker: The Man Who Made Washington Work," PBS Documentary, 2014, DVD.

493. Maureen Dowd and Thomas L. Friedman, "The Fabulous Bush & Baker Boys," *New York Times Magazine*, May 6, 1990, https://nyti.ms/3a1XIZp, accessed April 11, 2020.

494. "James Baker: The Man Who Made Washington Work," PBS Documentary, 2014, DVD.

495. David Chikvaidze, "Former Secretary of State James Baker is the Gold Standard," *The Columbus Dispatch,* Opinion column, April 29, 2020, https://bit.ly/371HMGC, accessed June 5, 2020.

496. "James A. Baker, III – The Velvet Hammer," Association for Diplomatic Studies and Training, https://bit.ly/2MRfwgm, accessed May 2, 2020.

497. "James Baker: The Man Who Made Washington Work," PBS Documentary, 2014, DVD.

498. Baker, PBS, DVD.

499. Baker, PBS, DVD.

500. Gwynne, "James Baker Forever," *Texas Monthly*, https://bit.ly/37jlPTB.

Index

For the purpose of this index, the following abbreviations are used for the names and titles indicated: **GHWB** = George Herbert Walker Bush; **GW** = George W. Bush; **VP** = vice president.